ISLAND SOCIETIES

Robin Cohen is an established scholar in development studies and sociology, known best for his writings on migration, diasporas and globalization. His books include *Migration and its enemies* (2006), *Global diasporas: an introduction* (1997, rev. 2008) and *Global sociology* (co-author, 2000, rev. 2007, 2013). He has long been fascinated by islands, an interest continued over many years through visits, research trips and residence in Mauritius, St Helena and the Caribbean. He was Professor of Sociology at the University of the West Indies, Trinidad and is now Emeritus Professor at the University of Oxford. This collection of his essays charts his intellectual journeys to islands, including the political economy of Mauritius and the Caribbean, critiques of colonial development models, forays into cultural social theory, and work on hybridity and creolization. Three essays are jointly authored with two colleagues: **Fitzroy Ambursley**, who currently works as a consultant to the World Health Organization and **Olivia Sheringham**, who is a post-doctoral research fellow at Queen Mary, University of London.

Island societies: protest and cultural resistance from below

Robin Cohen

Professor Emeritus of Development Studies
and Senior Research Fellow
Kellogg College, University of Oxford

including essays co-authored with

Fitzroy Ambursley and Olivia Sheringham

Oxford Publishing Services

Published in 2017 by

Oxford Publishing Services
34 Warnborough Road, Oxford, OX2 6JA

ISBN: 978 0 9955278 0 5

Cover photo by Jeffrey E.F. Friedl.

Contents

Acknowledgements

Robin Cohen warmly thanks Fitzroy Ambursley (who co-wrote one essay) and Olivia Sheringham (who co-wrote two essays) for allowing him to reproduce them in this collection.

Thanks too to Jason Cohen of Oxford Publishing services for his splendid work on the text and for the arresting cover.

Introduction: protest and cultural resistance from below

Robin Cohen

Islands are often in our imagination. In the tourist brochures they are 'romantic', 'idyllic', 'far-away' places where, for a couple of weeks, we can leave behind our stressful, humdrum metropolitan lives. They ring a musical bell too. Who can fail to respond to Harry Belafonte's beautiful lyrics and mellifluous voice in his famous song, 'Island in the sun'? It is all too easy to recall these lines:

> Oh, island in the sun
> Willed to me by my father's hand
> All my days I will sing in praise
> Of your forest, waters, your shining sand

The song evokes coral reefs, blue seas and piña coladas being served to tourists in colourful dress and straw hats. However, it needs little scratching beneath the surface to find that Belafonte, who identified closely with the struggles of oppressed people, referred in other parts of the song to much harsher realities. He sings of 'a heavy load' and a 'burning glow', mingling with sweat in the 'earth below'. This underside of islandness, this everyday life for many islanders, forms the leitmotif of this book. Here are the traces of transported populations, slavery, indenture, colonialism and the desperate need to create some means of survival in places that were often abandoned by the circuits of trade and capital as they flowed elsewhere throughout the world. Islanders' struggles were physical as, for example, when newly-freed

1

plantation slaves tried to scratch a living from little parcels of land. However, they were also cultural and spiritual. Island populations were often brought there from far-off places, so new languages and social practices had to be fashioned from diverse elements and half-remembered traditions. This process of diasporic remembrance and creative creolization is reflected in several of the essays reproduced here.

Life on islands was often precarious, and still is. Statistically, islands are much more prone to hurricanes, cyclones and other adverse climatic events. Now the effects of global warming threaten to *submerge* some islands completely or loom over the beautiful coastlines that support tourism and fishing. Islands became important for strategic or economic reasons – during the mercantilist period many sugar, cocoa and banana plantations were located there. Now these crops have moved to mainland sites. (By 2017 the five biggest sugar producers were Brazil, India, Thailand, Pakistan and Mexico, while the five main banana producers were India, Uganda, China, the Philippines and Ecuador.) Work on plantation islands was rarely pleasant, but with the relative decline of labour-intensive industries, secure well-paid employment has become increasingly uncommon. Emigration has been the solution for many islanders, sometimes generating a diaspora much larger than the home population on their islands of origin (this applies, for example, to Montserrat, Cape Verde and Puerto Rico). So, in addition to my consideration of the special internal features of island societies, some of the essays in this collection are concerned with my specialism in migration and diaspora studies.

In the colonial imaginary, islands could also be rather more threatening than they appear in contemporary depictions. For example, on certain South Pacific islands, the Caribbean, New Guinea and the Solomons, it was firmly averred that cannibalism was widely practised. Serious scholars have long suggested that much of this narrative was 'cannibal talk', i.e. invention or massive exaggeration (Arens 1979; Obeyesekere 2005). However fabulated, the association with unknown dangers fed a narrative of the island as a place of primeval battle to survive in the face of capricious natural phenomena and unfamiliar enemies. A popular UK radio show ('Desert Island Discs') sanitizes this danger. When the show's guests are exiled (virtually) to a remote island, they can select some music and a luxury they can take with them. They are then asked, 'how would you manage?' We immediately recognize the trope; the challenge refers to the character and activities of Defoe's fictional character, Robinson Crusoe, who was washed up on a desert island for 28 years and endured many adversities.

Through the fictitious Crusoe, islands became important reference points in the origins of social science, providing the foundation of much economic theory. Robinson Crusoe became the prototype of the gender-insensitive *homo oeconomicus* ('economic man'), an agent who makes rational calculations about scarcity and survival. Marxists used islands to expound their theories of primitive accumulation, exploitation and use-value. Anti-colonial and anti-racist discourses were grounded in the persona of Man Friday, a Carib (by inference), who also gets stranded on the island. Crusoe reduces him to a servant, cures his cannibalistic urges and appropriates his labour even as he persuades him to become a Christian. So mission and religious studies also get a look-in. Not to be outdone, feminists have wondered whether Robyn Crusoe might have done it better or more co-operatively than Robinson (Hewitson 1994). I like to think she would.

The etic and the emic

Much of the social scientific literature on islands has been developed from the point of view of the observer (the etic), often

3

to dispute some contentious philosophical point like whether humankind is hard-wired either to be co-operative or competitive. In this sense, islands fulfilled a similar function to 'a state of nature', a hypothetical invention used by seventeenth and eighteenth-century thinkers like Hobbes, Locke and Rousseau to anchor their moral and political philosophies. Suggestive and generative as many of these discussions may be, Godfrey Baldacchino (2008) has articulated a powerful critique of the widespread tendency (which is undeniable) to see islands solely from the outside, from the mainland, from the continent. Where, he asks, is the missing emic, the voice from within the social group? Though by no means defending a naïve subjectivity, Baldacchino (2008: 50) insists on hearing the voices of *both* the outside commentators and the islanders themselves:

> Were 'outsiders' not involved in the (problematic) task of commenting on and about islands, most of us would be facing the dire prospects of an absent script. The inclusion of the 'islander-as-subject'/ indigenous point of view cannot be ignored; but nor can it be construed as exclusive. If island(er)s are hybrid, glocal, shifting, defiantly unstable, and inherently undefinable, how then do we address and temper the enthusiasm to preserve their essence, their sense of place, however flexible it may be? How can island studies manage this 'nervous duality', defending, even celebrating, an 'inside' that is resentful of what is felt to be an overbearing 'outside'; when the outside is essential for island(er) survival, its representation, its very identity? All forms of understandings are needed for a fuller, deeper appreciation of the island condition: surely, island studies will only be richer by nurturing these.

This collection of essays is very much within the spirit of Baldacchino's intervention. The essays and reviews reproduced here were written over a long period, 1978–2017, and reflect my periods of residence, research and work in Mauritius, the Caribbean and the south Atlantic island of St Helena. There is a distinct shift in analysis from an early political economy optic to one much more preoccupied with cultural and social practices. However, throughout the essays, runs a common question – how do resistance and protest arise 'from below' and with what effect?

Unemployment and the illusion of revolution

In the case of Mauritius (Chapter 1), I address the widespread belief in the 1970s that unemployment was a 'natural condition' somewhat like the climate or the vegetation (though we know now that these too are heavily influenced by human actions). Instead, I argue that unemployment was created by the 'historic bourgeoisie' intent on maintaining and enhancing its dominant class position after the end of slavery. I suggest that 'Mauritian politics is essentially, historically and experientially, about how different fractions of the petty bourgeoisie seek to represent (and perhaps misrepresent) the rural proletariat, workers and unemployed against the claims and demands of the historic bourgeoisie'. Although often expressed in communal terms, I show how the political struggles in Mauritius were predicated on these class differences and alliances. In the period after independence the major opposition to the Labour Party (which had attained power in the period of decolonization) came from the Mouvement Militant Mauricien (MMM). This was a party with a multi-ethnic leadership, which organized trade unions in Afro-Mauritian, Indo-Mauritian and 'mixed' areas. The MMM also fought the election on a programme of limited nationalization, the return of Diego

Garcia ('sold' to the British who passed it on to the Americans as a base), and on severing ties with South Africa. In these policies and in stitching together an effective coalition between many rural proletarians, urban workers and intellectuals, the MMM constituted a progressive force which, however, was a long way off a revolutionary force. I argue that without a stronger challenge, the power of the historic bourgeoisie could not effectively be challenged.

In Chapter 2, a reflection on and appreciation of Ken Post's massive social history of Jamaica, the protests of the labouring classes are symbolically represented through the fictional characters of Quashee and Anancy. The first was the slave owners' name for any male slave, who was demeaned by being epitomized as a clownish, irresponsible, overgrown, child. Of course, the playing out this role could itself be an indirect form of resistance, a parody of the image the slave owner wished to believe. However, both embodied in the image and in its parody is the idea that Quashee had the capacity for sudden, atavistic and irrational violence – something that went bump in the night. The brutality of colonial repression in Jamaican history is driven by the fear a renegade Quashee evoked. Anancy is the more subtle figure, a spider man and 'trickster' who uses cunning and duplicity to run rings around the rich and powerful. Because Anancy seemed to enjoy playing the game rather more than leading his side to victory, the poor and the powerless could derive solace from his sly digs, but they could rarely find retribution or redress. Through his understanding of the pale pastels as well as the bold colours of protest Post has assembled a convincing picture of the failure of the rebellion of 1938, when a revolution briefly looked possible. He provides, I argue, a clear-eyed and sometimes brilliant piece of social history that remains and unrivalled account of the limits of protest in a colonial setting.

Even where sections of the political class take up the cudgels on behalf of the labouring poor, there are real constraints in how far island societies can break with the past. I alluded to this in the case of Mauritius. Chapter 3 considers a number of Caribbean cases which reveal, as Fitzroy Ambursley and I argue, a good deal of confusion and uncertainty in evolving the strategies, tactics and ideologies of fostering a socialist transformation. Could there be a possibility of 'socialism in one country', especially if the countries concerned were small, weak, isolated and located close to Uncle Sam's looming shadow? Was it possible for socialists to combine with progressive elements of the national bourgeoisie, even assuming that this class had developed some corporate identity and strength? And would not a tactical alliance with such an ally lead to a more permanent co-optation and ultimately betrayal of mass demands? Again would an alliance of revolution-ary intellectuals, workers and displaced peasants hold together long enough to capture the state apparatus and attempt the task of socialist reconstruction from the bottom up? Were the class organs of such an alliance – the trade unions, youth movements and socialist and communist parties – able to effect something more than an étatist or bureaucratic solution once they had achieved power?

Given the external constraints and internal weaknesses, it is perhaps unexpected that Nicaragua, Grenada, El Salvador and, more recently. Venezuela attempted the transformation to a socialist society at all. It is certainly not surprising that they failed. As I suggest in Chapter 7, perhaps the most predictable failure was that of Grenada. Payne, Sutton and Thorndike in *Grenada: revolution and invasion* (1984: 11) had shown how the New Jewel Movement (which was to form the core of the People's Revo-lutionary Government) uneasily combined 'elements of racial and national pride, Rastafarianism, "popular power" and participatory

7

democracy with social reformist zeal'. They argued that it was only in 1976–77 that any Marxist and socialist theory emerged. But this tiny protest against US hegemony was clumsily but brutally squashed by the US invasion in 1983. There remains the counter-example of Cuba, which has retained some level of revolutionary fervour since 1959, despite many predications of the end of this experiment. The venality of the Batista government, the incompetence of the US-supported invasion of the island and various futile attempts on Castro's life, as well as the sustained support of the USSR, can all explain the first 35 years of survival. After 1994, a more complex picture emerges. Thereafter, the Communist Party of Cuba has had to make various pragmatic adjustments to the market (especially in the recognition of private property and the encouragement of tourism), but has also retained core socialist principles in providing good health care and education provision, which have led to considerable support for the regime.

The dead hand of colonialism

As is shown in Chapters 4, 5, 6 and 8, many islands were linked to the emerging world system by mercantilist trade followed by fitful and often ineffective periods of colonial government. Chapter 4 comprises a detailed study of the education system on St Helena, which remains a British colony to this day. Even when the colonial government sought to establish a functioning and ambitious educational service, I show how it failed to realize its self-declared aims. Instead, as I demonstrate through interviewing and surveying the environmental perceptions, aspirations and expectations of a group of St Helenian schoolchildren, the colonial government provided an education for dependence. The background to this failure were the hopeless trading situation, the poor level of self-sustaining productive activities and the dulling effects of British colonialism itself. This is a society which lacks binding self-definitions, a people without a nationalism. The Governor and his officials could not inspire, galvanize or transform anything (including the educational system); first, because the raison d'être for the original existence of the island had disappeared; second, because British colonialism could not provide a legitimating ideology for its existence, and finally, because St Helenians have failed, so far, to come to grips with their own history and what is being done in their name. The impoverishment of St Helena is not only of the body, but of the intellect. I argue that neither form of impoverishment can be overcome until St Helenians start to make history themselves rather than being made by it.

In the second detailed study of St Helena (Chapter 6) I examine the contradictory pulls of welfare colonialism from the top and various forms of passive resistance from below. The social situation on the island itself encouraged stasis. This stems partly from the conservatism of the small settler element, but also from the difficulties islanders have experienced in forming themselves into effective political lobbies. The narrow basis of consultation, representation, and participation permitted by the government also allows little room for the expression of opinions and grievances. The Development Plan for the island for the most part bypassed the islanders. The colonial government was unable to harness private entrepreneurship to its stated task of reducing St Helena's dependence on the United Kingdom and, in the face of a challenge from this quarter, retreated to its prior position of trusteeship. It was also unable, despite formally adopting the modern goals of community development and self-reliance, to build in or activate the structures of consultation and participation that would have made the realization of these goals possible. Instead 'development' remained an abstraction, far removed from the needs and wishes of the people in whose name it was propagated.

As I further show in Chapter 6, realistic and quite modest demands from below, were met with stony indifference from above.

Chapters 5 and 8 are also predominantly concerned with the precarious situation inherited from the period of mercantilism and colonialism. Even where independence was achieved (as in Mauritius, the Cape Verdes, Equatorial Guinea, the Seychelles, and the Comoros) the burden of the past weighs heavily on them. Such islands were typically dependent on a monoculture and a plantation economy worked by imported slave labour and only the post-independent leaderships were only slowly able to diversify their economies. There are of course, examples of economic success in islands with colonial heritages – indeed, there are 7 such examples in the first 50 countries ranked by GDP per capita by the IMF in the projected 2017 ranking (http://statisticstimes.com/economy/gdp-capita-ranking-2017.php). However, the tendency is in the opposite direction. As I argue in Chapter 8, in the period of decolonization many new small island states were created with little attention to the minimal condition for economic and political viability. To the problems of autarkic economic development have now been added the internal political instability of many small states, augmented by regional or great-power rivalry for effective control over small countries. So captivating was the nineteenth century doctrine of self-determination and so determined were decolonizing powers to get rid of nearly all their possessions that the possibilities of thriving, or surviving, in the post-colonial world were systematically ignored or minimized.

The Caribbean: diasporas and identity

As is well-established, many islanders respond to a lack of opportunities at home by choosing to emigrate. Chapters 9 and 10

concentrate on migration from the Caribbean. While their populations abroad have often been described as a diaspora, both
chapters allude to the complexity of using this description in the
case of the islands of the Caribbean. In Chapter 9, I ponder on the
tricky question of whether Caribbean emigrants should be seen
as 'a diaspora of a diaspora', a clumsy expression that nonetheless
recognizes that many Caribbean people have roots in Africa, India
(or indeed other places). Should 'Caribbeans' (to deploy a newly
coined expression) abroad be seen a part of wider African and
Indian diasporas, or should they be treated as 'Indo-Caribbeans'
and 'Afro-Caribbeans' with hybrid identities? Again, has there been
sufficient distance, geographically, temporally and emotionally,
for a separate Caribbean identity to emerge, so that the expression
'Caribbean diaspora' can now be used unproblematically?

In Chapter 10 I show how this last view is challenged by those
who advocate, following Paul Gilroy's (1993) notion of a 'Black
Atlantic', that there are continuous cultural connections in a
virtual (and sometime actual) oceanic space between the
Americas, Europe and Africa. Formed during the horrors of transatlantic slavery, the 'Black Atlantic' links Africa and its diaspora
though the trauma of the Middle Passage, trade, voluntary
migration and movements such as négritude, Pan-Africanism,
Rastafarianism and Black Power. As Gilroy graphically argues, the
waves of the Atlantic have been supplanted by the airwaves as
music, dancing, carnival and religious inspiration crosses and
re-crosses all the points of African dispersion. Within the
Caribbean, as I argue in Chapter 16, this has resulted in a social
laboratory for the study of social identity. I argue that the
Caribbean was a nexus of the intersections and contradictions of
an early form of global capitalism, mercantilism where European
settlers, African slaves, indigenous populations, indentured
Indians and subsequent migrants from places as far afield as

China and Syria, found themselves trying to make new lives in small, often hostile, settings.

Creolization and cultural resistance

One of the key sociological features of islands – especially those that where there were few indigenous people or their populations were reduced by imported diseases – was that imported populations often developed shared Creole languages. However, creolization should not be understood merely as a linguistic concept. Syncretic faiths, like Shango, Santeria, Voudou and Rastafarianism, are examples of creolization, as are pooled and emerging practices like creolized music, dance, poetry, orature and folkways together with large public expressions of fusion such as carnivals, festivals and parades. Chapters 11, 12, 13, 14 and 15 document these developments in various island settings. Chapters 11 and 12 concern creolization and cultural politics in the islands of Réunion and Mauritius. Réunion is a 'DOM', a French overseas department that is legally treated as if it were a department in the 'metropole' (that is, mainland France). But as this review of Laurent Medea's (2010) account of creolization on the island demonstrates, formal incorporation into the French political structure, and thereby into the European Union has left the islanders in a cross-pressured situation. On the one hand, their standard of living and opportunities for education and upward social mobility are enhanced by the metropolitan link. On the other hand, resentment against metropolitan settlers has found expression in creolized culture – showing that Réunion is both French and not French at the same time. In Mauritius, with a partly shared cultural heritage as a French Indian Ocean island (before the British took control), creolization has developed in another direction. While still a unifying force in the island to some degree, as I show in my review of Rosabelle Boswell's *Le malaise Créole: ethnic identity in Mauritius* (2006) this remains true despite in increased ethnic assertiveness of those of Indo-Mauritian descent and the increasing use of 'Creole' to describe a stigmatized, marginalized section of the Mauritian population, descended from African and Malagasy origins. The 'Redlegs' of Barbados, discussed in Chapter 13, are another stigmatized group, though this time of European origin.

Chapters 14 and 15 discuss creolization more conceptually. In the first instance, Olivia Sheringham and I consider whether islandness and creolization have 'an elective affinity', a suggestive phrase coined by Max Weber, in which there is no clear causal direction (A causes B or vice versa), but nonetheless A and B go together well. Issues of scale, the vacillation of global connectivity with periodic isolation and the need to rely on one another seem to generate the preconditions for cultural cross-overs. It is thus no coincidence that creolization corresponds to the phase of mercantile capitalism, and takes place on islands and plantations where tropical products were produced by slaves or other unfree labourers. However, the collective process of identity formation results in a number of possible outcomes and trajectories. For the purposes of understanding how new cultures emerge, Olivia Sheringham and I see people bringing to the interaction some level of valorization of their past identities (where they are from), just as they embrace some elements of other cultures they encounter (where they are at). Shared identities thus emerge as a combination of part recovered, part experienced and part imagined possibilities, processes that we think are usefully conceptualized through the prisms of diaspora and creolization. This is the theme of our discussion in Chapter 15.

Conclusion

In the great sweep of social science, island studies is of relatively recent provenance. It has nonetheless created passionate

13

debates, albeit that these debates have, on the whole, been between friends – generally outside scholars who love (and are fascinated by) islands. Those close to islanders, and islanders themselves have had relatively less exposure. As Baldacchino suggested in the passage cited earlier, subjective, inter-subjective and external perspectives can make useful bedfellows in understanding islands. In this collection of essays, I have focused overwhelming on views from below. Political economy and understanding the heritage of colonial government have been a necessarily prelude and accompaniment to ethnographic analysis in the first half of the book. However, the focus then shifts from reactions to economy and the colonial order to patterns of cultural recovery and resistance. I hope too that this collection will provide some conceptual entry-points to other scholars of islands.

Note

While I have added or corrected some references and tidied up the text occasionally, the texts published in this book are very close to the original essays and reflect the issues of their time. Addenda to a number of the chapters give details of the original publication, provide ancillary information and include some retractions where I got it wrong.

References

Arens, William. 1979. *The man-eating myth: anthropology and anthropophagy*, New York: Oxford University Press.

Baldacchino, Godfrey. 2008. 'Studying Islands: on whose terms? Some epistemological and methodological challenges to the pursuit of island studies', *Island Studies Journal*, 3(1), 37–56.

Boswell, Rosabelle. 2006. *Le malaise Créole: ethnic identity in Mauritius*, New York: Berghahn Books.

Gilroy, Paul. 1993. *The Black Atlantic: modernity and double consciousness*, London: Verso.

Hewitson, Gillian. 1994. 'Deconstructing Robinson Crusoe: a feminist interrogation of "rational economic man"', *Australian Feminist Studies*, 9(20), 131–49.

Medea, Laurent. 2010. *Réunion: an island in search of an identity*, Pretoria: UNISA Press.

Obeyesekere, Gananath. 2005. *Cannibal talk: the man-easting myth and human sacrifice in the South Seas*, Berkeley: UCP.

Payne, Anthony, Paul Sutton and Tony Thorndike. 1984. *Grenada: revolution and invasion*, London: Croom Helm.

Robin Cohen
Oxford 2017

Chapter 1
The political economy of unemployment in Mauritius

Robin Cohen

States emerging from the decolonization process are preoccupied with solving a key indicator of underdevelopment, namely unemployment. Mauritius is an exemplary case to study in that, at its independence in 1968, it inherited a swelling population with limited opportunities for meaningful economic activity. However, there are two dimensions particular to Mauritius that influence the solution to this problem. The first is a competitive electoral system – a good index of development of course – but one that pits communal and class interests against one another, sometimes to negative effect. Would the progressive political movements on the island, which gained some electoral traction, be able to intervene effectively to enhance employment opportunities? The answer to this question was partly predicated on the second distinctive dimension of Mauritius – the existence of a powerful 'historic bourgeoisie', one that had dominated economic life and constrained upward social mobility on the island since the early days of settlement.

The December 1976 Election

Mauritius is one of the few developing states where electoral politics have to be taken seriously. Here, unlike in most other postcolonial states, it has proved difficult for the leadership of the 'independence party' to establish or consolidate its political and economy hegemony, even within Mauritian society. This is especially puzzling to observers who insist, as does Hugh Tinker, in an otherwise informative analysis of Mauritius, on viewing politics as electoral politics, and viewing electoral politics as communal politics.[1] The uncertainties of his analysis are clearly revealed in his reflections on the December 1976 elections in Mauritius, elections long delayed by the fearful ruling Labour Party. Ramgoolam's Labour Party – fighting the election in an alliance with another minor party, the Muslim Committee of Action (MCA) under the banner of the Independence Party – had good reason to be concerned at the possible outcome of testing its popularity at the polls.

The major opposition came from the Mouvement Militant Mauricien (MMM) a party with a multi-ethnic leadership, which organized trade unions in Afro-Mauritian, Indo-Mauritian and 'mixed' areas. The MMM also fought the election on a programme of limited nationalization, the return of Diego Garcia ('sold' to the British who passed it on to the Americans as a base), and on severing ties with South Africa. The MMM came increasingly, as Tinker notes, to represent the young and the poor. In December 1976, after the 'best-loser' seats were redistributed, the MMM won 34 seats to the Independence Party's 28. A smaller reactionary party, the Parti Mauricien Social Démocrate (PMSD), won 8 seats and a hasty defensive alliance was patched up between this party and the ruling party to prevent the MMM acceding to power.

---

1   This perhaps does some injustice to the author's numerous asides but accurately reflects his principal conclusions. Hugh Tinker, 'Between Africa and Europe. Mauritius: cultural marginalists and political control', *African Affairs*, 76(304), July 1977, 321–38, especially pp. 336–8.

Yet despite the electorate's display of confidence in a non-communal party, Tinker tentatively poses the question: 'Is it time to conclude that the politics of communalism is giving way to the politics of class in Mauritius?' He replies, even more cautiously, 'probably not' on the grounds that the MMM parliamentary team 'reflected the religious and caste opposition of the population as closely as did Ramgoolam supporters. Muslims still voted for Muslims, Hindus for Hindus and Creoles for Creoles.'[2] This last statement is more than dubious. Neither Ramgoolam's Labour Party nor its electoral allies, the MCA, showed many inhibitions in trying to manipulate Hindu and Muslim communal sentiments. Yet the MCA, an overtly communal party, managed to capture only one seat in an electorate 17 per cent of whom are Muslim,[3] while the remaining 27 Independence Party seats (38 per cent of the House) were won in a population more than 70 per cent of whom are Indians. Equally, while the PMSD has been represented by communal theorists as the party of the Afro-Creoles and the Franco-Mauritians, their joint representation in the population (28 per cent) was not reflected in the 11 per cent representation that the PMSD achieved in the House. The reader may also have noticed reference to a so-called 'best-loser' system. This system was invented especially for Mauritius by the 1966 Banwell Commission which was instructed to give 'the main sections of the population an opportunity of securing fair representation of their interests if necessary by the reservation of seats'.[4] The formula the Commission evolved fell short of reserving seats and

---

2   Tinker, 'Between Africa', p. 337.

3   Based on 1975 population estimates given in 'Mauritius', in *Africa: South of the Sahara*, London: Europa Publications Ltd., 1977, p. 587.

4   Mauritius: Report of the Banwell Commission on the Electoral System, Report no. 362, London: HMSO for the Colonial Office, 1966, p. 5.

the precise procedures it recommended need not detain us here. The point is that communalism is partially constitutionally *guaranteed* by the system: in December this worked out at 8 of the 70 seats in the Legislative Assembly.

For a society which is supposedly marked by the 'politics of communalism' the communal parties do not seem to have been doing that well – especially when the constitutional system pre-determined that 11 per cent of the Legislative Assembly had to be selected on communal lines. But even if it is by now clear that the support for parties does not mirror ethnic constituencies, I must also briefly consider Tinker's subsidiary thesis that the MMM had to take account of communal loyalties in its own selection of candidates (though notice how 'communal' is transmuted into 'religious and caste composition'). This seems to be saying no more than that the MMM was politically adroit enough to select a number of candidates with an appropriate background for their constituencies. None of the MMM members (to my knowledge) campaigned on an ethnic platform and quite a number were elected – including the MMM leader, Berenger – by an electorate of a dissimilar communal background. (Berenger, a Franco-Mauritian, comes from a cultural section representing about two per cent of the population so a communal electoral appeal would not have worked.)

In short, the December 1976 elections were not primarily about communalism. It would be foolish to deny that people in Mauritius, like people elsewhere in the world, have strong religious, ethnic or communal sentiments, but these were politically less significant in the context of three deep-rooted and related problems, problems which both accompanied and transcended the election campaign:

- The continuing social, cultural, and economic hegemony of the 'historic bourgeoisie'.

- The relationship of this historic bourgeoisie to the under-classes and its role in creating successive unemployment problems.

- The continuing incapacity of the ruling party to generate anything but the most demeaning employment for the huge latent, floating and stagnant surplus population.[5]

It is to these problems that I now turn.

The domination of the 'historic bourgeoisie'

By far the most useful class analysis of Mauritian society is that provided by Ram Seegobin and Lindsay Collen. In respect of the dominant class they argue that: 'in Mauritius the bourgeoisie is so highly developed that the state, in its totality, cannot do otherwise than reflect the interest of this dominant class. This means that any political party which comes to power through parliament, lands itself with a set of institutions which are far from useful in attacking the bourgeoisie.[6] In a subsequent article, they see a more complex conflict between the new 'state bourgeoisie' and the 'historic bourgeoisie'.[7] But it is clear in many accounts, and indeed by common observation, that any uppity

---

5   For an exposition of these concepts see Martin Godfrey, 'Surplus populations and underdevelopment: reserve army or marginal mass?' *Manpower and Unemployment Research* 10(1), April 1977, 63–71; or turn to the original, where Marx is particularly clear. See Karl Marx, *Capital*, part 7, chap. 25.

6   Ram Seegobin and Lindsey Collen, 'Mauritius: class forces and political power', *Review of African Political Economy*, 8, January-April 1977, p. 110.

7   Ram Seegobin and Lindsey Collen, 'Leta e Eleksion', *Lalit de Klas*, 1977. Original in Kreol. Typescript translation kindly provided by the authors.

cuckoo is going to have a difficult time displacing the far-from-dead dodo from its feathery nest.

What are the origins of this 'historic bourgeoisie'? What is its social character and what define the source of its continuing power? How has its formation and development affected the 'under-classes' of Mauritius? In 1720, French colonialists seized the island, interposed themselves as critical intermediaries in the Indian Ocean trade and set up a colonial economy based on sugar plantations worked by slave labour from Africa and Madagascar. Port Louis, the capital, became something of an entrepôt in Indian Ocean trade with slaves, spices, jewels, sugar, provisions and other goods being traded with British, French, Portuguese and Arab ships. At the centre of this trade were the French *colons* who were, at an early stage, engaged both in mercantilist exchange and direct production.

The *colons* showed their teeth in their brutal suppression of slave revolts which occurred sporadically from 1735–1835. The movement for emancipation was much accelerated by the French Revolution and there were even some Republican supporters in Mauritius who killed a naval commander, Comte MacNemara.[8] But Mauritius did not have its Toussaint who, beginning in 1791 led a massive and ultimately successful slave revolt in San Domingo.[9] In Mauritius, the *colons* were determined to hang on, and they were aided and abetted by the Governor. When, in 1796, two Commissaire Directoire Republicans arrived from Paris with instructions to free the slaves, the settlers sent them packing. This was not surprising. Many members of the historic bourgeoisie openly identified themselves as aristocrats who left

---

8   Seegobin and Collen, 'Leta e Eleksion', p. 9.

9   C.L.R. James, *The Black Jacobins: Toussaint L'Ouverture and the San Domingo revolution*, New York: Vintage Books, 1963.

France during the Revolution and found a refuge in Mauritius (these claims were often exaggerated).

In 1810 the island was captured by the British who, in the Capitulation Treaty, left the power of the *colons* intact. In the words of the treaty, the British were to 'respect' the *colons'* 'rights to property, their religion, laws and customs'.[10] Their rights to property included, naturally, their slaves. In 1807, the British parliament had abolished the trade in slaves as 'contrary to the principles of justice, humanity and sound policy', but so weak was the British presence in 1810 that the first Governor, Farquhar, did not even attempt to implement the laws against the slave trade of his home Parliament. When Hall, the next Governor, attempted to implement slave abolition he met with so much resistance that he was moved instead to abolish the Assembly, suspend the Chief Judge, the Procurer General and the Collector of Customs. Hall's bold actions were then overruled by London. His hands were tied and he found himself ruthlessly suppressing a slave revolt in 1822 at the insistence of the slave owners.

As Eric Williams argues, sugar plantation slavery without the continuous supply of slaves (cut off by the end of the slave trade) was not profitable in the West Indies. However, in the larger, more fertile, less exhausted areas of Mauritius, Cuba and Brazil, sugar cultivation with slaves still brought good returns.[11] This is why the *colons* opposed Hall and were later to bitterly oppose the Emancipation Act of 1830. They mobilized large demonstrations, with the permission of the Governor, started military training to suppress slave revolts and resisted the Colonial Office

---

10 Cited in *Maurice Diboute!* 2, Groupement revolutionnaire de Île Maurice, n.d. but 1975.

11 Eric Williams, *Capitalism and Slavery*, London: André Deutsch, 1964, 150–2.

representative, John Jeremie, who was sent out to enforce the abolition order. Riots and strikes fomented by the *colons* and the shutting of shops for 45 days forced Jeremie to leave the island. When he returned he did so under armed escort. It was argued that the 'rights' of the *colons* under the Capitulation Treaty had been violated and a settler representative went to Britain to protest. He returned with permission to start a newspaper, found a bank and a Chamber of Agriculture. Large sums of money were promised as compensation to the slave owners and they were to have independent representation in the Legislative Assembly, where the *Grands Blancs* would sit alongside the British colonial officials. As Ram Seegobin and Lindsay Collen argue, 'With a newspaper, bank, a Chamber of Agriculture, capital, and political power, the Mauritian bourgeoisie was born.'[12] It should perhaps be added that while these authors confine their consideration of 'capital' to the new compensation money, Mauritian sugar had been doing very well in London in the period 1810–30 at the expense of some of the older West Indian plantations,[13] while the Franco-Mauritians continued to participate in the more general mercantile trade between Europe and Asia. Their accumulation of capital was thus more generally based.

Hopefully, it is now evident why this is an 'historic bourgeoisie'. I could even advance the term 'haute-bourgeoisie', as it expresses more exactly the continuing cultural arrogance and assertiveness of this powerful group. Several members of this class casually evince an almost pre-1789 disdain for the plebeian British. A British colony since 1810, yet Mauritius still has no English-language daily newspaper, important provisions of the *Code Napoleon* continue to be in force, the children of the

---

12 Seegobin and Collen, 'Leta e Eleksion', p. 10.

13 Williams, *Capitalism and slavery*, p. 151.

Franco-Mauritians go to *lycées* and finishing schools and universities in Switzerland and France, while English is only partially established as an official language. As Tinker notes, 'Mauritius never ceased to be the Île de France.'[14] In terms of the patterns of ownership there are today [this chapter was written in 1978] 21 large sugar estates (producing 60 per cent of the crop) only two of which are owned by British capital ('Tiny' Rowlands Lonrho group) and one of which is government owned. The rest are owned nearly in their entirety by the historic bourgeoisie – who also own the sugar mills which process and bag the sugar, make the molasses, rum, cane spirit and other derivative produces. The concentration of ownership is even more startling – 13 families having a lion's share of the capital assets. The 452 medium planters and 30,000 small planters (producing the remaining 40 per cent of the crop)[15] have to send their cane for processing to the mills of the big planters, the point in the production chain where the profits are greatest.

The power of the top Franco-Mauritians effectively remained unchallenged by British colonialism. True, certain of the metropolitan shipping companies and import-export houses muscled in under the protective umbrella of the colonial government. But even such British-sounding companies as the Rogers Group (founded in 1899), which controls major areas of trading, shipping and aviation, are owned and managed by the Mauritian bourgeoisie. Most have diversified their interests in recent years, first into tourism and second, into manufacturing (the last being under the joint sponsorship of the state bourgeoisie). The Weal Group, for example, who own the two largest sugar estates, the combined output of which accounts for 24 per cent of the

---

14 Tinker, 'Between Africa', p. 323.
15 'Mauritius' in *Africa: South of the Sahara*, p. 584.

national figure, has invested in fancy hotels (La Pirogue, Touessrok, and Île-aux-Cerfs), a travel agency (Concorde), cattle breeding and industry.[16]

Tourism is of some interest in respect of the political implications of its expansion. It is now the second most important foreign exchange earner, tourist arrivals having increased from 27,650 in 1970 to 75,000 in 1975. The bulk of the tourists are white South Africans, who need to brown their hides, toughened by rejection in every other self-respecting country, in some exotic setting. Durban is only 1,240 miles away and daily flights to Johannesburg by South African Airways or Air Mauritius (the 'national' airline managed by the Rogers Group), make travel easy. Mauritius is a member of the Southern African Regional Tourist Council. It is also, however, a member of the Organization of African Unity, and Sir Seewosagur Ramgoolam, Prime Minister of Mauritius happened to be Chairman of the OAU in 1976. Among the more unusual events and delicious ironies surrounding the OAU conference in June 1976, the following can be recorded: South African tourists were banned for two weeks; embarrassed waiters were seen rubbing out the 'Made in South Africa' labels on the ashtrays placed in the hotels of the OAU delegates; African journalists covering the conference refused to pay their bills in the South African-owned hotel they were booked into on the grounds that a few miles away the conference had just passed a resolution supporting sanctions against South Africa.

Not that the bourgeoisie was much disturbed by this two-week wonder. Their ventures into tourism ineluctably tighten the links between the two countries, while 75 per cent of the tea crop

---

16 Advertisement in *The Times*, Special Supplement on Mauritius, 30 June 1976.

(Mauritius' second export crop) is bought by South African importers. Three weeks after the OAU conference, a visitor to the Mauritius Turf Club could read the following information in the Programme officiel des courses. The 34th race was for the OAU cup. A more tempting prize was offered in the race for the Coupe de l'Ambassade de France, while if you fancied on the 29th, your horse was eligible for the Jockey Club of South Africa Cup. If you wished to back South African horses or jockeys, a ubiquitous Chinese bookie could always be found to oblige. The unsuccessful punter could of course console himself to the strains of Offenbach, Chabrier, Strauss and Khachaturian, not to mention l'Hymne national de Maurice ('Motherland') played by the Mauritius Police Band. The list of Commissaires, Juges du Départ, Juges à l'Arriveé and Chronométreurs in the programme reads like the guest list for a dinner party for the historic bourgeoisie – M. Camille L. Nairac, M. P. Robert de Senneville, M. J. Paul Hein, M. L. Philippe Boullé, M. J. Philippe Ducler des Rauches, M. Roland Ducler des Rauches, M. J. Jacques Vallet, M. J. Raymond Hein, and so on.

The under-classes

It should now be evident that the historic bourgeoisie is not simply one 'communal group' among several. It is a historically well-anchored *class*, represents the higher levels of the social elite, the dominant cultural reference group and holds the overwhelming share of economic wealth in its hands. As one might expect, the dialectic counterpoint for such a concentration of agricultural, industrial, service, social, cultural and finance capital in the hands of a few is seen in the immiseration of large numbers of other Mauritians. The politics of unemployment are directly related to how the under-classes were formed in their encounters with the haute-bourgeoisie.

The first important moment was the final collapse of slavery under the impact of local slave revolts, pressures from Britain and the inducements of compensation. The former slave and slave-descended population basically went in three directions--in all cases as far away from the land as possible:

- The *créole-de-couleur* joined the *petits-blancs* (whites without property) to create one fraction of the petit-bourgeoisie including the bureaucrats and professionals (doctors, teachers, lawyers, civil servants, and the like).[17] (This group is not nearly as powerful numerically or socially as its Caribbean equivalents.)

- Small numbers of freed men joined groups of runaways to establish small fishing communities in remote parts of the coast. These self-employed fisher folk still survive today but their livelihood is being threatened by imported fish, foreign and local Mauritian fleets, and prawn farms established by the bourgeoisie. Their capacity for self-reliance and competition is certainly limited and most of the young men in the fishing communities can be regarded as unemployed.

- The former slaves drifted into Port Louis and to a lesser extent to Curepipe and Moka, much smaller urban concentrations. There they became proletarians (mainly factory workers and dockers) and members of the relative surplus population, particularly what Marx identified as the stagnant and pauper sections of this population.[18]

---

17 Seegobin and Collen, 'Mauritius: class forces', p. 110.

18 For Marx, the stagnant section of the relative surplus population 'forms part of the active labour army; but with extremely irregular employment. Hence it furnishes to capital an inexhaustible reservoir

In other words, the first 'employment problem' in Mauritius occurs as a result of the unwillingness of the slaves to labour, even for wages, in the brutalizing conditions of the post-emancipation sugar plantations.

A new under-class was needed and this the newly formed haute-bourgeoisie was to find in the 'latent' population of the Indian subcontinent. Although small numbers of Indian slaves had been purchased in the French ports of India before 1810 and there were also a small number of artisans and Chettyar merchants, the bulk of forebears of the present Indian population were imported as indentured labourers between the period 1843 and 1880. It would be churlish not to point out, as I have taken issue with Tinker earlier, that his writings are by far the most authoritative and important accounts of how the agricultural (rural) proletariat of India was recruited and harnessed to the task of plantation labour in Mauritius, Fiji, Natal and the Caribbean.[19] For the plantation owners this was clover. Why they ever bothered to suppress those nasty slaves or protest about their emancipation, they hardly knew. Bhojpuris, Dhangars and Tamils proved pliable labourers and the estates boomed under the new order. But sugar plantations, like all capitalist enterprises, are subject to the normal laws of concentration of capital, cyclical depression and the need to continually habituate workers to the debilitating and alienating conditions of production.[20] The

---

of disposable labour-power.' The pauper section is divided more complexly into three sub-sections. See *Capital*, part 7, chap. 25.

19 See, in addition to Tinker, 'Between Africa', Hugh Tinker, *A new system of slavery: the export of Indian labour overseas, 1830–1920*, Oxford: Oxford University Press, 1974.

20 A general discussion of habituation can be found in a yet unpublished paper by Jeff Henderson and Robin Cohen, 'Work, culture and the dialectics of proletarian habituation', 1977. [The

large estates numbered 200 in 1850, 50 in 1910 and 21 in 1978. With each change in the pattern of ownership and major fluctuation in the world demand and price for sugar, so were there changes in the composition of capital and the consequent reorganization of production. Sections of the rural proletariat were fired, displaced, and pushed off the land they had occupied as tenants or squatters. This was Mauritius's second 'unemployment problem'.

It was one of the contradictions of the ruthless production methods and the back-breaking work that the destabilizing aspects of plantation life had to be paralleled by the creation of an intermediary group, who could supervise, placate or control the labourers and who had something to gain from the system themselves (though not, of course, so much that they could challenge the hegemony of the historic bourgeoisie). Thus, the owners usually worked through *sirdars* (overseers or foremen) and job contractors. This was the origin of another fraction of the petty bourgeoisie. As Seegobin and Collen write:

> These sirdars and job-contractors controlled the working class in exchange for access to land, and a higher wage for lighter work. This extra cash was increased by ending money at high rates of interest to labourers. At the end of the nineteenth century when many sugar estates were selling their marginal land, the sirdars and job-contractors began to buy up land.[21]

---

paper was subsequently published in *Papers in Urban & Regional Studies*, No. 3, 1980, 3–34.]

21 Seegobin and Collen, 'Leta e Eleksion', p. 12.

The stabilization of the plantation system also required that, after 1880 (when recruitment from India virtually creased), the cost of reproduction of labour be met internally. This encouraged the growth of a small planter class whose demands for land were partially assuaged while the cost of the biological reproduction, nutrition, child care and socialization of the estates' future labourers (both part-time and full-time) could be met, not from wages, but from the modest profits the small planters earned from selling their cane to the estate owners' mills. It was as if the latent relative surplus population had been transferred from Chota Nagpur, Lucknow, Patna, the United Provinces and Trichinopoly to within the boundaries of Mauritius itself. The excess supply of labourers could be hired as and when the season demanded it (cutting is only possible for 125 days of the year) and for the rest of the year, or whenever the demand for sugar was low, they could be left to vegetate on their small plots. There are now at least 30,000 of these small plots, often on marginal land.

From the point of view of the historic bourgeoisie, a careful balance had to be struck between stabilizing the small planter class over and above the numbers of permanent employees of the big estates, but not stabilizing them so greatly as to prevent men, women and children coming forward for temporary or seasonal work. Small planters were part-time proletarians, a 'peasantariat' who tried to obtain their own patch of land. These were the people who were thrown about by what Marx called the faux-frais of capitalist production. The best form of social insurance in these circumstances was to have children, preferably male children who could be used as domestic labour on the small farm or join the cutting gangs on the big estates when their family income was depleted.

Two extraneous circumstances reinforced this social tendency to increase the population. The first was the 'baby boom' which accompanied the return of Mauritian soldiers from the war in

1944. The second was improved public health measures after the Second World War. The death rate more than halved between 1946 and 1950 and dropped by about another third by 1964.[22] The result was a rapid increase in the post-1945 population which greatly alarmed colonial officials, government planners and visiting experts. These joined together in a shrill cacophony of Fabian self-righteousness and finger-wagging good sense to pro-duce three major reports, the Luce Report (1958), the Titmus et al. Report (1960), and the Meade et al. Report (1961).[23] In the wide range of evidence they assembled and the sweep of their recommendations, these reports can be seen as representing the high point of Fabian intervention anywhere in the Empire. The economic and social policies they set out still inform the character of official political debate. Sydney Webb's spiritual descendants had answered the call to solve Mauritius's third 'unemployment problem', overpopulation.

Mauritius's fourth and final 'employment problem' is still maturing. It stems from the attempts by the historic bourgeoisie

---

22 Christos Xenos, 'Mauritius: Country Profiles', in *Report issued by the Population Council and the International Institute for the study of human reproduction*, Columbia University, September 1970, 2–3.

23 R. W. Luce, *Report on employment, unemployment and under-employment in the colony*, Sessional Paper no. 7, Port Louis: Mauritius Legislative Council, 1958; R. M. Titmus et al., *Social policies and population growth in Mauritius*, Sessional Paper no. 6, Port Louis: Mauritius Legislative Council, 1960; reprint ed., London: Frank Cass and Co., 1968; and J. E. Meade et al., *The economic and social structure of Mauritius*, Sessional Paper no. 7, Port Louis: Mauritius Legislative Council, 1960; reprint ed., London: Frank Cass and Co., 1968. A tepid attack on Meade's neo-classical approach to economics can be found in John King, 'Mauritius, Malthus and Professor Meade', *Communications Series of the Institute of Development Studies* (Sussex) 49 (January 1970).

to stretch sugar production to its absolute limits. The Lomé agreement signed by the African, Caribbean and Pacific countries with the European Economic Community, served to stabilize a 500,000 ton annual quota at a price equivalent to European beet production, about £180 a ton. Not surprisingly, a spokesman for the Mauritius Chamber of Commerce told The Times correspondent in 1976: 'We are delighted with Lomé.'[24] In 1976 the bourgeoisie saw another chance to increase sugar production – mechanization. In the short-term (perhaps two to three years) destoning and bringing marginal lands into production would employ several thousand labourers. But the real thrust of the bourgeoisie's strategy is large-scale mechanization to reduce the labour component (60 per cent of the cost of production), without which it cannot hope to compete in the long term with the highly successful Australian producers. Mechanization and increased technological inputs are taking several forms: increasing the milling capacity by factory modernization; using chemical ripeners to increase the sucrose content of early maturing varieties of cane; introducing better yielding varieties and fertilizers, and controlling pest diseases and weeds. (The local Sugar Research Institute, generously funded by the bourgeoisie, has pioneered these developments.) Finally, planters are introducing mechanical cutters and grabbers where the land permits this. The effects of these measures will be to displace many cane cutters and estate and mill workers. The cane of the small planter will also become uncompetitive.

'Solving' the unemployment problem

While government officials only dimly apprehend the possible dimensions of the new unemployment problem that the

---

24 *The Times* Special Supplement on Mauritius, 30 June 1976.

bourgeoisie is creating in its lust for profit maximization, strenuous attempts have to be made to reduce the unemployment problem confronting post-independence governments. It is necessary first to give some rough indicators of the size and characteristics of contemporary unemployment. At the time of the last census (1972) there were 41,700 who declared themselves unemployed, compared with 292,600 (1972 figures) in regular employment. The unemployed are thus about 19 per cent of the active labour force. But unemployment is highly skewed in respect of age. It is estimated that 55 per cent of the age group 15–19 is unemployed, while the 20–24 age group has 26 per cent of its members unemployed. The Government's Five Year Plan argues that to achieve the planned full employment by 1980 the growth in employment will need to be 4.7 per cent per year. On the Government's own assumptions, employment in the manufacturing sector will need to grow at about 17 per cent a year between 1974 and 1980. The actual (1974) and target (1980) employment objectives can be seen in Table 1.1. The targets require that 76,000 jobs be created by 1980, a 32 per cent increase

Table 1.1: Official employment objectives (000s)

Sector	1974	1980
Agriculture (including tea and sugar manufacturing)	75.0	81.0 (+8%)
Services (including tourism)	80.0	99.5 (+24%)
Construction	16.0	30.0 (+87.5%)
Manufacturing	30.0	77.0 (+157%)
Other	39.0	28.5 (-27%)

Source: Mauritius: Five Year Plan, Port Louis: Mauritius Government Printer, May 1976, 8–10.

in employment 25 opportunities, and a 20.6 per cent growth rate in the manufacturing sector.[25]

At first sight such dramatic employment targets look like pie in the sky; and at second sight, as I shall argue, the image remains, both in respect of the quantity of jobs created, and (what is also politically significant) their quality. What factors have led the Government and planners into such wild optimism which is unusual, if not unique, in developing countries? These factors, and my own reservations about government thinking, are specified below:

Factor 1

The population growth has slowed down significantly. Fertility rates started dropping after 1964 partly as a result of the massive concentrated effort by foreign aid agencies to assist the local family planning bodies, the Family Planning Association and Action Familiale (a Catholic group offering free thermometers and complicated temperature charts). By 1969 the FPA and AF had received US$ 432,000 in foreign assistance (from eight or nine different bodies) and US$ 297,000 from the Government of Mauritius.[26] Though the family planning organization are loud in trumpeting their own claims for the slowing-down in population growth, the most important factor explaining the maintenance of the drop, is the high participation of young women (16 to 24 years old) in the new industries. They constitute 85 per cent of the workforce in these factories and if they are to hold their jobs, they have to avoid getting pregnant – thus decreasing their overall

---

25 Figures from 'Mauritius' in *Africa: South of the Sahara*, pp. 584, 587; Tinker, 'Between Africa, Asia and Europe', p. 331 and Mauritius: Five Year Plan, Port Louis: Mauritius Government Printer, May 1976, ii, pp. 8–10.

26 Xenos, p. 10.

fertility span. The Government's assumption that population growth will stabilize thus seems valid. But it is important to note that the increasing racist immigration laws in Britain will virtually cut off one fairly widely-used escape valve. Government officials continue to assume an annual figure of 3,000 emigrants.

Factor 2

A rural development programme, financed by the World Bank, and started in 1974 is intended to create temporary work for 7,400. But the long-term effects of this are unclear.

Factor 3

The Travail Pour Tous ('work for all') programme was begun in 1971 and some 18,700 'development workers' were engaged on government-created construction and reclamation projects by 1974. The projects are generally very poorly selected and managed and morale among the workers is abysmal. Quite a number of the work-gang leaders are part-time thugs for the Labour Party and its new-found ally, the PMSD. With low output and high levels of pilfering Travail Pour Tous is becoming increasingly expensive to administer. Tasks are performed with such a notable lack of enthusiasm that it is only with some degree of poetic licence that this can be considered a form of 'job creation' at all. Public criticism of the programme is high, especially insofar as it is used as a reward for the Party's tame lumpen elements. It would seem an invalid assumption made by the Government that such workers can be integrated in normal government departments (one proposed strategy) or that the programme can continue at its present level.

Factor 4

Tourism, according to M. R. Franchette, the Director of Tourism, has provided increases in gross earnings of 800 per cent from

1968. Employment has also risen from perhaps 3,500 (1968) to 9,000 (1976). But 65 per cent of the tourists are South African whites. To plan increases in tourist numbers without a discussion of the long-term prospects of affluent white supremacy or indeed the growth of anti-apartheid sentiment within the country, needs further consideration.

Factor 5

Population stabilization, the rural development programme, the Travail Pour Tous programme and job creation via tourism are all but molehills compared with the mountain of employment that the Government projects for the manufacturing sector (See Table 1.1). It is to this, the central plank of the employment strategy, that we have to pay more attention. The strategy is based on export-oriented manufacturing, with, in its original formulation, envious glances being cast to Hong Kong and Puerto Rico.[27]

Nowadays, export-oriented manufacturing has become the new conventional wisdom, the new El Dorado for developing countries, paraded about in the ILO, UNDP and other international bodies with such an air of discovery that one might think they have never heard of South Korea, Taiwan, China or Hong Kong. To be sure there is a 'new wave' of developing-country manufacturers and one must credit the Mauritian bourgeoisie, this time in alliance with the Labour Party (the leading section of the state bourgeoisie), for being quick off the mark in establishing the Mauritian Export Processing Zones (EPZs). The concessions given to capital, foreign and local, are virtually incredible in their generosity. Here, I can do no more than list (verbatim) some of the many concessions offered to investors:

---

27 Meade, *The economic and social structure of Mauritius*, p. 126.

- total exemption from import duties on goods constituting capital (e.g. machinery, spare parts);
- total exemption from import duties on raw material and semi-finished products (not alcohol or tobacco);
- exemption from corporate tax for a minimum of ten years and a maximum of twenty years;
- no tax on dividends for five years;
- freedom to repatriate profits and dividends;
- grant of permanent residence permits to entrepreneurs and shareholders according to the importance of the investment;
- loans at preferential rates to help import raw materials;
- possibility of renting premises for industrial use;
- favourable labour laws to help export industries achieve their objectives; and
- guarantees against nationalization.[28]

Short of lying on its back and shouting 'Take me', it is difficult to see what else the Government of Mauritius could have done to encourage the entry of foreign capital. But flies have a habit of appearing in even the most unguent of ointments. First, though the EPZs are highly successful in economic returns (the value of total exports from the EPZs increased from 3.9 million Mauritian Rupees (R) in 1971 to R196.2 million in 1975),[29] employment increased from 1,000 in 1971, the first year of operation, to only 14,000 in 1976. Second, the EPZs attracted a number of fly-by-

---

28 For a full list, see Conditions for Setting-up Industrial Undertakings: Mauritius, Brussels: Commissioner of European Communities, 200 Rue de la Loi, 1040 Brussels, 2nd ed., 1974.

29 'Mauritius', *Africa: South of the Sahara*, p. 586.

nighters – Japanese firms manufacturing nearly all the product at home, but interested in getting under the EEC's tariff wall by using Mauritius's Associated Status, and 'runaway shops' which are unlikely to stay for longer than the best of the concessions obtain. Third, successful Mauritian exports like knitwear into France, are meeting the opposition of the Lyon manufacturers who may successfully organize against Mauritian imports. Fourth, many other developing countries are now getting into the act. The expensive long-distance freight between Mauritius and its markets might weaken its competitive position vis-à-vis its competitors. Fifth, 85 per cent of the employment in the EPZ is of women most of whom are new to the employment market. Thus the standing problem of unemployment is barely touched at all. In short, the EPZs, though successful financially, are not likely to generate anything like the volume of employment projected in the Five Year Plan.

Factor 6

As argued before, government assumptions in its employment targets take no account of the possible redundancies flowing from modernization, mechanization and increased technical inputs into sugar. To indicate an increase of 4,000 employees in agricultural employment over the plan period (Table 1.1) seems to be unduly optimistic.

To summarize: the assumptions about population stabilization seem valid, though one has to take account of the increased difficulty of emigration; the Development Workers' Programmes are poorly conceived and managed; employment in tourism has probably peaked; the EPZs are likely to be less successful in job-creation than the Government hopes for; finally, Mauritian sugar producers may lay off agricultural workers and make small planting unviable as they modernize against Australian competition. There are therefore some serious doubts about the presumed quantity of jobs to be created.

But, as important, is the fact that government planners, like many development advisers assume too glibly that the masses can be driven into their units of production like oxen, there to remain dumb with gratification whatever the pay or conditions of work. Space does not permit discussion of the riots, disturbances and strikes of the 1930s and 1940s where the agricultural proletariat fought for better conditions.[30] Suffice it to say that dock workers have a strong union and militant tradition, the rural proletariat is being increasingly organized by unions supporting the MMM (or indeed more radical groups, including Maoist tendencies) and slowly but surely, unionization and organization in the EPZs is undermining the 'favourable labour laws to help export industries achieve their objectives' that Ramgoolam promised his foreign investors. It is thus by no means clear that workers will willingly hump stones off marginal lands, act as pimps, waiters and whores to racist tourists, work in idiotic and meaningless tasks in the Development Works Programme or spend long hours in badly ventilated factories with poor sanitary and safety conditions for a low wage packet. Unemployment is not 'solved' by writing a Five Year Development Plan.

Back to the political arena: a concluding note

The explicit assumption of this paper is that the 'unemployment problem' cannot be detached from class forces and class relations and in particular from how the hegemonic class – in Mauritius, the historic or haute-bourgeoisie – seeks to establish, maintain and enhance its class position vis-à-vis the under-classes.

---

30 But see, for example, Government of Mauritius, *Commission of Enquiry into the Disturbances Which Occurred in the North of Mauritius in 1943*, Report published on behalf of the Government of Mauritius by the Crown Agents for the colonies, London, 1943.

Mauritian politics is essentially, historically and experientially, about how different fractions of the petty bourgeoisie seek to represent (and perhaps misrepresent) the rural proletariat, workers and relative surplus population against the claims and demands of the historic bourgeoisie. Dr Ramgoolam, of course, performed several roles. During the Second World War, he was the guarantor of the loyalties of Indian labourers to the Empire when the bourgeoisie was not far from being Vichyist and a number of Indian nationalists were pro-Japanese.[31] He was also an *interlocuteur valable* between the Governor and his subjects, especially necessary after the 1943 riots of sugar workers. One suspects it was easier for the Governor to talk to him (a doctor trained in London with moderate, Fabian views) than it was for him to interact with the haute-bourgeoisie. Indeed, in the negotiations leading to independence, some Franco-Mauritians raised the possibility of re-joining France, while many more opposed the idea of independence. But the Labour Party Ramgoolam built up also was primarily a party which drew its support partly from urban workers (Creole and Indian) and mainly from rural proletarians and small planters. Class oppression was often expressed in communal terms but it was no less real for that reason – nor, of course does that make the Labour Party 'a communal party'.

Other sections of the established working class (particularly the dock workers) and much of the relative surplus population were to find their petty-bourgeois leadership in the form of the populist rhetoric and 'Bonapartism'[32] of Gaëtan Duval, the leader of the PMSD. Duval has all the vigour of an exciting, though slightly debauched, man of the people in marked contrast to the

31 See Tinker, 'Between Africa', p. 329.

32 The reference here is to Marx's *18th Brumaire*, where Marx acidly describes Louis Napoleon as the 'chief of the lumpenproletariat'.

diminutive, sober, retiring Ramgoolam – blind in one eye since infancy. But charisma is not enough: so the bourgeoisie has to finance Duval's campaigns and make common cause with him, using him to nurse Creole fears about 'Hindu domination'. While Duval can still be effective in pleading the cause of individual workers, constituents and unions he will have a following, but the electorate has shown that it cannot always be fooled by populist rhetoric. The PMSD held 27 seats in 1967, 15 before the December 1967 elect and 8 after it.

What of Berenger and the MMM? Leftists in Mauritius often represent him as yet another petty-bourgeois figure who will travel the same road as Ramgoolam. Some say he is pretty far along it already. Certainly, his opportunistic manoeuvrings within the party, and his 'come hither' signs to Ramgoolam, are strong indications that this is the case. Yet the MMM undoubtedly represents a progressive force, in its stitching together of an effective alliance between many rural proletarians, urban workers and intellectuals, in its relationships with certain trade unions, and in its foreign policy. All of this does not, however, constitute a revolutionary force. Without a stronger challenge, the power of the historic bourgeoisie cannot effectively be challenged, nor can the 'unemployment problem' effectively be solved.

Addendum

This paper was first published as 'The politics of unemployment in Mauritius', *Manpower & Unemployment Research*, 11(1), April 1978, 3–18. It was clearly a political intervention directed, at that time, against the technocratic language that development experts used to describe and solve unemployment. I insisted that unemployment was not a natural condition simply 'found' in developing countries as they had implied, but one that had historical origins and class dimensions. I do not regret my use of

Marxist analysis which yielded key insights, though the constant iteration of the word 'bourgeoisie' now looks a bit tedious. I was also, as it turned out, too harsh on Hugh Tinker, who I subsequently met and grew to like and respect. His views were more complex than a first reading of his article indicated. Again, I was trying to counteract the conventional wisdom of the time – virtually every established social scientist simply assumed that ethnicity and communalism explained everything in Africa and 'the Third World' (as it was called then) more generally. Though I was right to question Tinker in 1976–78, communal sentiments did indeed make a much stronger appearance in the 1990s and noughties. Finally, I was too pessimistic about the capacity of the post-independence government to tackle unemployment. In fact, employment opportunities in manufacturing, tourism and service industries have placed Mauritius in a virtuous league of middle-income countries with relatively low of unemployment (7.4 per cent in July 2015). This is partly the result of population decline (which I anticipated) and the intervention of some of the progressive forces whose provenance I described in the article. I need to concede, however, that conventional market strategies also were deployed to good effect and the pay-off from tourism proved much more sustainable than I had assumed possible.

Chapter 2
Althusser meets Anancy: structuralism and popular protest in the history of Jamaica

Robin Cohen

L. Althusser: Marxist philosopher in the French Communist Party.

Anancy: Jamaican spider-man of popular legend who uses his superior cunning to outwit the rich and powerful.

This review article is primarily an appreciation, and in only a limited way a critique, of Ken Post's three major books interpreting Jamaican history from the 1930s to the end of the Second World War. The books are: Ken Post. 1978. *Arise ye starvelings: the Jamaican labour rebellion of 1938 and its aftermath*, The Hague: Martinus Nijhoff, pp. 502 (hereafter *Arise ye starvelings*) and his two volumes jointly titled *Strike the iron: a colony at war, Jamaica 1939–45*, New Jersey: Humanities Press in association with the Institute of Social Studies, 1981, pp. 567. As the pages of the last two volumes are numbered in sequence, I shall refer hereafter to *Strike the iron*, followed by a page number. My task is primarily expository at this stage, largely because for a book of such imagination and ambition, *Arise ye starvelings* was met with an astonishing lack of scholarly and political discussion. The author clearly is concerned that such a fate will befall his current two volumes, for he briefly repeats some of the theoretical formula and conclusions of *Arise ye starvelings*. It is heartening to note that, despite initially meeting some stony ground, Ken Post announces that he still intends to plough the same furrow. These first thousand pages are to be part of a series on the modern history of Jamaica.

It is perhaps worthwhile hazarding a few guesses about why *Arise ye starvelings* failed to take off. An inappropriate publisher, the price of the book and lack of commitment in promotion no doubt have something to do with it. Post has had to suffer what many writers would recognize as a common plight, the alienation of the product of his mental labour-power. Indeed, this should be of no surprise to a socialist intellectual – a book, once it has entered the mode of distribution, is as much connected to the direct producer as is a typewriter or a plug spanner. Yet this cannot be the total explanation – for other outrageously priced books have met at least a critical, if not popular success. Has the marketing appeal of 'The International' failed? I suspect that the period of the Spanish Civil War was indeed probably the last time the lines from which Post's titles are derived, were widely sung, at least in the Anglophone world. Who now would instantly recognize:

> Arise! ye starvelings from your slumbers
> Arise! ye criminals of want...

Or the later lines:

> Each at his forge must do his duty
> And strike the iron when it's hot?

However, these remarks sidestep the principal problem with Post's writings on Jamaica, i.e. that they appeal to no single readership. But this commercial weakness is the obverse face of

Post's formidable academic strength. The books essentially combine a fundamental and hard-headed reconstruction of structuralist social theory, an analysis of popular protest fairly close to the traditions established by the English social historians, a commentary on the contours of development/underdevelopment in a peripheral social formation (he calls Jamaica 'a colonial instance of British capitalism' in *Strike the iron*: 2) and, finally, a more conventional history of decolonization and the growth of nationalist and socialist sentiments and practices.

The uses of structuralism

For those interested in his theoretical contribution, Post will not satisfy the metatheorists concerned only to examine the internal logic or, more usually, the inconsistencies of Marxist theory. Not that he cannot trade the apt quote or bon mot with the best of them. The footnotes are littered with references to Vol. III, *The Grundrisse*, Gramsci, Męszaros, Hindess & Hirst, Ollman, Meillassoux and, most influentially, Althusser and Poulantzas. But Post's task does not become overdetermined by the siren of pure theory. His is a more instrumental, rawer purpose. Given a particular expository and political problem, how can you make a reconstructed Marxist theory work for you? The result is, for me, a wholly appropriate and satisfactory wielding of a conceptual meat cleaver, where many others have hesitantly used a cheeseparer. Others again, like Thompson, have woven an elaborate spider's web (to change the metaphor) wherein to trap the theoretical gadflies of our age. For those who found the literary intricacies and political barbs of Thompson's *Poverty of Theory* just a little 'over the top', Post's meat cleaver approach might provide some relief.

However, be warned. At first sight the whole Althusserian/ Poulantzian beastie appears intact. The 'social formation' characterizes and is characterized by 'modes of production'. 'Structures' define 'practices' and their 'instances' by 'specifying both the ways in which they bring together actors and means of productions and their spatial structures' (*Arise ye starvelings*: 15). The 'power bloc' must be distinguished from 'the ruling class', 'the state apparatus' and the bureaucracy which staffs it (*Arise ye starvelings*: 61). On closer examination, the decisive breaks with Althusserianism become apparent. Post hacks off a limb or two with no compunction and no regrets. Some blows are aimed in the direction of ostensibly restoring a dogmatism. For example, the author bluntly asserts that of the three practices he considers – economic, political and what he calls cognitive – 'economic practice is indeed the major determinant' (*Arise ye starvelings*: 17). This allows Post to break directly with the sort of causal democracy he sees in Althusser. I quote:

> Althusser always seems in danger of attenuating determination by the economy to the point where it not only becomes distant from immediate action in society but ceases to have a direct connection with it. It is necessary to read Capital again and to give preference to the original over the exegesists. [For Marx] ... the economy always plays the principal role; but the totality of structures in a particular social formation is articulated in such a way that economic practice is given its full expression by the structures and contradictions of other practices. Althusser is quite correct to point out the complexity of determination, but we must not follow him into a sort of pluralism, in which economic factors share a place with others, which is equal in all but a payment of lip service to 'the last instance'.
>
> (*Arise ye starvelings*: 70, Note 4)

Elsewhere, Althusser's central failing is more pithily exposed – Althusser is said to mistakenly insists on a totality without a centre. Is it too glib to suggest, as Post, a good materialist, does not, that those whom the gods wish to destroy are enjoined to imagine a whole without a core and autonomous parts which none the less rotate dominance amongst themselves (see *Arise ye starvelings*: 17)? Post's orthodoxy on the issue of the economic does not, however, produce a blind adherence to a formula at the expense of an analysis. He carefully specifies the senses in which he sees economic practice as determinant (*Arise ye starvelings*: 17) and, far from neglecting political and cognitive practices, devotes the bulk of his narrative to these aspects.

Post's instrumental use of theory also leads him to reject flatly Poulantzas's characterization of the state, even though he adopts some of his vocabulary ('power bloc'). The state is not a general 'factor of cohesion'. Poulantzas virtually idealizes the state into a Hegelian absolute, exaggerates its role in reproduction and fails to separate contradictions arising in all parts of the social formation as a result of class struggles appropriate to the totality (*Arise ye starvelings*: 72, Note 28). Post is only marginally kinder to Mao Zedong, who made 'important though underdeveloped suggestions' (*Arise ye starvelings*: 27) on the nature of contradiction. Mao distinguishes between primary (principal) and secondary contradictions, the primary and secondary aspects of a single contradiction and between antagonistic and non-antagonistic contradictions. For Post, both Mao and Althusser use such distinctions pragmatically rather than dialectically. He worries away at a formulation which expresses the dialectic aspect ('A contradiction is a relationship between two moments each of which is a condition of existence of the other', *Strike the iron*: 4), but also hierarchizes and distinguishes, in structures and practices, moments and classes, those contradictions that are necessarily contradictory, those that may be antagonistic but are derivative and those that are secondary and non-antagonistic (*Arise ye starvelings*: 27–30). Though the theory is challenging, I did not always find the exemplars that convincing. For example, while there is a succinct and insightful discussion of why the relationship between Jamaican peasants and workers was non-antagonistic, why the relationship between the petty bourgeoisie and capitalists was decisively antagonistic seemed to me to be less clearly established (*Strike the iron*: 23–5).

I am, however, straying into the narrative itself slightly prematurely. Perhaps it is only necessary to conclude this discussion of Post's theoretical interventions by saying that he directs his cleaver with equal force at definitions of the 'mode of production', where he disposes in a few pages (*Arise ye starvelings*: 21–5) of the ridiculous confusions that sought to identify separate modes for each country or culturally specific zone (like the Andean mode, the Kenyan mode). He also includes a complex discussion on the nature of 'determination' (*Arise ye starvelings*: 51–74), on distinctions he introduces between 'conjunctures', 'conjunctions' and 'rhythms' (*Strike the iron*: 5–8) and on questions of 'consciousness' (*Arise ye starvelings*: 53–60, *Strike the iron*: 37–43). As if this were not a rich enough diet, there are comments on how consciousness becomes 'refracted' and 'concentrated', on how classes are 'segmented', 'stratified' and 'fractionalized' and much, much more. Enough, in short, to keep a couple of theoretically-inclined graduate students discoursing for a year or three.

Post as social historian

As indicated earlier, Post's account, despite its structuralist appearance, is also close in style and spirit to the social history often exemplified by Thompson's *Making of the English Working*

Class or, in more recent years, by the work of The History Workshop. Of course, as those of us who have worked in peripheral zones with large illiterate populations have found, there is a special difficulty. Grassroots evidence has to be garnered from a variety of sources, often from testimony hostile to the class interests of the popular classes. In Post's case, given that the events he describes are within the living memory of many Jamaican workers and peasants, I had hoped for somewhat more in the way of oral history and interviews with some of the participants in the events he describes – particularly the rebellion of 1938. But Post's talents as a historian lie rather in extracting the fullest possible measure of significance from archival material (in the Public Records Office, Jamaica and Washington), down often to the most minute comment on the flimsiest of memoranda. He has also extensively used newspapers and party and trade union records as well as the papers made available by leading Jamaican leftists like Richard Hart (himself engaged on a history of the slave period in Jamaica), to situate and document worker and peasant struggles.

Virtually the whole of *Arise ye starvelings* centres around one set of events (a 'break event' as Post calls it) between April and June 1938 when workers and peasants struck, rioted and demonstrated. 'What happened' is described in just nine pages (*Arise ye starvelings*: 276–84). Why it happened and how to analyse its significance and consequences fills the other 500 pages of *Arise ye starvelings* and a good deal of *Strike the iron*. Briefly, a riot on the Frome estate of a British company, the West Indies Sugar Company on 29 April 1938, was followed by a strike. One hundred police rushed in, killing four people, wounding 14 more and arresting 85. Following a long-established tradition of protest dating from the slave period, cane was fired at three of WISCO's estates. Public meetings and marches in Kingston followed and late in May dock workers, then public-sector workers in Kingston, came out on strike, overturning stinking garbage and blocking the streets of the city. Elsewhere in Jamaica, in Spanish Town and in the rural estates, telephone lines were cut, the police stoned, roads blocked and fires started.

It was, in short, the closest Jamaica had ever come to experiencing a revolution, combining conflicts between capitalist agriculture and a debilitated independent peasantry, between capital and labour, and involving a temporary and partial alliance between worker and peasant, employed and unemployed. Yet, as Post insists, a revolution it was not. Indeed, one of the starting points of his analysis is that Marxism must be able to give an adequate account of failure as well as success, of refracted forms of consciousness, of the capacity of capital to recover, of the limits to particular courses of action by rebellious workers and peasants. This task is approached exhaustively and one after another of the economic, political and cognitive practices of each of the classes and intermediate strata are dissected and mounted onto the explanatory frieze. Of all these procedures, the most rigorously and elegantly executed are those concerned with the cognitive practices of the dominated classes. Thank goodness Post has had the good sense to ignore or reject 'the ideological level', a phrase advanced particularly by Althusser. It is unclear why Althusser adopts 'ideological' as a general term, when Marx quite clearly reserves it principally for a specialized discussion of how the bourgeoisie seeks to legitimate itself? Indeed, Althusser uses the notion in precisely the classical way in his seminal essay contrasting the repressive with the ideological state apparatus. It is possible that the functionalist tone so evident in Althusser and Poulantzas is signified by their use of the 'ideological level' and derived from their understanding the social formation largely in terms of the views and actions of the dominating classes?

Post resists my simplifications, but perhaps I should also be a little cautious in embracing a term so rooted in individualist and developmental psychology as cognitive practice. Despite an initial caution, Post fashions it well enough for the purposes of examining the various states and forms of consciousness of the Jamaican poor. Would that he had abandoned the notion of 'false' and 'true' consciousness in his theory as he had largely in his analysis. Therein Post allows a more inclusive vision. Racial, religious, nationalist and class consciousness are all characteristic forms of opposition – but, of course, with varying degrees of significance – to the Jamaican instance of the capitalist mode of production.

As his central example of race consciousness, Post provides an informed view of Garveyism. Indeed *Arise ye starvelings* opens with an account of the (real) debate in Kingston in 1929 between Garvey and Otto Huiswood, a Surinamese who had joined the Communist Party (USA), on the motion that 'The Negro problem can only be solved by International Labour cooperation between white and black labour'. Is there anything new under the sun? His discussion of the religious consciousness amongst Jamaican peasants and workers is even better, with a rich account of Bedwardism, a religious movement with strong political overtones. Bedward was said to have told a crowd of 1,000 in 1895, that: 'We ... are the true people; the white men are hypocrites, robbers and thieves; they are all liars. Hell will be your portion if you do not use up and crush the white man. The time is coming, I tell you the time is coming.' In addition to Bedwardism, Post includes a sensitive portrayal of Rastafarianism (on which he was one of the earliest of contemporary commentators in an essay published in 1970), which lays great emphasis on the influence of events in Ethiopia itself, like the crowning of Haile Selassie and the Italian invasion, on the way in which the movement developed in Jamaica.

51

The question of nationalism, a form of consciousness of course shared with other classes, including the indigenous bourgeoisie, is best left until I consider Post's treatment of the People's National Party (PNP). What has to be, at least briefly, summarized here is his discussion of the extent to which class consciousness developed before, during or as a consequence of the events of 1938. Let me perhaps start by citing his slightly later and cautious judgement published in *Strike the iron*. On the one hand, in the aftermath of 1938 there was 'a growing inability of the power block to reproduce false consciousness and the acquiring by workers and peasants of a capacity for collective class action through organization, which implies the existence of defined goals, shared beliefs, hierarchies of authority and leaders' (*Strike the iron*: 38). On the other hand, he considers that while 1938 forced important changes in political organization and in class alignments, 'it did not produce a distinctive and autonomous politics of labour on the part of the workers and their clear alliance with the peasants' (*Strike the iron*: 48).

Why, again, did 1938 stop short of a revolutionary trajectory? If we confine ourselves to the cognitive practices of the subordinate classes, it is not so much that they were victims of false consciousness, for as we have seen, religious, racial and nationalist cognitive practices were in many ways complementary to class consciousness. But these forms had inherent limits as means of cognitive opposition to the power bloc in Jamaica. Further, these limits became clear in the context of two other interrelated problems.

One concerned the question of the leadership of the workers' movement; the second, what might be described as the dialectic between Quashee and Anancy. The leadership issue hinged essentially around two elements: the backroom, but essentially limited, influence of the left (which Post none the less minutely documents) and, by contrast, the overwhelming dominance of Alexander Bustamante – at the time of the rebellion the Treasurer of the Jamaican Workers' & Tradesmen's Union and later to become boss of the Bustamante Industrial Trade Union (BITU). Busta was a complex figure – a moneylender who started his political life in Jamaica at the age of 50 in defence of (wait for it!) beekeepers. A man with more than a touch of braggadocio, hubris and egotism, he was also capable of being swayed by a crowd into radical, even wild, sentiments, yet simultaneously representing himself to the power bloc as a moderating influence. Post presents a rounded picture of Busta (*Arise ye starvelings*: 250–61) showing how he was able to convince workers that what was often in his own interest, or what served to dampen down class conflict, were simply cunning means of deceiving the employers or the government. That he, in short, was Anancy in modern guise – darting, biting and stinging at the monolithic monster that oppressed Quashee for whom he petitioned and fought, but with whom there was final identification.

Who then was Quashee? Originally, this was the slave owners' generic name for any male slave, but it came to be associated with a Jamaican version of the 'Coon' or 'Sambo' (see *Arise ye starvelings*: 112, Notes 71, 72) – a clownish, irresponsible, overgrown child. Of course, playing out this role was itself a form of resistance, but in Jamaica Quashee had a more sinister side. As Post puts it: the rich and powerful feared Quashee for they suspected or believed that 'the clown masked a savage and the irresponsibility an irrational violence' (*Strike the iron*: 39). But neither side of Quashee was a remotely adequate foil to his oppressor. Quashee the Sambo, expressed largely a privatized, individualized mimicry of the superordinate class but one which could not galvanize his own class. Quashee the Atavist invoked spine-chilling fears in the dead of the night, but in the cold light of dawn could not organize, command the sources of legitimized violence, nor seize the instruments of production. Quashee perforce could not represent himself. He had to be represented. And in 1938 this meant by the tricky Anancy whose cunning and duplicity could not altogether be trusted to work solely against Quashee's enemies and who seemed to enjoy playing the game more than leading his side to victory.

Some of the last strokes of gloss are my own, but it is from such subtle pastels and bold colours that Post assembles his picture of the revolutionary failure of 1938. It is a sustained, almost merciless and sometimes brilliant piece of social history and it is this aspect of Post's work for which most praise is due.

Development and underdevelopment

Post's writings can be used to illuminate debates about development/underdevelopment and can be read also at the level of a conventional history of decolonization. Certainly the contribution to the development debate is indirect. A.G. Frank, a guru of the trade, merits only one footnote where, in typical style, he is cleaved down to size:

> Frank's insistence on underdevelopment as a creation of capitalism is acceptable, but he fails to distinguish between phases in the emergence of metropolitan capitalism, a phenomenon which he also totally fails to grasp on the theoretical level. ... To adopt Frank's views would be to label both slave Jamaica and 18th century Britain with the blanket term 'capitalist', thus obscuring the crucial changes in Britain and its colony.
> (*Arise ye starvelings*: 45, Note 16)

But this general attack is an aside, and one in which Post even makes the uncharacteristic slip of identifying a 'British' mode of production. His main contribution to the development field is to occupy long-recognized lacunae in the analysis of under-developed social formations. In particular, he goes a long way towards developing a class analysis – with historical depth and sociological precision – relevant to such areas. Not that Post is pursuing quite so lonely a task in this respect. Leys, Shivji, Mamdani, Bartra, Shanin, Rey, Kitching, Stavenhagen and many others have made notable contributions to this task. In this respect, Post is simply adding to the climate of opinion that seeks a more fine-combed, situationally specific and sociologically informed view of peripheral societies than that provided for us by radical trade theorists (Emmanuel 1972; Amin 1974; Frank 1967), whose work has often acted as a surrogate for such an analysis. Just to make this point a little clearer – this is not a general denunciation of the three authors just mentioned. Rather, I simply suggest that, while their work is essential to understanding some of the dynamics of modern imperialism, it cannot be substituted for the kind of internal analysis that Post undertakes.

He summarizes the problem in this way. Classes are imbedded in a structure that is 'fluid and forming rather than fixed and frozen'. In Jamaica, the distinctive relationships and some of the determinants of formations are particularly difficult to describe given the impingement of metropolitan influences. Thus, he has to take account of 'classes with a common historical origin in the same mode of production', as well as combinations of classes 'whose constituent elements originated in different historical periods and from different modes of production'. Thirdly, given the uneven development of classes, he has to take account of strata, fractions and segments within a class. Finally, he deals with strata and social categories that may have some class-like characteristics but are strictly speaking not themselves classes

(*Strike the iron*: 12). This comprehensive vision somewhat separates Post's class analysis from some of the sympathetic authors mentioned, whose views are often more narrowly identified with their analysis of a particular class – Shanin for the peasantry, Leys for the indigenous bourgeoisie, Shivji for the bureaucratic bourgeoisie. Post generously spreads his vision across four classes – the capitalists, the workers, the petty bourgeoisie, and a set of 'middle strata' located between the capitalists and the other classes. Perhaps the only note of dissent I would sound is that I found his analysis of the petty bourgeoisie (that very muddy class as Bechhofer and others have recently reminded us), somewhat confusing, somewhat too derivative of Poulantzas's discussion, and not sufficiently clearly separated from the middle strata (*Strike the iron*: 25–6).

Post has also filled a gap in the development literature by providing a case study detailing the texture of metropolitan/satellite relations. Many discussions of underdevelopment fail precisely because of their inability to find an appropriate level of analysis. Using a geographical unit clearly does not answer the legitimate objections to such a focus argued by dependency or world systems analysts. At the same time the global determinism and formal chains of causality derived from such perspectives ignore the situationally specific, while grossly underrating the political and cognitive (to use Post's term) practices of the actors concerned.

Thus, in Post's account, while it is always important to refer to the world situation (perhaps particularly so, for *Strike the iron* deals with the war period), the 'rhythm' of the war and of underdeveloped colonial capitalism proceed at different rates (*Strike the iron*: 245). The first rhythm ultimately 'asserted a dominance' over the rhythm based on the 'long-term decline of British imperial capitalism and its ruling class' and the short-term rhythm based on the Jamaican structure of production, its sources of public finance, its capacity to export and its labour market (*Strike the iron*: 6). The war rhythm dramatically escalated, as German U-boats sunk allied oil tankers and cargo ships in the Caribbean. By mid-1942, with precious oil being diverted to metropolitan war purposes, and with the Jamaican economy crucially dependent on imports and exports, the island was plunged into a social and economic crisis which propelled constitutional change (*Strike the iron*: 245–305).

But the compelling force of changes at the global level is never allowed to explain everything. Instead, we have a careful account of how the war permitted the USA to insert itself, and ultimately substitute itself, for Britain's metropolitan control. The personalities and practices of colonial officials and contending sections of the British power bloc are likewise documented. Finally, the class alignments, electoral contests and the institutionalization of class struggles on the island itself are all analysed, particularly in the final volume of *Strike the iron*. Before discussing briefly how Post handles these themes, I cannot resist quoting a story Post recounts about the period when US capital was about to make significant inroads into the Caribbean. So weakened was British imperialism that Churchill permitted the USA to buy, lease or develop bases all over the Anglophone Caribbean for an unequal exchange of 50 old destroyers. So blind were some colonial officials to the loss of their power in the Caribbean that they totally misjudged Charles W. Taussig, Roosevelt's confidante and Caribbean expert who organized a mission to the Caribbean in December 1940. While Taussig was cabling Washington that 'if the President should decide to assume active leadership in world social and economic reconstruction, the British islands of the Caribbean would undoubtedly fall into line', the Colonial Office official in charge of Development and Welfare spent his time sneering at the Americans spouting mere 'bilge' and their use of an excessive amount of chewing gum (*Strike the iron*: 138, 139). Though such minutiae do not constitute a theory of the transition from metropole to metropole (the germs of one are rather in Post's notion of differential rhythms), at least they are an improvement on the total absence of such a problem in Frank's original metropolitan/satellite model.

The beginnings of decolonization

I have characterized this last aspect of Post's work as perhaps the most conventional and therefore requiring less comment by me. Yet in terms of its weight, a final chapter of *Arise ye starvelings* and the good part of *Strike the iron* concerns itself with the rise of the nationalist parties, the People's National Party (PNP) and the Jamaica Labour Party (JLP), the evolution of official colonial policy to Jamaica, the movement of the labour movement to a position of alliance with the parties, and the electoral and other contests held to establish who should ultimately inherit the colonial state.

No doubt much of the material will be of great interest to specialist historians in that it combines US, British and Jamaican sources and neatly contrasts the often divergent conclusions that emerge, but I did find myself skipping lightly through some of the text. Being more than somewhat selective, let me identify and briefly comment on six of Post's major historical themes:

- Post shows how the state – in the form of the colonial bureaucracy – sought to use the war as a way of solidifying the population behind its rule (*Strike the iron*: Ch. 4). On the whole I had always assumed that this legitimating function had been easily achieved. While there was initially little enthusiasm for open expressions of loyalty, an American intelligence report in 1942 wrongly claimed that 'the natives are unruly, very anti-Government, and anti-American. An open break is expected at any time and violence and bloodshed feared' (*Strike the iron*: 248).

- Post is excellent on demonstrating how the passing of the Colonial Welfare and Development Acts in 1940 was linked with an attempt to control class conflict through economic and social measures. Moreover, he argues that incorporation through welfare, was rehearsed in the colonies before it was applied in the metropole after 1945 (*Strike the iron*: Ch. 5).

- In his analysis of the PNP, he argues that, despite the alliance with the BITU and the formal declaration of the belief in socialism, the middle and rightist leadership of the party (and the left for tactical reasons also) saw no incompatibility between such an alliance or such an ideological espousal and the process of a negotiated package of self-government within the British Empire (*Strike the iron*: Ch. 7 et seq.).

- Post makes a convincing case for arguing that as early as 1942, with the failure to support the left (who were incarcerated by the government), and the alienation of the peasantry, the workers' movement had effectively abandoned the terrain of class struggle to electoral and constitutional struggle (*Strike the iron*: Chs. 10 & 11). This was to determine the basic character of Jamaican political struggle until the 1960s and 1970s.

- In a like manner the PNP, despite its 'socialism', saw no problem in first arguing for self-government (a phase in which capitalists, workers and peasants were seen to be united) to be followed later by socialism. As if espousing the cause of national capital were not enough, even the left in the party were quite willing to see participation by US companies like Colgate Palmolive, if they were able to help solve the unemployment problem. And this openness to North American capital came just at the moment when Alcoa and Reynolds were plotting, scheming and leaning on the British to let them have the lion's share of Jamaica's newly discovered aluminium wealth. The root of post-colonial domination lay therefore in these early tactical errors.

- Post's account concludes with an account of the electoral contest of December 1944 in which the JLP, a populist and recently established party set up by Bustamante, rather to most observers' surprise, trounced the PNP (*Strike the iron*: Ch. 18). By the end of the war the political balance rotated uneasily between the Labour Government in Britain, the still considerable effective power of the colonial bureaucracy and the leadership of the JLP (*Strike the iron*: 539). In short, the spirit of 1938, of independent initiatives by workers and peasants, had evaporated in the fog of constitutionalism and in the mists of bourgeois nationalism.

A final word

What was a surprise to observers in 1944, as it was also to those who witnessed the 1981 election in Jamaica, was the way in which radical and even revolutionary sentiments could be deflected into a party like the JLP. This is less surprising when we think of the dialectic between the two faces of Quashee on the one hand and Anancy (symbolically Busta, the BITU, the JLP and now Seaga) on the other. It is Anancy who ultimately seizes the political initiative and seeks to represent, or misrepresent, the popular will. But as Jamaican folklore sometimes hints, Anancy does not appear entirely fortuitously. As Post might say, the conditions of his emergence are structurally determined by a conjunction ('the coming together of class elements which have been developing at different rhythms', *Strike the iron*: 7). It is in the coupling together of a critical and instrumental structuralism with the richness of a good social history, that Post's central achievement lies. Even those with no interest in Jamaica could profit by sampling the result.

References

Post, Ken. 1978. *Arise ye starvelings: the Jamaican labour rebellion of 1938 and its aftermath*, The Hague: Martinus Nijhoff.

Post, Ken. 1981. *Strike the iron: a colony at war, Jamaica 1939–45*, New Jersey: Humanities Press in association with the Institute of Social Studies. 2 volumes.

Addendum

This review article was published first in *The Sociological Review*, May 1982, 345–57, a journal, which under the imaginative editorship of Ronnie Frankenberg, carried unusual items rather than the humdrum stuff designed for resumes that seems to dominate so many other professional journals. For a time (1966–8), Ken Post was the supervisor of my doctorate which, like his own first work, was on Nigeria. Later, and more coincidentally, I also worked at the University of the West Indies (though he was in Jamaica and I followed a few years later in Trinidad). Our friendship, and overlapping interests and career patterns have not, I trust, influenced my considered position that he was one of the most original and scholarly academics working on international labour studies and the developing world more generally. The very length, detail and complexity of his work inhibits any easy summary, but I hope this extended review of his Jamaican books will provide some appreciation of his important contribution. Sadly, Ken Post died on 13 March 2017 in The Hague, aged 82, just as I was completing this book. My obituary can be found online.

Chapter 3
Crisis in the Caribbean:
internal transformations and
external constraints

Fitzroy Ambursley and Robin Cohen

This chapter is a slightly amended Introduction to a book (Fitzroy Ambursley and Robin Cohen (eds.) *Crisis in the Caribbean*, 1983) drawing together analyses of some of the most salient political developments in the circum-Caribbean after 1979. Since that year, we argued, there was a qualitative heightening of class contradictions in most countries and a growing crisis of US foreign policy in the region. The Grenadian revolution of March 1979 and the overthrow of the Somoza dictatorship in Nicaragua four months later were the decisive elements in the overall situation. These popular struggles shaped the context of subsequent events, such as the military coups in El Salvador and Suriname, the political turmoil during the October 1980 elections in Jamaica and the murder of Walter Rodney in Guyana. Indeed, one could say that 1979 opened up a new period in the Caribbean, a period exhibiting four main characteristics:

1. The consolidation of revolutionary governments in Grenada and Nicaragua, providing a more radical model of political transformation than those of either the former Manley regime in Jamaica or the government of Forbes Burnham in Guyana [Burnham came to power in 1974].

2. The political impact of the Grenadian and Nicaraguan events in bolstering the strategic position of the Cuban state and providing it with more consistent and durable allies in the Caribbean.

3. The emergence of the oil-based economic power of Venezuela and Mexico as a new and complicating factor in the determination of US foreign policy in the region. While the growing influence of these two countries was viewed, quite correctly, with some apprehension by smaller countries in the Caribbean basin, Mexico and Venezuela also adopted a posture which, on certain key questions, clashed with the policies of the US State Department. The opposition which both regimes, along with other members of the Organization of American States (OAS), expressed to any direct US intervention during the revolution in Nicaragua was the most important example of this. However, the huge external debts that Mexico had incurred by mid-1982 limited the extent to which it could oppose the US.

4. The strengthening of political and military ties between Washington and the traditional pro-US parties in the region in the wake of events in Grenada and Nicaragua. Electoral contests and political debate in a number of the smaller territories evinced a much sharper polarization between radical and conservative programmes. At the same time, the contradictions of dependent development continued to manifest themselves even in more stable and economically 'successful' territories such as Barbados, Trinidad and Tobago, and Puerto Rico.

While Washington's counter-offensive scored certain victories – the most significant being the electoral success of the Jamaica Labour Party (JLP) in Jamaica – the general context remained quite explosive with the possibilities of further revolutionary advances on the Central American isthmus in El Salvador and Guatemala. Hence, whatever the vicissitudes of the political situation from month to month and from country to country, we noted that the crisis in the Caribbean was going to be both protracted and fraught with a good deal of uncertainty.

The countries selected for our book were chosen to convey the full dimensions of the regional economic and political crisis. We included studies from each of the four principal linguistic domains. Three were ostensibly stable territories (St Vincent, the French Antilles and Trinidad and Tobago). Another chosen set of countries (Jamaica, Guyana and Suriname), while being prone to a good deal of internal violence or dramatic shifts in government, had nonetheless undergone no radical structural transformations. Finally, the book included those countries in the region (Cuba, Grenada, El Salvador and Nicaragua) that had experienced a revolutionary trajectory of some significant degree.

Internal transformations

The locus of underdevelopment

Most of the case studies in *Crisis in the Caribbean* sought to explain Caribbean underdevelopment mainly in terms of class relations and of the insertion of these countries into a subordinate relationship with the capitalist world economy. As such, they offered more complex and multiform explanations of the region's impoverishment than those offered by the then fashionable 'plantation-economy' theory. Although one of protagonists of the model of the pure plantation, Beckford, moved beyond this framework (Beckford and Witter 1982), the paradigmatic basis of much Caribbean scholarly writing was set by this perspective (Beckford 1972; Levitt and Best 1978). The plantation-economy thesis is, in essence, a Caribbean version of dependency theory. Many studies based on it contained valuable material on the misallocation of resources engendered by estate production for export, while a number of writers in this school made acute observations about the exploitative nature of the connection between the periphery and the metropole. But such studies were often vitiated by their failure to take into account the role played by indigenous ruling classes in propping up and defending the dependent capitalist system. Moreover, as a number of the studies contained in this volume indicate, there has been a progressive shift by the dominant classes of the Caribbean, and by the metropolitan interests that supported these classes, away from purely agricultural production. Thus, an attempt to conceptualize these societies primarily in terms of the plantation unit bears little relation to the dynamics of capital accumulation in the region.

The parasitism, the retrogressive and surrogate nature of the local ruling class were stressed, in particular, in the chapters on El Salvador and on Jamaica by Dunkerley [*Crisis* Ch. 6] and Ambursley [*Crisis* Ch. 4]. In criticizing the political programme of the Partido Comunista de El Salvador (PCS), Dunkerley pointed to the absence of an independent industrially based national bourgeoisie. He argued that the economic boom of the 1960s was sponsored by the landed oligarchy in concert with foreign capital, but that the continued hegemony of the oligarchy and its direct control over the state apparatus had thwarted attempts at land reform and frustrated plans to increase consumer demand through income redistribution.

A similar line of argument was put forward by Ambursley in his assessment of the Manley era in Jamaica. He highlighted the critical role that foreign investment in bauxite played in the Jamaican economy and the extreme dependence of the local bourgeoisie on inflows of capital, raw materials and fuels. Although Manley's attempt to renegotiate the terms of the island's domination by imperialism could hardly be thought of as radical, it nonetheless unleashed a chain reaction which pitted the local capitalist class against the People's National Party (PNP). Ambursley again emphasized the importance of the character of the ruling class in explaining the sustained depression of the Grenadian economy under Gairy [*Crisis* Ch. 9]. He drew attention to the preponderance of the comprador bourgeoisie and showed how its pre-eminence was cemented by the lending policies of foreign-owned commercial banks, by tourism and by the stagnation of domestic agricultural production. The corrupt and idiosyncratic nature of the Gairy regime merely added a new dimension to the inertia and limited horizons of this class. Thus, while there is an evident crisis of accumulation in the region, it stemmed as much from the underdeveloped, compliant and frequently corrupt nature of the local ruling classes, as from a structural and largely outdated abstraction like 'the plantation economy'.

The crisis of the state

The central feature of the state in the 'Third World' is that it provides the basis for primitive accumulation for the native bourgeois classes, since both the internal social structure and external capital limit the scope of independent development in the productive spheres. The expanded role of the state in numerous countries of the capitalist periphery does not necessarily reflect any radicalization of these regimes, but corresponds rather to the exigencies of national capital accumulation and to the realities of the world economy. While, on the one hand, the local capitalist class can only develop with the assistance of the bourgeois state, on the other hand, foreign capital has increasingly adopted a strategy of allying itself with the local bourgeoisie through 'joint ventures' patent and licensing agreements, loans and credits. Four of the chapters in Crisis addressed themselves specifically to this question.

Thomas explained how the expansion of the state sector in Guyana, to encompass some 80 per cent of the local economy, was the outcome of two distinct but complementary stratagems: firstly, an aspiration on the part of the petty-bourgeois elements inside the People's National Congress (PNC) to use the state apparatus as an instrument of 'class creation'; and, secondly, a move by the multinational sugar and bauxite-alumina companies to alter the terms of their domination of Guyanese society. The net result of the government's commercial 'repurchase' of these companies was to turn national assets into a national foreign debt. A heavy premium was thereby placed on all subsequent foreign-exchange earnings. Thomas sharply criticized commentators who saw the growth of state control as a move to the left by the PNC regime. His principal thesis was that the advent of state capitalism led ineluctably to an increase in government repression, since it was basically designed to foster the development of the petty-bourgeois and bourgeois forces aligned to the PNC.

Nanton's chapter on St Vincent [Crisis Ch. 10] also focused on the increase in dependency that is brought about by the expansion in the activities of the peripheral capitalist state. He showed how the increase in state intervention generated unintended and far from beneficial consequences, even for the incumbents of state. The economy in general, and the agricultural sector in particular, had been badly mismanaged, while government ineffectiveness triggered a growth in labour unrest, a brief separatist rebellion and a significant political challenge from the left.

The chapter by Blérald [*Crisis* Ch. 7] on the French Antilles addressed itself partly to the crisis of capital accumulation and the attempt by the colonial state to resolve this crisis by restructuring and re-orientating the economies of Martinique and Guadeloupe. This was effected mainly through a redistribution of income and a massive increase in public expenditure. Blérald, however, isolated a number of obstacles to the state's modernization drive. These included the vigorous opposition mounted by the monopoly transport companies and the comprador bourgeoisie, the disastrous effects which a rationalization policy would have on the already high level of unemployment and the limitations which the capitalist world recession had imposed on the state's ability to increase public spending. Blérald also pointed out that while the granting of autonomy to the two *départements* could have facilitated the consolidation of the industrial wing of the bourgeoisie, this option was ruled out because of the dependence of the ruling class as a whole on metropolitan France for the instruments of state coercion.

Finally, Ch. 11 by Sandoval on Trinidad and Tobago, then the most dynamic economy in the Commonwealth Caribbean, traced the role played by the state in promoting capital accumulation by both local and foreign interests. He pointed out how the spectacular increase in oil revenues after 1973 permitted the implementation of a strategy of industrialization devised in the 1950s, but which, until the oil bonanza, had encountered numerous difficulties. The principal effect of the oil boom was to enable the state to enter into joint ventures with the multinational companies which dominated the oil and natural gas industries, and, at the same time, establish autonomous enterprises of its own. Local capital was also drawn into the process. Several established trading firms developed important manufacturing and assembly activities, and managed to extend their operations into the neighbouring islands through Caricom. Sandoval [*Crisis* Ch. 11] concluded by pointing out that reductions in income from the oil sector placed a big question mark over the government's economic strategy.

Given that Sandoval concentrated his discussion on economic factors, the social and political tensions apparent in Trinidad and Tobago are accordingly de-emphasized. His attention to the modern period also presented the 1970s as a sort of *belle epoque* in the country, a characterization which may have been true. However, the oil boom itself generated a number of contradictions, the most notable of which were economic bottlenecks, an exhaustion of infra-structural capacity, corruption and mismanagement. The crisis of the state in Trinidad and Tobago began long before the difficulties in the oil industry.

Culture, race and national identity

The racial and cultural heterogeneity of Caribbean societies and their long years of subjugation by European powers made ethnicity and national identity important foci of their class struggles. This dimension was integrated into several of the case studies, which counterpoised a Marxist treatment of this subject matter to the thesis of cultural pluralism – the theoretical starting point of much academic writing about the Caribbean. (For the *locus classicus* of this tradition see Smith 1965.) Ambursley's chapter on Jamaica contained a brief discussion of Ken Post's work [see Ch. 2 of this book], which has made a seminal break with the prevailing literature on this and many other questions. Ambursley also proposed that the PNP's ideology represented a bourgeois adaptation of popular Jamaican racial and cultural motifs, which were interlaced with Fabian and nationalist shibboleths.

The issue of national identity and cultural imperialism was,

69

however, most acutely addressed in the French islands, much of Blérald's chapter being anchored upon an analysis of the ideological–cultural system of oppression. He pointed to the material basis of the French state's policy of 'genocide by substitution', whereby Antilleans were encouraged to emigrate to France, ostensibly as a solution to the unemployment problem, only to see Europeans take up key posts and settle in the Antilles. Blérald argued that the cultural sphere constitutes the terrain where the crisis in the relations of oppression is most marked and lists the gamut of publications and organizations that have emerged in opposition to assimilationism. The reassertion of a unique cultural identity can be considered (more negatively) as a displacement of a classical nationalist struggle or (more positively) as the expression of a political challenge in a context where the objective basis for economic independence is limited.[1]

Hira's chapter [*Crisis* Ch. 8] on Suriname was also concerned with the cultural level, in that he draws attention to the overlapping of racial categories with class boundaries, and examined the effects that this had on the tenor of class struggle. He explained the mass exodus of people to Holland on the eve of Surinamese independence as solely an expression of the 'disillusionment of the masses in the economic and political system'. This could, however, be extended. For example, he took no account of either the debilitating effects of the colonial incubation, or the internalization of Western lifestyles and consumption patterns by the Surinamese populace. Despite this shortcoming, the last chapters mentioned show the outlines of an alternative form of cultural analysis to that presented by pluralist theorists.

---

1   For an up-to-date account of the struggle for cultural autonomy in the French Antilles, see Robin Cohen and Olivia Sheringham *Encountering difference*, Cambridge: Polity, 2016, Ch. 7.

Pitfalls of the 'non-capitalist path'

The downfall of the PNP government in Jamaica, the revolutionary victories in Grenada and Nicaragua and the army officers' coup d'état in Suriname, all raised a number of theoretical issues concerning class alliances and revolutionary strategy in the Caribbean. Initially, we introduced this topic by considering the theory of 'non-capitalist development' or 'socialist orientation', which was adhered to by the official communist parties and their supporters in the region. The theory also influenced (or at least provided an ideological sanction for) parties such as the PNP and the New Jewel Movement (NJM). Contrary to the assertion made by its principal Caribbean advocates (Gonsalves 1981; Jacobs and Jacobs 1980) and even certain writers who have made valid criticisms of it (Thomas 1978; Halliday and Molyneux 1981), the theory of non-capitalist development has no real basis in the writings of Marx, Engels and Lenin. As Lowy (1981) has recently pointed out in his philological study of their texts, Marx and Engels's theoretical prognoses on the bypassing of capitalist development in Russia during the 1880s envisaged this process taking place only under proletarian hegemony and linked to a proletarian insurgency in the advanced capitalist countries of Western Europe. Likewise, Lenin's deliberations on the possibility of averting capitalist development in backward countries, made at the Second Congress of the Comintern and in other writings, stressed the necessity of establishing independent organs of the working class and poor peasants. He also noted the importance of material assistance from more advanced countries under the dictatorship of the proletariat (Lenin 1971; 1971a).

In short, the then current theory of non-capitalist development used quotations from the works of Marx, Engels and Lenin, but arrived at conclusions wholly at variance with the major content of their arguments. Elaborated in the 1950s and 1960s by the Soviet theorists Ulyanovsky (1974), Solodovnikov and Bogoslovsky (1975) and Andreyev (1977), the theory raised the objective possibility of superseding capitalism in contemporary underdeveloped countries, yet suggested that in order to accomplish this, a new stage of development must be traversed that is neither capitalism nor a transition to socialism. Furthermore, this allegedly non-capitalist path can involve, as Ulyanovsky in effect concedes, a long-term strategic alliance with the local bourgeoisie (Ulyanovsky 1977: 26).

As Löwy (1981) points out, the real origins of official communist 'stagism' as required by the theory of non-capitalist development are the neo-Menshevik theses advanced by Stalin during the 1920s. Whereas Stalin's writings did, however, have a certain logical consistency, in that the injunction to enter into a broad strategic alliance with the bourgeoisie was justified as a means of consummating the bourgeois democratic revolution, the theory of non-capitalist development mystifies the objective nature of the process it describes with vague talk of 'bypassing the capitalist stage'. Indeed, such have been the contradictions involved in the application of the theory that it underwent a semantic evolution and was rebadged as 'socialist orientation'. Halliday and Molyneux (1981: chapter 7) explained how the reversals suffered by Soviet foreign policy in Egypt and Somalia (two of the countries that were considered to be classic examples of the non-capitalist road) led the Soviet theoreticians to re-examine the theory and suggest a refinement which they termed 'states of socialist orientation'. A perusal over the list of countries Halliday and Molyneux identified in Soviet literature as 'socialist orientated' would suggest that, as with the non-capitalist path, the terminology was instrumental and reserved for regimes with close economic and political ties with the Soviet Union, whatever the objective basis for such a label might be. (The list includes, for example, such diverse countries as Ethiopia, Guinea, Benin, Malagasy, Congo, Tanzania, Angola, Mozambique, Guinea-Bissau, Cape Verde, Sao Tome, Algeria, Syria, South Yemen, Libya, Afghanistan, Burma, Nicaragua and Grenada.) The emphasis in the theory of socialist orientation upon such factors as 'the relative autonomy of the state', 'the revolutionary potential of military officers' and 'popular committees' served merely to occlude the objectively capitalist nature of most of these countries and their continued symbiosis with the capitalist world economy (for a more extended critique of the theory see James 1982).

Within the official communist movement, the decision to designate a country as non-capitalist or socialist-oriented was taken by the Central Committee of the Communist Party of the Soviet Union (CPSU). Apparently no such decision was taken about either the Manley regime in Jamaica or the Burnham government in Guyana. Nevertheless, at least three Caribbean proponents of official communist orthodoxy (Gonsalves 1979: 2; Jacobs and Jacobs 1980: 83) have placed these regimes in this taxonomy. Moreover, the official communist parties in both these countries pursued a political line fashioned largely by the ideological parameters of the socialist-orientation thesis. In his chapter on Jamaica, Ambursley argued that given the innumerable ties that bound the Jamaican bourgeoisie to foreign capital, the Workers' Party of Jamaica's (WPJ) search for a 'national patriotic bourgeoisie' was illusory and only led the party into becoming loyal but mistaken supporters of the PNP regime. In its endeavour to 'push' the PNP along a non-capitalist path, the WPJ refrained from mounting any serious opposition to Manley, even to the point of joining PNP henchmen and security forces in breaking up a mass protest movement in 1979.

The PNP experiment in 'Democratic Socialism' was a tightly controlled affair. It sought to ameliorate some of the more naked forms of oppression of the Jamaican working class and attempted to accomplish this by redistributing a greater proportion of the surplus value extracted by foreign capital towards a particular fraction of the local bourgeoisie. The socialist and anti-imperialist pronouncements of the PNP, Ambursley argued, were designed to increase its appeal among the oppressed and provide a camouflage for its pro-capitalist policies. In the theory of non-capitalist development it found a ready-made ideology which the left wing of the PNP integrated into its populist rhetoric. Manley himself preferred not to use this particular terminology and in his recent book depicts the PNP's abortive development strategy as a 'third path'. This, he claims, was a distinct and median course between the Puerto Rican model and the Cuban revolution (1982). Manley's contention that his removal from office was due to a CIA conspiracy is a matter of the truth, but not the whole truth. Nor should it evoke too much sympathy, coming as it does from a man who was baptized into Jamaican politics in 1952 as the willing accomplice of a US-inspired operation that decapitated the Marxist tendency in the Jamaican labour movement. The economic policies of the Manley regime could in no way be construed to have represented a serious challenge to the local capitalist class or to foreign domination. Most of the battered remnants of the PNP's reform programme still in existence in 1980 were discarded by the Seaga regime without significant popular opposition. On balance, Ambursley argued, the WPJ strategy of alliance with the PNP only facilitated Manley's unprincipled balancing act between the classes. It also left a gaping hole for the JLP to build a right-wing opposition movement and carry out its electoral coup d'état.

We have already mentioned Thomas's warning that the extension of state control in Guyana should not mislead us into thinking of the Burnham regime as left-wing. Yet here too the advocates of the non-capitalist path made precisely this error. The main proponent of the notion that the regime was undergoing radicalization was the Guyanese communist party, the People's Progressive Party (PPP). In 1975, the PPP adopted a policy of critical support for Burnham and this helped consolidate the PNC regime. The pusillanimity of the PPP's politics, indeed, promoted the emergence of the Working People's Alliance (WPA), which offered a more resolute and proletarian-anchored strategy of political opposition to the PNC. The PPP's pursuit of an alliance with the PNC was greeted with a good deal of scepticism, since it was widely acknowledged that the Burnham regime was the most repressive and despotic in the English-speaking Caribbean and, in 1980, was responsible for the brutal murder of one of the region's leading revolutionary thinkers, Walter Rodney.

Class alliances and revolutionary strategy

The chapters by Weber [*Crisis* Ch. 5] and Dunkerley [*Crisis* Ch. 6], on Nicaragua and El Salvador respectively, highlighted a number of pitfalls in the official communist practice of seeking to establish long-term inter-class blocs. Weber (1981) pointed out how the Partido Comunista de Nicaragua (PCN) was outflanked on the left by the Frente Sandinista de Liberation Nacional (FSLN), because of the former's step-by-step overtures towards the Somoza dictatorship. A similar fate also befell the PCS in El Salvador. Dunkerley explained how the PCS's desperate search for reformist elements within the various client military regimes and its dogged commitment to electoralism led the party into a political impasse. The principal guerrilla movements, the Fuerzas Populares de Liberation (FPL), the Fuerzas Armadas de Resistencia Nacional (FARN) and the Ejercito Revolucionario del Pueblo (ERP), either emerged out of, or developed their politics through, a sustained critique of the policies of the PCS. The PCS was obliged to abandon its gradualist strategy and joined with guerrilla groups in forming the Frente Democrático Revolucionario (FDR) and its military wing, the Frente Farabundo Marti para la Liberation Nacional (FMLN). Dunkerley suggested that the PCS was, nevertheless, still pursuing a stagist orientation within the revolutionary camp. Both Nicaragua and El Salvador thus provided a certain parallel with events in Cuba during the 1950s, where the official CP (the Partido Socialista Popular, PSP) was supplanted by the July 26 Movement as a result of its conciliatory attitude towards Batista.

The popular insurrections that took place in Grenada and Nicaragua pose a number of complex questions about class alliances and revolutionary strategy. This is because both events were led by political formations other than orthodox CPs and yet, in both cases, political alliances were entered into with the bourgeoisie which remained intact for a long time. Of course, the official communist movement was not the only protagonist of class alliances with the bourgeoisie in the capitalist periphery: such ideas have been peddled in various complexions by a plethora of movements and parties. Indeed, the attraction of particular tenets of official communism to a host of regimes in the periphery had its basis in a political convergence with respect to the complex issue of class alliances. Hence, in the case of Nicaragua and Grenada, our analytical task was to ascertain whether the popular-frontist pronouncements of either the FSLN or the NJM led to a neo-bourgeois or petty-bourgeois deflection of the revolutionary process. Both in his book (Weber 1981) and in his chapter included in *Crisis*, Weber advanced the view that FSLN alliance politics were different from those of the Stalinist front, in that they were based on conflict and on FSLN hegemony. In spite of the non-Somoza bourgeoisie retaining its economic power and its ties with foreign capital, a transition to socialism was, he argued, in progress because of the FSLN leadership's commitment to such a course and because of the control the revolutionary movement over the coercive apparatuses of the state. However, in his chapter on El Salvador, Dunkerley took issue with what he considered the subjectivism of Weber's analysis. He regarded the possibility of a state capitalist ossification of the revolution as equally, if not more, likely than a transition to socialism. In any event, he perceived great dangers in the revolutionary movement of El Salvador adopting the 'Nicaraguan model' and characterizes the Sandinista regime as a popular front.

In a revised and updated version of his original study of Grenada, Ambursley expressed reservations about the NJM's adherence to the theory of 'socialist orientation', but argued that a socialist revolution along the lines of the Cuban revolution would be out of the question. This is also a revision of an earlier study which he made of the first year of the revolution (Ambursley 1981). On account of the objective and subjective constraints, the PRG has been prudent to leave important areas of the island's economy in the hands of the bourgeoisie. This enabled the regime to stimulate economic activity, build up the defence capacity of the island and provide for the self-organization of the masses. Due to the caution which it has exercised, the PRG has successfully thwarted US attempts to isolate it and scored a series of propaganda victories over Washington. [In the event, President Reagan decided he could tolerate the prospect of a 'second Cuba' no longer. The US military invaded in October 1983 with over 8000 troops and displaced the PRG.]

In his own account, Manley pointed to the 'mixed-economy' approach being followed in Grenada and Nicaragua as a vindication of the development path that he tried to chart, since, despite the armed seizure of power that took place in these two countries, the NJM and the FSLN have also seen fit to align themselves with the private sector. He argued that the difference between these two processes and the PNP strategy was mainly a matter of emphasis (Manley 1981; *Socialist Challenge* 9 July 1981). Manley had some telling remarks about the nature of the political struggle in these two countries, though his claim that these developments somehow represent an *ex-post-facto* verification of 'Democratic Socialism' was not very convincing. For it is clear that the FSLN and the NJM did not represent the same class interests as did the PNP, and that the Sandinista and Bishop regimes – until its removal – effected a greater degree of popular participation than the PNP achieved at any time during its eight years in office.

In showing that the main impetus for the February 1980 coup d'état in Suriname came from the industrial wing of the bourgeoisie, the chapter by Hira described an additional dimension to the problem of class alliances and revolutionary strategy. The bourgeois forces grouped in the Partij Nationalistische Republiek (PNR) (Party for a Nationalist Republic) had for some time expressed dissatisfaction with the comprador-bourgeois government of Henk Arron and had conspired with a dissident caucus of non-commissioned army officers to seize state power. The right-wing origin of the military putsch immediately became evident as the new regime moved to impose press censorship, curfews and a ban on political meetings. The radical inclinations of the army officers had given rise to tensions within the insurrectionist fraction of the bourgeoisie and this saddled the National Military Council regime with an element of marked instability. The regime's attempt to make economic concessions to the masses, in an extremely unfavourable international climate, added fuel to the government's crisis. Suriname thus presented a significant divergence from Grenada and Nicaragua, for although a component of the bourgeoisie supported the uprisings that took place in these two countries, unlike in Suriname, the primary thrust came from revolutionary 'Jacobin' forces which mobilized the working class and poor peasants.

Finally, to conclude this section on class alliances and revolutionary strategy, a word on Soviet and Cuban foreign policy in the Caribbean is in order since, on the one hand, the Cuban model (or elements thereof) have been embraced by various political formations and, on the other hand, all radical developments in the region have been regarded by US strategists and their supporters as emanating from Moscow and/or Havana. On the contrary, our chapters have shown that the principal challenge to the neo-colonial status of the region has not in fact come from the official parties tied to Moscow. Soviet policy, as carried out by these parties, has neither been subversive nor expansionist. Furthermore, as Ambursley argued in the case of Jamaica, there is evidence that the Soviet Union advised Manley to remain in the Western camp because of its unwillingness to provide him with economic assistance.

Equally, Cuba has for the main part supported the strategy of the CPs in the region. The precise international policy to be pursued by a revolutionary government with the geo-political and economic circumstances facing Cuba is undoubtedly a complex matter. Nevertheless, it is necessary to stress that since the period 1968–70, Cuban foreign policy underwent a distinct shift away from unconditional support for revolutionary movements in Latin America and the Caribbean and evolved around three specific axes. Firstly, an alignment with the basic international orientation of the Soviet Union. Secondly, an opening towards reformist bourgeois governments which the Cuban leadership has described as 'anti-imperialist' and 'revolutionary'. And finally, an abandonment of the strident criticisms that Castro himself made of the official CPs of Latin America and a growing rapprochement with these parties. Resolutions adopted at the Havana conference in June 1975 sanctioned these shifts of policy (Castro 1972; Petras and Laporte, Jr. 1971: 331–71). This evolution was certainly facilitated by Cuba's growing economic ties with the Comecon countries and by the sustained isolation of the revolution in the American hemisphere, but we do not believe that it was inevitable. In any event, Cuban foreign policy in the Caribbean had been laden with contradictions and cannot adequately be described as consistently internationalist – as has recently been argued by Taber (1981).

In his report to the Second Congress of the Cuban CP held in December 1980, Castro expressly used the notion 'socialist orientation', and the political ramifications of this theory appear to have underlined much of Cuban policy in the region. Both Michael Manley and Forbes Burnham were given the Jose Marti award and eulogized by the Cuban regime as 'revolutionary leaders'. The Cubans also endorsed the alliance strategy of both the WPJ and the PPP. Events in Grenada and Nicaragua have, of course, met with an enthusiastic response from the Cuban leadership and this deepened the rift between Havana and Washington. While adhering to the theory of 'socialist orientation' the Cuban government gave support to the political path chosen by these two revolutionary states. However, according to Dunkerley (198z: 212), the Cuban intervention in El Salvador was designed to coax the guerrilla movement into establishing a long-term bloc with the reformist opposition. Surprisingly, the Cubans themselves also seem to be the source of a currently fashionable misconception that the Cuban revolution itself went through a process of 'non-capitalist development' (Gonsalves 1981: 31; Halliday and Molyneux 1981: 176). But this is entirely erroneous.

Within the space of less than a year, the alliance between the *Fidelistas* and the bourgeois wing of the July 26 Movement had proved untenable. In the face of Castro's determined effort to introduce revolutionary socialist measures, the Cuban bourgeoisie turned to counter-revolution and is now found in Miami, Florida.

In summary, then, it is true that the revolutionary experience of Cuba and the accomplishments of the Castro regime provided a source of inspiration to political forces throughout the region. But the main radical developments in the Caribbean cannot be attributed either to Soviet or to Cuban foreign policy, which in theory and practice seems to have a restraining influence.

The transition to socialism and socialist democracy

Despite our foregoing remarks on Cuban foreign policy, Beauvais's chapter [*Crisis* Ch. 3] on Cuba registered some of the social and economic advances that a planned collectivist economy could bring about in the Caribbean. It also highlighted a number of contradictions and tensions inherent in the Cuban attempt to build socialism. He took care to separate those objective factors that militated against the development of the Cuban revolution from the impediments that he saw as resulting from the economic and political decisions of the Castro leadership. Beauvais's analysis, in effect, represented a more nuanced version of the 'Sovietization' thesis, advanced by writers such as Mesa-Lago (1974), Gonzales (1976) and Goure and Weinkle (1972). According to this line of argument, the qualitative strengthening of Cuba's external links with the Soviet Union, particularly after the political and economic setback of 1970, led to the wholesale Sovietization of Cuban society.

Previously distinctive aspects of socialist transformation in Cuba had either been discarded or refashioned in the image of the Soviet Union. Beauvais, like the Sovietization theorists, was cognizant and critical of the growing use of Soviet economic doctrines in Cuba and considers that the adoption in 1975 of the new System of Management and Planning in Cuba provided fertile ground for the reproduction of some of the deleterious aspects of Soviet planning. Nevertheless, while there was definitely an objective trend towards bureaucratization, Beauvais argues that a bureaucratic caste, which had interests antagonistic to those of the masses, had not yet consolidated itself in Cuba. He cited the democratic aspects of the Cuban political system, *poder popular*, as well as the high level of political consciousness and mass mobilization, as evidence that the Cuban revolution had not regressed to the level of the 'degenerated workers' states' of Eastern Europe. Nevertheless, he viewed the organization of power in Cuba as paternalistic and thought it unlikely to guarantee any genuine exercise of power by the masses. It is above all the absence of democratic planning, self-management of the units of production and distribution, free public discussion and the possibility of open debate within the party and mass organizations that had given rise to the 'low economic consciousness of the workers'. He argued that the technical reforms introduced in the 1970s, although an improvement on some of the inefficiencies of the early years of the revolution, provided no real alternative to a democratic self-organization of the proletariat. Beauvais thus arrived at a different conclusion from that of Fitzgerald (1981), who had also made an interesting critique of the Sovietization thesis. Fitzgerald's submission was that the introduction of Soviet-derived planning mechanisms not only made Cuban society more functional, but had also afforded greater and more stable participation by the masses.

The question of popular power was also touched upon in the chapters by Weber, Ambursley (Grenada) and Thomas. Like

Beauvais, Weber considered the Cuban system inadequate as a method of proletarian rule and expresses reservations about the FSLN emulating certain aspects of this system. Ambursley described the Parish Council system in Grenada and suggested that it was a practical unit because of the tiny size of the island. However, he pointed out that it did not yet correspond to the proposals set out in the 1973 manifesto of the NJM. Significantly, Thomas concluded his chapter on Guyana with a quotation from Rosa Luxemburg, the legendary communist leader of the Polish and German labour movements who, perhaps more than any other classical Marxist thinker, ruminated upon the relationship between socialism and democracy. We may reflect that in Guyana, as in many states of the Caribbean basin, the choice facing the masses will increasingly be posed in terms of socialist democracy or no democracy at all.

External constraints

Foreign domination of the Caribbean

Whatever choices are open to the people of the Caribbean, they are tightly constrained by the historical domination of the region by external forces. During the mercantilist period, the islands were little more than plantation outposts of the core economies, the effective control of the area being determined by the relative strengths of British, French, Dutch, Portuguese, Spanish and, in the Virgin Islands, Danish, mercantilism.

Despite the general success of the movements towards independence and self-government in the post-war period, the process of dismantling external hegemony is far from complete. Puerto Rico passed from Spanish hands to US control in 1898, the Danish Virgins were simply purchased for $25m by the USA in 1917, while US marines occupied Haiti for 20 years (1915–35).

[After the earthquake of 12 January 2010, when many were killed or left homeless, the country – which had a turbulent history after its successful rebellion against colonial France – has become more and more dependent on international aid and US support.] While general decolonization has been effected by the British, the UK continues to govern the Turks and Caicos and the Cayman Islands, though these are seen as residual and minor colonial responsibilities, which are seen as best shed, rather than shouldered. Although this is the prevailing view in the British Foreign Office, the case of the Falklands/Malvinas shows how even the faintest prospect of colonial vainglory in the remotest spot can be used to stir reactionary and chauvinist sentiments, when that will turn to the advantage of a discredited politician.

As far as the territories in this book are concerned, the French Antilles have, if anything, been more tightly integrated into the web of metropolitan control, having the status of departments of France. The material advantages of this status have constantly dogged the attempts by progressive elements in Martinique and Guadeloupe to advance their case for political independence. Consequently, as we have indicated, Blérald's contribution depicted the struggle for transformation in the French Antilles as much in cultural as in political or economic terms. The political struggle was also much blunted by successive concessions to 'autonomy' and by Mitterand's public disagreement with Reagan at such events as the Cancun summit in Mexico. Mitterand both rejected the notion of development through private capital transfers and unfettered market forces and advanced the cause of a 'North–South dialogue' and a 'New International Economic Order'. For all that, Guadeloupe and Martinique remain as firmly under Paris's political thumb as they ever were.

Unlike the French Antilles, Suriname held some independent status since 1975 and, technically, enjoyed a similar relationship to the kingdom of the Netherlands as does Holland, but the country is critically dependent on Holland for aid, technical expertise and investment. Holland also continues to dominate the former Dutch Caribbean on such critical matters as defence, foreign affairs and definitions of nationality and citizenship. So powerful was the ideological grip of the metropolitan power that virtually half the population of the country went to Holland as the country approached independence. Despite a careful attempt to install a pro-Dutch ruling group at independence, it was difficult constantly to prop up the discredited regime of Prime Minister Arron whose government, as Hira shows in his contribution, was constantly under the threat of collapse from its own decline in morale, following a wave of corruption charges and the growing strength of the left in the army, the trade unions and other popular forces. In the event, the right in the army triumphed in a pre-emptive coup designed to nip the movements of the left in the bud.

In the case of St Vincent, Britain continues to have an influential voice in the island's affairs, despite the discarding of the status of an associated state in 1980. The regime's dependence on foreign aid was particularly manifest during an emergency following a volcanic eruption on the island. As Nanton showed, the ruling party was able to use its connections with its 'special friends' – Canada, the United States and Britain – to ensure its electoral victory. By the same token, Cato's ruling party was able to tar its opponents on the left (organized for the most part under the banner of YULIMO) as tools of the Soviets or the Cubans and ready to propel St Vincent along the much-feared path of Grenada.

The US imperial tradition

Though we have described the continuing importance of French, Dutch and British influence in the Caribbean, there is no doubt that the major foreign threat to the Caribbean comes principally not from the European powers, but from the US, whose policies in the region both follow a long imperialist tradition and showed some alarming shifts. The most rabid imperialist doctrines were openly advanced by Roosevelt (Beale 1956: 39) at the turn of the century, while the cases of Haiti, Puerto Rico and the Virgin Islands, already mentioned, show that the USA had little hesitation in acquiring new territories or intervening when it felt its regional interests to be threatened. The cavalier treatment of the peoples of the region by the USA was later to be followed by military interventions (for example, in the Dominican Republic and Nicaragua), occupation (for example, of the Panama Canal), attempts to destabilize regimes through covert means and finally, the use of international agencies (like the IMF in Jamaica) to undermine the legitimacy of reformist governments. Even in the period before the Second World War, when the right of the Republican Party under Senator Taft advanced the notions of 'Splendid Isolation' and 'Fortress America', as Davis (1981: 32–6) makes clear, what the right really wanted was isolation from European squabbles. The doctrine of 'Manifest Destiny' was always applied to the Caribbean and (to a lesser extent) in the Pacific. Kennedy's adventurist and abortive invasion of the Bay of Pigs in 1961 and the invasion of the Dominican Republic in 1965 were thus part of a long tradition of wielding a big stick in the area whenever US economic or strategic interests appeared to be threatened.

Why then has the Caribbean occupied so central a place in the expression of US imperialism? First, as Maingot has argued, parts of the USA are in fact *in* the Caribbean even if not precisely *of* the Caribbean. This has meant that the USA has always conceived the Caribbean as *mare nostrum*. Second, in its strategic definitions of thirty-one essential trade routes, several of the major routes pass through the Caribbean and all pass the busiest border, Cuba. In particular, Trade Route Number 4 (so designated by the Merchants' Act of 1934) makes heavy use of the Windward Passage between Cuba and Haiti (Maingot 1979: 255, 256).

But if these two factors may be seen as determining the longstanding strategic significance of the region to the US, since 1959 a number of new economic and political factors increased the US sensitivity to its interests in the area. The US military and naval control of the area had been much extended during the Second World War when Churchill abandoned naval bases in the area in return for US strategic support in the Second World War. In addition, the Second World War had marked the period when British capital effectively collapsed as the dominant force in the region and American capital became predominant. This, however, was insufficient to stop the July 26 Movement in Cuba. The USA was unable to invade Cuba successfully, subvert it internally or assassinate Fidel Castro (though CIA attempts were numerous and often bizarre, including the issuing of a 'contract' to the Mafia). What are the main factors determining the interactions between the Caribbean and the USA?

- First, the successful emergence of Cuba as a socialist state in the region – and one that was to have considerable influence on progressive forces.

- Second, US investments in the area began to expand and, by the early 1980s, constituted some US$ 4.5 billion (excluding Puerto Rico). By the 1970s, 55 per cent of Caribbean exports and 43 per cent of imports went to and from the US. In terms of value, the US exported goods worth US$ 2 billion in 1977. Though this level of economic investment and trade is small in world-wide terms, it is nonetheless disproportionately great if we bear in mind the relatively minor economic importance of the region in the world economy (Maingot 1979; Palmer 1979).

- Third, since 1973 the issue of Caribbean oil became a matter of vital concern. There are major oil refineries in Mexico, Venezuela, Puerto Rico, Trinidad and Curacao, all of which refine oil, often not from the region, for the US market. So, while the Middle East and the Gulf were important in respect of oil supplies, the Caribbean was an equally sensitive zone in terms of the sea routes through which oil is imported and the refining capacity of the region.

- Fourth, the first two named countries, Venezuela and Mexico, developed an increasing stake as oil producers in their own right. Prior to 1973, when Venezuelan oil was expensive in relation to Middle Eastern oil, this was of no great importance. However, since 1973, Venezuelan oil became competitive in US markets and it is only since that date too that Mexican oil reserves came on stream on any large scale. This has given to Venezuela and Mexico a certain degree of strategic leverage in the region though, in the case of Mexico, this is limited by its huge accumulation of debts to Western, and particularly American, banks. Both countries have nonetheless played an important mediating role (insofar, for example, as Mexico provides diplomatic and economic support for Cuba) and both show a certain capacity to intervene in their own right – as 'sub-imperial' powers.

- Fifth, American concern for its Caribbean borders reflected regional shifts within the USA away from the north-east and towards the southern rim. This shift in power was recently engagingly described by Sale (1979). The leisure industry, defence and space programmes, agribusiness and new manufacturing industries all became increasingly concentrated in the southern rim and lent a new significance to the Caribbean ports and industrial areas of New Orleans, Miami and Houston. At a political level, so Sale's argument runs, Nixon and Carter's elections to the presidency (and, we may add, Reagan's) all symbolize the 'power shift' he described. It is not without significance to the evolution of US policy in the Caribbean basin that the coalition of southern business interests set up overseas branches in Guatemala and Nicaragua and were influential in seeking to torpedo the Panama Canal legislation (Black 1982).

The liberal phase and its demise

By the time of Carter's accession to power, the stage was set for the USA not only to uphold its traditional interests in the area, but also to advance them in new and more pervasive directions. Carter's foreign policy was, however, dictated by more complicated ends than simply wielding a big stick. The failure of US attempts to unseat the Manley government in 1976 played an important role in pushing the Carter administration to introduce changes in its foreign policy in the Caribbean. In that year a Caribbean Task Force began functioning in the State Department. Its fundamental brief was to keep West Indian experiments in socialism from drifting to the radical left and to do so through political, rather than military, means. This approach was also supported by the House Sub-Committee on Inter-American Affairs headed by Dante Fascell, the Democratic representative from Florida. In addition, the liberal foreign-policy group, whose views were reflected in the Linowitz Report, favoured such a policy. The report reflected some new foreign-policy imperatives: the need to respect diversity in ideology and economic and social organization, the independent role of Latin American and

Caribbean nations in international fora and the global significance of US Latin American and Caribbean relations. The report emphasized co-operation with Latin American nations and the provision of aid to development agencies. Less emphasis was placed on bilateral aid. In spring 1978, a 'Group for Co-operation in Economic Development' was launched to implement such a multilateral approach in the Caribbean under World Bank sponsorship.

Various international agencies (the IMF, the Caribbean Development Bank and the Inter-American Development Bank) were to co-ordinate aid activities in the region (Maingot 1979: 298). This softly-softly approach was to be reflected in other ways too. Foreign Service in the Caribbean had traditionally been a repository for political appointees, but Carter soon began to appoint career diplomats, particularly to the ex-British Caribbean. In 1977 Andrew Young visited the area and emphasized Carter's doctrine of human rights and the USA's new concern for the area (Khan 1979: 29–53). In that year, too, there was a growing entente with Cuba, with hints of the possible establishment of diplomatic relations and a more relaxed attitude to the Manley regime in Jamaica. This phase of American policy in the region was not to last long, but was perhaps best expressed by Terrence Todman, the Assistant Secretary of State for Inter-American Affairs.

> We no longer see the Caribbean in the same stark military security context that we once viewed it. Rather, our security concerns in the Caribbean are increasingly political in nature. The threat is not simply foreign military bases on our doorstep. It is possibly an even more troublesome prospect: proliferation of impoverished third-world states whose economic and political problems blend with our own.
>
> (cited Maingot 1979: 293)

This more sophisticated view of the region was to be dealt a death blow by three events. The first was the victory of the revolutionary forces in Grenada on 13 March 1979. While a meeting of the Caribbean foreign ministers held the next day denounced the revolutionary change in government in Grenada as 'contrary to the traditional methods of changing governments in the region', it nevertheless 'reaffirmed that the affairs of Grenada are for the people of the territory to decide and accordingly there should be no outside interference' *(Trinidad and Tobago Review May* 1979). This stance by American allies restrained direct US intervention for a while. The second decisive event happened only four months later, when the revolution in Nicaragua reached a decisive phase. Again, the OAS restrained the USA from mediating, but this time the patience of the USA for 'diversity in economic and social organization' was wearing thin. Finally, Carter's human rights policy came under strong attack from the US right as the Cuban refugee crisis escalated. At first, the administration were able successfully to use the refugee crisis to score a propaganda victory over Cuba. But Castro was able to turn the tables initially by announcing that all who did not agree with the aims of the revolution would be free to go and second, by emptying the prisons of Cuba and sending minor criminals to the embarkation point. The large numbers of Cubans involved soon aroused the wrath of racists in Florida, while the poor conditions under which many refugees were admitted and housed turned the propaganda victory rather sour. Under the weight of the Grenadian, Nicaraguan and Cuban crises, Washington's policy took a massive lurch to the right.

Its first move was to provide greater economic and military assistance to its traditional allies and at the same time strengthen its capacity to undertake rapid military action. In July 1979 the State Department's AID authorized US$ 8.4m as a loan on soft terms to the Barbados-based Caribbean Development Bank. This money was designed for the ailing economies of the small territories of the Caribbean like St Lucia, Dominica and Antigua, intended to prevent 'another Grenada' (*Financial Times* 17 July 1979). Next, using the pretext of the discovery of Soviet troops in Cuba, a military task force was set up in Key West Florida, while US marines were deployed at Guantanamo Bay, Cuba, in October 1979. This was followed by the Solid Shield exercises in May 1980. State Department officials warned that co-operative security arrangements would be necessary in the region and that the failure to effect these would 'leave the field open for Cuba' (*Caribbean Contact* July 1980). Barbados, the Bahamas, Guyana, Haiti and the Dominican Republic received particular attention from the so-called International Military and Education Training fund. Barbados was identified as a special friend in the region and there was even talk of that country becoming a sort of Iran in the Caribbean. This message was received with some unease by the Prime Minister, Tom Adams, who pointed to the fate that befell the Shah. However, Barbados did indeed act in a minor way in this capacity in December 1979, when it responded to a request from Milton Cato to put down a rebellion in Union Island in the St Vincent Grenadines, an event described by Nanton in his chapter in *Crisis*.

Economic sweeteners and security assistance

The outlines of a much tougher stance towards the Caribbean basin were thus already present in the last year of the Carter administration, but with Reagan's accession to power the attempts to secure a policy consistent with Reagan's campaign themes of 'Resurgent America' accelerated. It is perhaps important to emphasize that Reagan failed to entirely subordinated the 'liberals' in the foreign-policy establishment; Haig's departure caused some strains and there were considerable unresolved tensions between various business, military and political lobbies with interests in the Caribbean, some of which are mentioned below. Nonetheless, the main lines of US foreign policy in the area were now clear. For those countries which appear to be 'soft on communism' or linked themselves to the Soviet Union or Cuba, immediate economic and diplomatic sanctions were applied. By contrast, Washington's 'friends' were provided with special economic packages and privileged access to the US market even though, in conformity with the doctrine of Reaganomics, private capital was predominant in effecting this economic relationship. Finally, for those countries which were held to be fighting the communist menace, military assistance was provided irrespective of the means whereby popular insurrections or democratic dissent were contained.

The pattern of economic sanctions directed against regimes that were held to be adopting the wrong international stances again predate Reagan's election, though in the case of Jamaica this pressure gained renewed emphasis with Carter's demise. In fact the IMF, whose pattern of lending was essentially influenced by the US, started proffering its poisoned chalice to Jamaica as early as 1976; by 1980 an attempt to swallow its contents had resulted in the destabilization and electoral defeat of the Manley government. The IMF made eight major demands to the Jamaican government over the period: (i) an attack on excessive wage increases; (ii) pressure to change what they saw as an overvalued exchange rate; (iii) pressure to reduce the fiscal deficit; (iv) pressure to reduce monetary expansion; (v) an attack on Jamaica's trade restrictions and payments; (vi) pressure to reduce state intervention in the economy; (vii) pressure to reduce price controls; and (viii) pressure to increase business confidence (Girvan et al. 1980: 118–19).

It is doubtful whether any reformist Third World government

with the basic economic problems that Jamaica experienced would have been able to resist such an onslaught, particularly since it was questionable whether Manley's regime had any consistent or continuous mass support for its programme. In the event, it vacillated, resisted some measures, partially accepted some, but was ultimately forced to go along with all the principal IMF demands. The assault on living standards for the working class, not to mention the related problems of violence and insecurity, propelled a significant section of the urban poor into the hands of Seaga's populist Jamaican Labour Party. Seaga lost no time in linking himself firmly to the tougher US line. He called for closer co-operation in Caricom to 'halt the expansion of communist imperialism' and again dwelt on this theme at a conference of US businessmen held in Miami on 23 November 1980. 'Like minds', he said, should fight 'Marxist adventures' in the region (*Latin American Regional Reports* 5 December 1980). Six months later the *rapprochement* with Jamaica was complete. If the US government did not want to fund some of Jamaica's economic programmes directly, it was sufficient that Reagan gave the go-ahead to private US interests. As Seaga (a former US-trained economist and IMF official) stated to *Newsweek*, 'I knew the President was strapped for money ... but his connections with the US business community were an untapped resource'. Apparently that community was responsive. According to one 'involved' businessman, 'with names like Rockefeller and Reagan singing duets about how wonderful Jamaica is, those wallets should be there and open in no time' (*Newsweek* 20 July 1981).

While the USA had little difficulty in gaining the unswerving loyalty of Seaga, other economic sweeteners appeared to be more difficult to package. The creation of a so-called Mini-Marshall plan for the region, drawing in the regional powers of

Mexico, Venezuela and Canada, although trumpeted with a great flourish, ultimately ran into difficulties. The plan was fully unveiled in a meeting in the Bahamas in July 1981 between General Haig and the foreign ministers of Canada, Venezuela and Mexico. It followed an intervention made to Haig by Prime Minister Seaga in January 1981 who argued that the small, weak, dependent territories of the Caribbean would fall 'like dominoes' to Cuba's influence, unless some US$3 billion was poured into the area each year (a trebling of the previous level of aid). The plan ran into some immediate difficulties, largely occasioned by Haig's heavy-handed demands. The Venezuelans and Mexicans had separate and somewhat contradictory interests to advance. The Canadians refused to go along with American insistence that Grenada should be cut off from all aid and indeed agreed to provide a considerable level of aid to the island. The attempt to isolate Grenada even aroused the wrath of the twelve members of the Caribbean Economic Community, including Jamaica and Barbados, who attacked the USA for offering a $4m grant to the Caribbean Development Bank, only on condition that none of the money be used in Grenada. In addition to these difficulties, there were reported inter-agency tussles in Washington as to how the Mini-Marshall aid should be allocated and spent (*Financial Times* 1 July 1981, 10 July 1981, 14 July 1981). By February 1982, even the nomenclature had changed – 'Mini-Marshall' had been replaced by the Caribbean Basin Initiative (CBI). By the time the CBI had been diluted by congressional lobbies, the total aid package of US$350m was spread thinly, with the special interests of Puerto Rico partly protected, a maximum of US$ 75m established for each recipient and other restrictions (*The Weekly Gleaner* 11 August 1982; *Financial Times* 27 *May* 1982). While not a completely damp squib (the package bought the loyalties of some smaller territories in the Caribbean archipelago), the emergency relief included for those countries with foreign-exchange difficulties was of little significance where (as in Central America) the foreign debts had grown twice as fast as the GDP or where (as in El Salvador) medium- and long-term loans had grown at ten times the GDP (Black 1982).

Reagan's policies for the 'Caribbean basin' were not, however, simply confined to opening up the area for a dose of 'Reaganomics'. The new administration had clearly signalled a fundamental reassertion of the USA's mission to contain the spread of 'world communism'. Perhaps the most blatant expression of this was made by Jeane Kirkpatrick, Washington's ambassador to the UN, who derided the ridiculous idea that 'forceful intervention in the affairs of another nation is impractical or immoral' (cited Chomsky 1981: 150). Like a diviner reading the entrails, one can also discern shifts in foreign policy and gain an insight into the mentality of planners by examining a key article that appears from time to time in the journal *Foreign Affairs*, the publication sponsored by the establishment's Council on Foreign Relations. Just such an article was Robert W. Tucker's 'The Purposes of American Power', which Chomsky has dissected in a recent analysis (Chomsky 1981). According to Tucker (1980/81), a scholar whose credentials appear to be well recognized by Reagan's foreign-policy advisers, the USA has every right to control the fate of the nations of the Central American area. This 'right', he claimed, is based on two fundamental principles:

1. Central America bears geographical proximity to the United States, and historically it has long been regarded as falling within our sphere of influence. As such, we have long exercised the role great powers have traditionally exercised over small states which fall within their respective sphere of influence. We have regularly played a determining role in making and unmaking governments,

and we have defined what we have considered to be the acceptable behaviour of governments.

2. In Central America our pride is engaged. ... If we do not apply policy of a resurgent America to prevent the coming to power of radical regimes in Central America, we have even less reason to do so in other areas.

In short, Tucker succinctly summarized the Reagan administration's abandonment of any pretence at Wilsonian 'Ideals' or 'Human Rights' in favour of the pursuit of 'Resurgent America'. Though there were occasional offstage noises by minor officials that perhaps such an open reassertion of power was embarrassingly explicit and in need of some sugar-coating, there is no doubt that Tucker correctly reflected the mood of the hawks in the administration. The primary test case for this political group was Central America where, it was thought, the shame of the Vietnam war could be exorcized, the compliance of the Western allies could be tested (only France and Mexico have publicly dissented on Nicaragua), and a useful contrast could be made with the soft-bellied period of the Carter years. As Black argued, 'The sclerotic American far right selected Central America – above all rapid victory in El Salvador – as a test case for reaffirming international will and Pax Americana' (Black 1982). One of Reagan's officials likewise claimed that an assertion of raw military power in the area was a signal to the electorate and to the USSR that the USA 'will take the necessary steps to keep the peace anywhere in the world' (*Guardian Weekly* 8 March 1981).

This odd notion of 'keeping the peace' included trebling military aid to the bankrupt regime in El Salvador to US$ 66m in 1981–82 and authorizing $19m for covert action against the Sandinistas in Nicaragua in November 1981. The USA also engineered border incursions into Nicaragua from neighbouring territories and tightened up the trade and financial embargo with Cuba (*International Herald Tribune as* April 1982). Even the small island of Grenada whose limited experiment in participatory democracy might have been tolerated by another imperial power, or at another time, did not escape the wrath of Washington. As Prime Minister Bishop plaintively complained in a published letter to Reagan, the USA has 'cut off our traditional aid possibilities both regionally and internationally with a view to strangling our fledgling economy and to subverting the political, economic and social process which we have instituted' (*Caribbean Contact* March 1982). Bishop also had good reason to express concern about the mercenaries being trained in the USA for deployment against the regional enemies of the USA. The USA's rather wilful ally, Israel, also sold arms to El Salvador and Nicaragua, which, so one newspaper surmised, 'Congress and public opinion in the US prevents Washington itself from supplying' (*Financial Times* 3 February 1982).

Conclusion

When we used the overworked word 'crisis' to describe the current situation in the Caribbean, we did so not simply as a form of journalistic licence, but in at least three specific senses. There was, we argued, a manifest crisis at the level of the state. In its baldest contrast, the choice facing the peoples of the Caribbean was that between socialist and capitalist paths to development. But within the former category, only the Cuban state had so far been able to record a measure of lasting success in combining redistributive principles with demands for popular participation. However, the Cuban experiment, despite lasting for a long time, needed to effect some unity of purpose with the two other declared revolutionary states in the area, Nicaragua and Grenada.

Within the other states surveyed, there were large divergences and contrasts. Some smaller islands had been unable to shake off the heritage of mercantile, colonial or metropolitan control. In the case of the French Antilles, the terrain of culture and identity had, in consequence, become the battleground for self-assertion. Other states embarked on a policy of dependent semi-industrialization, sometimes concealed behind a socialist rhetoric, sometimes in a more open alliance with foreign capital. Yet none of the capitalist states in the region escaped the internal crises born of massive unemployment, poor housing, health and educational services, political instability and dependence on an ailing world economy. Some sought to prop up their discredited regimes by military alliances and injections of capital from Washington and the aid agencies, but this solution only acted as a temporary palliative, rather than a permanent cure.

It is perhaps overstretching the term 'crisis' to say that the progressive forces in the region were experiencing a crisis in how to analyse and combat the conditions of underdevelopment. Yet there was certainly a good deal of confusion and uncertainty in evolving the strategies, tactics and ideologies appropriate to a socialist transformation. Could there be a possibility of 'socialism in one country', especially if the countries concerned were small, weak, isolated and located close to Uncle Sam's looming shadow? Was it possible to combine with progressive elements of the national bourgeoisie, even assuming that this class had developed some corporate identity and strength? And would not a tactical alliance with such an ally lead to a more permanent co-optation and ultimately betrayal of mass demands as a number of our contributors argued? Again would an alliance of revolutionary intellectuals, workers and displaced peasants hold together long enough to capture the state apparatus and attempt the task of socialist reconstruction from the bottom up? Were the class organs of such an alliance – the trade unions, youth movements and socialist and communist parties – able to effect something more than an *étatist* or bureaucratic solution once they had achieved power?

Finally, we noted a rapidly escalating crisis directly linked to the assertion of US power in the region. Bankrupt and murderous juntas like those of El Salvador and Guatemala were granted both the physical means and diplomatic support to suppress popular movements in their countries. Elsewhere, driblets of aid and rivers of 'security assistance' were poured in to tie countries just escaping from colonial rule even more firmly to the apron strings of the State Department. And where the carrot of aid was too tentatively grasped, the stick of military intervention was raised in an ever-present threat. While a more detailed analysis of the elements that go up to make US foreign policy in the area would have revealed a number of countervailing pressures, there was no doubt that the hawkish elements were sufficiently in the ascendant to promote interventionist and sometimes wild schemes for the maintenance of US hegemony in the region. As long as open military involvement remained a serious possibility, it was difficult to predict the exact contours of mass struggle in the territories of the Caribbean basin. But despite the turn to the right in Jamaica, some challenges to US hegemony surfaced in Cuba twenty years ago, and emerged in Nicaragua, Grenada and El Salvador more recently.

References

Ambursley, F. 1982. 'Whither Grenada? An investigation into the March 13th revolution one year after', in S. Craig (ed.), *Contemporary Caribbean: a sociological reader*, vol. 2, Trinidad and Tobago, Susan Craig, 425–63.

Ambursley, F. and Robin Cohen (eds.) 1983. *Crisis in the Caribbean*, London: Heinemann.

Andreyev, I. 1977. *The non-capitalist way*, Moscow: Progress.

Beale, H. K. 1956. *Theodore Roosevelt and the rise of America to world power*, New York: Collier Books.

Beckford, G. 1972. *Persistent poverty: underdevelopment in plantation economies of the third world*, London: OUP.

Beckford, G. and Witter, M. 1982. *Small island ... bitter weed: struggle and change in Jamaica*, London: Zed Press.

Black, G. 1982. 'Central America: crisis in the backyard', *New Left Review* September–October.

Castro, F. 1972. 'The Latin American communist parties and revolution', in M. Kenner and J. Petras (eds.), *Fidel Castro speaks*, London, Penguin.

Chomsky, N. 1981. 'Resurgent America', *Socialist Review*, 11(4), July–August, 135–54.

Cohen, Robin and Olivia Sheringham 2016. *Encountering difference*, Cambridge: Polity.

Davis, M. 1981. 'The rise of the new right', *New Left Review*, no. 128, July–August.

Dunkerley, J. 1981. *The long war: dictatorship and revolution in El Salvador*, London: Junction Books.

Financial Times, Various issues.

Fitzgerald, F. 1982. 'The direction of Cuban socialism: a critique of the sovietization thesis', in S. Craig (ed.), *Contemporary Caribbean: a sociological reader*, vol. 2, Trinidad and Tobago, Susan Craig, 243–74.

Girvan, N., Bernal, R. and Hughes, W. 1980. 'The IMF and the Third World: the case of Jamaica, 1974–80', *Development Dialogue*, vol. 2, 113–55.

Goldthorpe, John et al. 1963. *The affluent worker: political attitudes and behaviour*. Cambridge: Cambridge University Press.

Gonsalves, R. 1979. 'The importance of the Grenadian revolution to the eastern Caribbean', *Bulletin of Eastern Caribbean Affairs*, 5(1), March–April, 1–11.

Gonsalves, R. 1981. The non-capitalist path of development: Africa and the Caribbean, London: One Caribbean.

Gonzales, E. 1976. 'Castro and Cuba's new orthodoxy', *Problems of Communism*, March–April.

Gouré, L. and Weinkle, J. (eds.) 1972, 'Cuba's new dependency', *Problems of Communism*, March–April.

Guardian Weekly, 8 March 1981.

Halliday, F. and Molyneux, M. 1981. *The Ethiopian revolution*, London: New Left Books.

International Herald Tribune, 21 April 1982.

Jacobs, W. R. and Jacobs, B. I. 1980. *Grenada: the route to revolution*, Havana, Casa de las Americas.

James, W. A. 1982. 'The non-capitalist path of development and the Caribbean: A critique and an alternative', paper presented at the annual conference of the Society for Caribbean Studies, High Leigh, Hertfordshire, May 1982.

Khan, J. 1979. 'De la matraque à la morale: la relance americaine dans les Caraibes', *Alternatives-Caraibes*, 1(1), 29–53.

Latin American Regional Reports, 5 December 1980.

Lenin, V. I. 1971. 'Report on the national and the colonial questions', in *Selected works in three volumes*, vol. 3, Moscow, Progress Publishers.

Lenin, V. I. 1971a. 'Preliminary draft theses on the national and colonial questions', in *Selected works in three volumes, vol. 3*, Moscow, Progress Publishers.

Levitt, K. and Best, L. 1978. 'Character of Caribbean economy', in G. Beckford (ed.), *Caribbean economy: dependence and backwardness*, Kingston, ISER: University of the West Indies.

Löwy, M. 1981. *The politics of combined and uneven development*, London: New Left Books.

Maingot, A. P. 1979. 'The difficult path to socialism in the Caribbean', in Richard R. Fagen (ed.), *Capitalism and the state in US–Latin American relations*, California: Stanford University Press.

Manley, M. 1982. *Jamaica: struggle in the periphery*, London: Third World Media.

Mesa-Lago, C. 1974. *Cuba in the 1970s*, Albuquerque: University of New Mexico Press.

Newsweek, 20 July 1981.

Palmer, R. W. 1979. *Caribbean dependence on the United States economy*, New York: Praeger.

Petras, J. and Laporte Jr., R. 1971. 'Total system change: a decade of revolutionary government in Cuba', in *Cultivating revolution: the United States and agrarian reform in Latin America*, New York: Random House.

Sale, K. 1979, *Power shift: the rise of the southern rim and its challenge to the eastern establishment*, New York: Pantheon.

Smith, M. G. 1965. *The plural society in the British West Indies*, Berkeley: University of California Press.

Socialist Challenge, 9 July 1982.

Solodovnikov, V. and Bogoslovosky, V. 1975. *Non-capitalist development*, Moscow, Progress Publishers.

Taber, M. 1981, 'Introduction' in *Fidel Castro speeches: Cuba's internationalist foreign policy 1971–80*, New York, Pathfinder.

Thomas, C. Y. 1978. 'The "non-capitalist path" as theory and practice of decolonization and socialist transformation', *Latin American Perspectives*, 5(2), 10–28.

Trinidad and Tobago Review, May 1979.

Tucker, R. W. 1980/81. 'The purposes of American power', *Foreign Affairs*, winter, 241–74.

Ulyanovsky, R. 1974. *Socialism and the newly independent nations*, Moscow: Progress Publishers.

Ulyanovsky, R. 1977. 'Foreword' in I. Andreyev, *The non-capitalist way*, Moscow: Progress Publishers.

Weber, H. 1981. *Nicaragua: the Sandinist revolution*, London, New Left Books.

Weekly Gleaner, 11 August 1981.

Addendum

Much of this editors' introduction to *Crisis in the Caribbean*, published in 1983, was written in the midst of a fervent debate on the left raising the possibility of a socialist transformation of the many countries emerging from decolonization. What accounted for this interest? For a start, the left intelligentsia in Europe and the USA (certainly those associated with the New Left) were totally disillusioned by the Soviet Union. A few veteran communists, like Eric Hobsbawm, clung on to old loyalties, but Soviet attempts to contain popular revolts in Hungary (1968) and Prague (1968) were the final straw. That the Soviet experiment was a deeply corrupted form of socialism was not news to Trotskyists, some of whose views are represented here. Equally, the old expectation that the working class in Western countries could be a revolutionary agent was dispelled by long experience, even though the argument that it had fully acquired middle class aspirations and loyalties was challenged by John Goldthorpe et al. (1963).

So progressives' hopes turned to what was then called 'the Third World'. Certainly, the anti-colonial rhetoric of the times promised social transformations of a more fundamental kind than subsequently proved possible. The orthodox left theory that justified these hopes was grouped around the idea that there could be a 'non-capitalist path' (bypassing the need for an industrial revolution) or that a decolonizing state could effect a 'socialist orientation'. Fitzroy Ambursley and I fiercely attacked this theory, pointing out that it was primarily a legitimating device for Soviet foreign policy. I am surprised now at the passion we brought to this argument, given its inherent implausibility, but those were ardent times when, we felt, getting political analysis right truly mattered. Fitzroy was deeply engaged in internationalist politics though emotionally linked to his Jamaican heritage, while I had been turned off the endless iterations of the 'non-capitalist path' in discussions of the South African Communist Party, which I felt were distractions from the core anti-apartheid struggle (with which I was somewhat involved).

This debate now looks more nostalgic than pertinent to current issues, but the book also contained the first systematic analysis of comparative political developments across the region and apposite assessments of the limitations to Caribbean revolutionary experiments in the shadow of the US. In the end, as we feared, the flirtations with revolution in the tiny state of Grenada, were crushed by a clumsy, but effective, US military invasion. By way of a curious footnote, this book was written and published before the US invasion, but its title, *Crisis in the Caribbean*, played into that newsworthy event, and the book sold quite well.

Chapter 4
Education for dependence: aspirations, expectations and identity on the island of St Helena

Robin Cohen

The Falklands/Malvinas crisis highlighted some of the development problems associated with Britain's remaining colonial possessions. This chapter concerns the equally remote island of St Helena in the South Atlantic Ocean, 1,700 miles from Cape Town and 4,606 miles from London, where another remnant of the British Raj lingers on. With the first Charter being given to the East India Company by Cromwell in 1659, St Helena is Britain's oldest, and may be one of her last, colonial possessions. For the 5,000 St Helenians who live on the island, their attitudes towards the metropole are extraordinarily complex – compounded, as they are, from the reality of total economic dependence, a history of loyalty and affection for the mother country (kitsch portraits of the Royal Family adorn many mantelpieces), cynicism and hostility directed at the often well-intentioned colonial officials and a sense of resentment and helplessness in the face of the adverse circumstances that confront them.

The adverse circumstances include the fact that the islanders survive, virtually entirely, on budgetary support and development aid provided by the British government. Since the collapse of the flax industry in the mid-1960s, due to competition from artificial fibres, the island has been unable to develop any form of export. Large areas of the arable land (only about a third of the total surface area of forty-seven square miles) are still covered with carefully planted, but now useless, crop. Production for local needs, in respect of market gardening and fishing, is at a very low level. Partly this is because of objective factors (including low and unreliable rainfall and low-powered boats that have to hug the small leeward side of the island when fishing). The small producer has also been driven out – only three full-time farmers remain – both by market forces (starting with the collapse of demand for fresh produce for passing ships with the invention of the steamship and the opening of the Suez Canal) and by the operations of the Agricultural and Forestry Department. Historically, the role of the department had been to protect the forests and support extension work (like undertaking local research and generating seedlings), but since 1965, and now under the name of the Agricultural Development Authority, it attempts virtually monopolistically, to supply fruits, vegetables, meat and dairy produce to the local market.[1] This it notably fails to achieve, the quantity of imported frozen meat and milk/milk powder, for example, went up from 504 to 1,313 cwt in the first case and 838 to 1,092 cwt in the second case over the period 1965–70,[2]

---

1   For accounts of the historical role of the department in St Helena see Norman Humphrey, *A Review of Agriculture and Forestry in the Island of St Helena* (London: Crown Agents on behalf of the Government of St Helena, 1957) and C. W. Lynn, *Review of Agriculture and Forestry in the Island of St Helena* (St Helena: Government Printing Office, 1966). The Agricultural Development Authority was created in April 1975 in the present Development Plan. See, Government of St Helena, *Development Plan, 1974–79 Part One* (St Helena: Government Printing Office, n.d., but 1975).

2   *St Helena Development Survey Part Two* (Typescript copy in author's possession, n.d., but 1974) p. 19. This section of the report on Agriculture, was written by J. R. Goldsack.

precisely when the Agricultural and Forestry Department was changing its principal role, becoming the major employer and producer on the island and gaining much higher levels of British government assistance. Reactions to the apparently insurmountable problem of finding meaningful productive employment in the face of such a poor level of economic performance will be addressed later in the chapter.

The traditional response of the islanders to such a lack of economic opportunity has been emigration, overwhelmingly to South Africa and to the United Kingdom, the two ends of the sole line of communication, cargo ships carrying only 12 cabin passengers each 4–6 week trip. Even this modest service is now under threat and the island could be without regular communication. In addition to the practical difficulties of leaving the island, racist legislation in South Africa and the United Kingdom has slowed down the rate of emigration. In the case of South Africa, most St Helenians were classified as 'Coloureds' – since 1948, hardly the most comfortable of denotations. In the UK, the Commonwealth Immigrants Act of 1968 has been enforced, in almost certain violation of an ancient Charter signed by Charles II (1673) which promised St Helenians full rights of citizenship, 'as if they had been abiding and borne within this our realme of England'. (Unfortunately, no St Helenian has yet challenged the ruling in the UK court of law.) The application of immigration controls has adversely affected a common form of mobility among young women – domestic service for a couple of years, followed by permanent settlement in the United Kingdom. Emigration is thus difficult, and, one must add, beyond the means of many islanders. Considerable numbers of young men do, however, travel as deck passengers to the island of Ascension, 700 miles North-West of St Helena. There they work as contract labourers to Pan Am, NASA, Cable and Wireless, the BBC and a few small concerns, which have bases on the island. Employment in Ascension, however, provides only a partial, temporary and, so it is reported, diminishing, solution to unemployment in St Helena.

Enough has been said to indicate the severe environmental constraints within which the educational system is set and the attitudes of St Helenian schoolchildren formed and generated. What pattern of education is possible in such an adverse context? What are the stated aims and the actual achievements of the school system? How do children perceive their immediate and wider environment? What are their aspirations for their future way of life and their expectations in respect of employment? How do these aspirations and expectations match the previous pattern of social mobility and employment? How finally, do St Helenian schoolchildren conceive of themselves and define their identity in relation to other peoples and other societies? Because of their sensitive character, a number of these questions are unassailable to the heavy bludgeon of an attitude survey, so a number of techniques were employed to discover the views of a sample group of 85 school children. These included informal classroom discussion, a mapping exercise, essay writing, and discussions and feedback from teachers, the methodology being described in more detail below. By trying to probe the answers to such questions amongst the schoolchildren of St Helena, it might be possible to infer a more general answer to the question that overwhelms the visiting sociologist. How is it possible for people to learn to cope with such total dependence, so little in the way of productive activity, and so great an isolation from the rest of the world?

The educational system

The ambiance of education in the eight Primary, three Senior and one Secondary Selective School on the island is, as one might expect, overwhelmingly British. The children use British text-books and readers and write examinations set by the Royal Society of Arts and 'O' levels for the General Certificate of Education. Every pupil at 14, takes a General Schools Certificate, a lower equivalent to a School Leaving Certificate, an index of a basic proficiency in English and arithmetic.

With the only exception of the Educational Officer himself (Canadian-trained), the Assistant Educational Officers and teachers are all trained in the UK or through in-service training programmes run by local officers with occasional assistance from a visiting UK tutor. A large proportion of the GCE entrants are, in fact, teachers attempting to obtain the requisite number of five 'O' levels before proceeding to the UK, for a one-year course, leading to a locally recognized Certificate of Education. Though a few teachers have been trained in Birmingham, Nottingham and Leicester, for the most part training is carried out under a 'link' scheme, sponsored by the Overseas Development Administration with the Cheltenham College of Education. Out of the total of over seventy teachers and pupil teachers only five are men. The low pay and status attached to the teaching profession (in 1974/5, a certified teacher started at £696 per annum)[3] are the usual reasons cited for the low number of male entrants to the profession, but the sexual division of labour also appears to have generalized psychological support. Administrators complain that the predominance of women, particularly teachers, means that there are always numbers of teachers away on maternity leave. The temporary gaps cannot be easily filled, first, because the few potentially available supply teachers are deterred by the low pay

---

3 Government of St Helena, *Estimates of Revenue and Expenditure for the Year 1974/7* (St Helena, Government Printing Office, n.d., but 1974) p. 11.

and second, because a scheme to use VSO (Voluntary Service Overseas) teachers has ended – not, allegedly, for educational reasons, but because of the sociable habits of VSO teachers. If this allegation is correct, and it is widely believed, it reflects the caste-like attitudes of white colonial officialdom, apparently disapproving of too much fraternization among the British citizens of St Helena who are somewhat darker and more ethnically diverse than their metropolitan counterparts. Teachers, in summary, are predominantly young women, who are poorly paid and often inadequately trained, while schools often are short staffed, at least for temporary periods.

Pre-school playgroups started in Jamestown, the capital, in the mid-1960s have, since 1972, attracted about 120 children, while enrolment in infant, primary and secondary schools for children aged 5–15 numbers over 1,258, over one quarter of the population. The teacher-pupil ratio is 1:18, a favourable ratio by UK standards, but one that has to be set within the context of an inadequate level of training and the frequency of leaves. At present the critical selection is carried out at the secondary level, where academically proficient children, are enrolled in the Secondary Selective School at Ladder Hill. A proposal for a more comprehensive system, first suggested by the Department in 1971, was given a much greater impetus first by the Development Plan and second by a report prepared by E J Dorrell, formerly Director of the Oxfordshire Educational Authority in 1974.[4] In the five-year Development Plan for the island due to run to 1979, the

---

4   The department paper 'Educational Development in St Helena' October 1971 is referred to on p. 6 of Basil George's, *Education for Growth: School and Community in St Helena* (Mimeographed Paper, Bristol, 1977, 9 pp.). See also E. J. Dorrell, *St Helena: the Educational System: Report of a visit undertaken on behalf of the Ministry of Overseas Development* (Dec. 1974).

capital cost for the comprehensive school is estimated at £200,000, which assumes an eventual intake of 400 pupils, the numbers going up as the school-leaving age is raised. The general proposal which included the idea of reorganizing the school system into First School (5–8), Middle School (9–12) and a single comprehensive school (13+) has now bogged down in a series of counter-proposals (a) to situate the comprehensive school at Ladder Hill by upgrading the existing facilities, (b) to purpose-build a new school at Half-tree hollow (Government Development Plan), (c) to build a purpose-built school linking it with an agricultural college on Francis Plain, which provides good playing fields but is relatively far from a centre of population or (d) a recent proposal to retain a selective system, with some modifications (the Education Office).[5] As with everything else in St Helena, the wheels of decision and implementation grind exceedingly slow, though it is interesting to notice an active participation in the debate by locals whose normal political posture tends to be quiescent.

It is necessary also to mention that other than the formal school system, there is some further and specialized education on the island. Saturday morning classes, run by the Department of Education, are attended by 130 people, many of them teachers, while a former ship's captain runs erratically-held navigation classes. A splendidly eccentric British expatriate woman, who claims to be a cousin of the Queen, runs speech, deportment and etiquette classes for young women. This is more practical than it sounds, as female St Helenians are highly valued by those members of the British aristocracy who can still afford to employ a large domestic staff. A few full-time craftsmen informally take on

---

5   The alternatives are summarized in Basil George, *Education for Growth*.

young apprentices. But the most important educational develop-ment, outside the school system, is the development of a Technical Trades Centre. Though only small numbers have enrolled, 12 in 1974 and 10 in 1975, the scheme has been highly successful in providing a range of skills in building and allied subjects, to a group of school-leavers who previously left school at fifteen to confront a highly adverse employment market. Most of the graduates of the Trades Centre go on to almost certain employment and shortened apprenticeships in government departments, predominantly the Public Works Department (known, cynically, as the Please Wait Department). A scheme run by the Agricultural and Forestry Department for young men in the 15–18 age group, called the Young Farmers' Scheme, has been less successful in educational terms and is more accurately seen as a welfare/social control scheme, rather than an educational project.

Educational objectives and the employment market

A number of critical statements issued by the Educational Department, or other officialdom, can be taken to indicate the planned objectives of the educational system. The 1971 state-ment of the Department states that the Education Department aims to provide 'an education suited to the ages, aptitudes and abilities of all children between the ages of 5–15 years, planned to give them the knowledge and *skills needed for life in St Helena* and an understanding of the problems of life in a small com-munity, and to *prepare them for life outside* should they leave the island'.[6]

---

6   Government of St Helena, *Development Plan 1974/1979 Part One* p. 11 [Emphasis added].

A more recent document (1972), consulted in the Education Department, Jamestown, is both a good deal fuller and considerably more idealistic in its aims. It states [emphasis added]:

- A resourceful people will accept responsibility for development of themselves and their community, use individual and collective initiatives to identify their problems and seek realistic solutions to them. ... Such a people will be *less dependent-minded* and more able to make positive contributions to themselves and the wider world community.

- A co-operative people will plan together and work together to build a better community for themselves and their children. They will rise above more selfish concerns and *organize co-operative enterprises to achieve socially-desirable ends.*

- A skilled people will meet the requirements of their developing community with competence and confidence in their ability. They *will also be better prepared for emigration.*

- A culturally aware people will be *conscious of their rich and varied heritage* and their social environment.

- Investment in *the creation of a 'new' people* characterized by the above qualities is a noble, and ultimately economic, expenditure of resources for the mother country.[7]

In the same document the school is seen quite explicitly as 'a major agency for social change' in St Helena. Other observers

---

7 Education Department of St Helena, *Projected Development, 1973–77* p. 5. [Emphasis added].

either are more sceptical, or see the role of education as much more marginal. For example, Ian Shine, in the course of undertaking a medical and genetic study, based on his period as a Medical Officer of Health, has this to say about education:

> Until recently, although few people were illiterate, the standard was poor mainly because of the scarcity of good teachers, many of them being untrained teenagers. Most of the thirteen schools are new, spacious and pleasant, but few pupils have achieved a single pass at O-level in the GCE, which would not seem to be due to a lack of native intelligence as far as one can judge on the basis of daily performance. For example, most, men are able to farm, fish, play the guitar, cut hair, make an efficient watering can from a margarine tin, mend shoes and build their own houses.[8]

If the descent is not from the sublime to the totally ridiculous, it is certainly to the highly prosaic level of everyday living. Another author, Margaret Stewart Taylor, again with a somewhat different appreciation of the possibilities of the life style after school pronounced herself impressed by a letter she had seen written by a young woman of 16 from a senior school: 'I was impressed', she writes, 'with the way the girl expressed herself, as well as by the good composition and neat writing'. She also refers to the evening classes given in Jamestown which provide 'instruction in crafts as well as pursuing academic studies'. These academic studies, however, appear only to have fitted her imaginary character 'Peter' for an unskilled position, for, she immediately goes on:

---

8 Ian Shine, *Serendipity in St Helena: A Genetical and Medical Study of an Isolated Community* (Oxford: Pergamon Press, 1970) pp. 20, 21.

Peter might get employment with Diplomatic Wireless Service as a labourer, or with Cable and Wireless Ltd. He might go to Ascension as an employee of the latter, or be recruited by the Americans for road-making or other work at the satellite tracking station established there. Ascension Island might well be the goal of Peter's ambitions. He would have seen his uncle returning on leave, wearing jazz-patterned shirt, tight trousers and pointed shoes.[9]

Exciting as the prospects may be for 'Peter' to emulate his sartorially inventive uncle, the reality that confronts him or his female counterpart after leaving school is far different. A more accurate gauge of his prospects can be gathered from examining the records of school leavers from three (out of the total of four) senior schools from which data were compiled (Table 4.1). The schools concerned are Harford Senior School, Country Secondary and the Secondary Selective (the last taking mainly girls with a stronger academic record). In each case the first 'occupation' (if we can so deem unemployment) is compared with the 'last recorded employment'. This reflects a three-year period in the case of students graduating in 1971 (about a quarter of the sample), a two-year period in the case of students graduating in 1972 (another quarter); and anything from three months to one year in the case of students completing their studies in the years 1973/74 (the remaining half of the sample).

The immediate prospects for the 15 to 16 year old school leavers are indeed grim. Well over half of the senior school graduates can expect to be unemployed immediately after leaving

---

9   Margaret Stewart Taylor, *St Helena: Ocean Roadhouse* (London: Robert Hale, 1969) pp. 131, 132–3.

Table 4.1: Occupations of school leavers from three St Helenian schools, 1971–4 (%)

	First Employment			Last Employment		
	HSS	CS	SS	HSS	CS	SS
Unemployed	60	53	30	41	39	19
Labourers	18	32	0	31	33	3
Clerks	0	1	25	0	1	26
Domestics (St H)	13	6	3	12	12	4
Domestics (UK)	1	0	2	1	2	
Teachers	2	0	19	3	0	17
Apprentices	1	4	15	1	6	13
Shop Assistants	2	1	5	2	1	2
Work on Ascension	0	0	0	6	3	0
Housewives	0	0	0	0	0	3
Nurses	0	0	2	0	0	2
Gardeners	1	1	0	1	1	0
Police	0	0	0	0	0	2
Public Health	0	0	2	0	0	2
Fishermen	0	0	0	0	1	0
Unknown	2	1	0	2	1	5
Percentage*	99	100	101	101	99	100

*Rounding errors where not 100

Key and numbers:

HSS=Harford Senior School   N=126, Males=73, Females=53
CS=Country Secondary   N=105, Males=61, Females=44
SS=Secondary Selective   N=69, Males=25, Females=44

Sources: School Records, Records of Education Department, Information from Teachers.

school, a proportion that drops only slightly after three years out of school. In the case of the elite school, the Secondary Selective, just under one third of its graduates can expect immediate unemployment, though this figure drops to 19 per cent after a period out of school. In fact, the critical period of unemployment can be easily identified as between 15–18 years. At fifteen, the school system ends for all young people, other than those attending the Senior Selective School, who stay on for another year.

At eighteen, which is the minimum age permitted for employment on Ascension, numbers of young men go to work as migrant labourers, accompanied by only a small number of young women. Out of a rough total of 450 'Saints' on Ascension, approximately 110 men in the age group 18–20 and 120 men in the age group 21–25 are on Ascension at any one time.[10] Thus while Margaret Stewart Taylor projects a somewhat fanciful image of the delights of the island (which in fact is a grim volcanic rock with 'clinker crawling' as virtually the only recognized sport), it is true to suggest that prospects of a young man (though not a young woman) spending some time working on Ascension are good, provided something of a work ethic remains after spending three years of boredom, frustration and unemployment on St Helena. The pattern of a stagnant pool of 'relative surplus population' which only gains employment, and overwhelmingly of course unskilled labour, over a number of years, is confirmed by longitudinal data compiled in 1973 by the Chief Education Officer. Here, in Table 4.2, only the returns for 1968 school leavers are listed:

---

10 These figures fluctuate with the available economic opportunities on Ascension. In 1956, the total number of St Helenians on Ascension was 336; in 1966 the number had reached 476; while a 1973 estimate was 450. See Government of St Helena, *Censuses of the Population of St Helena Island and Ascension Island, 1956, 1966* (St Helena: Government Printing Office, 1956, 1966) pp. 10 and 14–15, and *St Helena Development Survey: Part Two* (Typescript) p. 11.

Table 4.2: Employment after five years for 1968 school leavers

	Males	Females
Employed immediately	8	8
Unemployed for full five years	3	13
Unemployed over four years	0	1
Unemployed for three years	1	1
Unemployed for two years	7	4
Unemployed for one year	7	1
Employed (year of engagement unknown)	19	8
Married*	0	4
Not known	2	1
Total	**47**	**47**

*That this should be regarded as a form of 'employment' is revealing.

Source: Chief Education Officer to Development Advisor, Memo, 1st June 1973

In the past some sort of precarious balance was maintained between the rate of emigration and the number of jobs genera-ted on the island or on Ascension. Now, however, the rate of emigration has dropped dramatically. Over the period 1950–72, there was a net in-migration from South Africa, following the application of laws of apartheid to St Helenians, while the sudden drop in emigration to Britain, after the (probably illegal) appli-cation of the Commonwealth Immigrant Act of 1968, can be evidenced as follows. From 1950–54 (261 migrants to the UK), in 1955–59 (492), 1960–64 (261), 1965–69 (92), 1970 (12), 1971 (19), 1972 (11). Such is the falling rate of emigration that the

planners now estimate an annual population increase of between 60–100 and an annual employment gap of up to 70 males
alone.[11]

Let us now return to the stated aims of the educational
department in the light of the nature of the employment market
confronting the St Helenian school-leavers. First, the aim to
'prepare [St Helenians] for life in the world outside' seems to
have been formulated when emigration was a more practical
policy for many St Helenians than now appears to be the case.
While it is doubtful that any adequate preparation of this kind
has indeed been undertaken in the schools (see later
discussion), the government planners curiously repeat the
solution of emigration in the face of their own figures. 'Sadly',
they write, 'it would seem that the seeking of more employment
opportunities overseas, on both a temporary and a permanent
basis, should be actively encouraged and sponsored by the
Government.'[12] This solution has been strongly opposed by the
St Helena Labour Party, a party which under the vociferous
leadership of G. A. D. Thornton, has considerable influence on
public opinion in the island, though it has so far failed to gain
representation on the island's Legislative Council. In the party's
major statement, The St Helena Manifesto, the policy of
depopulation is hotly attacked: 'We say No! Depopulation is a
defeatist and negative "solution" to the problems of St Helena.
If the plan cannot claim to absorb the expected increase in
population then the plan is a failure before it begins.'[13]

---

11 St Helena Development Survey Part Two (Typescript) pp. 8, 9.
12 Cited in St Helena Labour Party, The St Helena Manifesto
   (Jamestown: St Helena Labour Party, November 1975) pp. 13, 14.
13 St Helena Labour Party, The St Helena Manifesto, p.14. The
   intervention of G. A. D. Thornton, a British-born but South African

Second, the aims of the department include preparing children for the 'skills needed for life on St Helena'. But what are these skills? Hair cutting, making watering cans, building houses (not in fact taught in the schools), selecting jazz-coloured shirts, accommodating to the long periods of unemployment or employment as unskilled labourers? These appear to be the skills demanded of school leavers.

Third, in its more idealistic formulation, the Department of Education talks of fostering 'less dependent-minded' people, able to 'organise co-operative enterprises to achieve socially desirable ends'. These will be a 'new people' who are 'conscious of the rich and varied heritage'. Stated in abstract terms, one could hardly wish for a more far-reaching and humanistic statement of the purposes of education.

But the products of the education system, seem to show, as shall be argued, that almost the opposite effect has been achieved. Overwhelmingly, the education system does not provide school leavers with an accurate or meaningful cognitive map of the world outside and so does not equip them for emigration. The school does in a sense equip St Helenians for the skills needed in St Helena i.e. how to survive in a situation of utter dependence and economic adversity, while exercising the minimum of skill and creativity. What it does not provide is the fostering of the capacity to transform the environment. There are no 'new people' being created on St Helena, individuation and not

based businessman, in the political and economic affairs of the island is a subject of considerable controversy. Since 1975 he has been banned from the island, which could account for the Party's poor showing in the 1976 elections. Background information to this complicated dispute can be found in reports in *The Guardian* (15/4/74), *The Times* (22/4/74), *The Guardian* (18/10/75) and *The Guardian* (21/11/77).

co-operation is the norm; while many St Helenian schoolchildren (and by inference their parents) are self-conscious, ignorant or ashamed of what is indeed 'a rich and varied heritage'. These assertions are addressed more fully below in respect of the separate treatment of environmental perceptions, aspirations and expectations and self-conceptions of 'identify' by St Helenian schoolchildren.

Environmental perception

In the first test, that of 'environmental perception', an attempt was made to assess what knowledge of, or images of the world outside St Helena were evinced by a group of school leavers. The sample comprised eleven young women, 15 or 16 years of age, in the Secondary Selective School and another set of 42 respondents, divided roughly equally by sex, drawn from two other senior schools. In this case the children were normally fifteen years old. In all cases the students were in their final year of instruction, so could reasonably be expected to have absorbed what was available in the school in the way of 'preparation for the world outside'.

As phenomenologists have been at pains to point out, we all perceive the world somewhat differently, variation stemming from such factors as past experience, access to information, social relationships of dominance and disadvantage, expectations by other parties, or the extent of networks and communication links. This insight was explained to the students both in general and by the use of everyday examples. For instance it was shown how individuals may variously define a blackboard eraser in terms of its function, its shape, its colour, the materials it was made from, and so on. When the idea of selectivity and variability in perception was understood, a flat outline map of the world – unmarked except for the barest geographical details – was given to each student. Two degrees of familiarity were assumed. In the first set, students were asked to mark locations, distances and times of travel to places that were assumed to be relevant to their experience and knowledge. In the second set, a higher degree of unfamiliarity was assumed (though no question was thought excessively opaque or obscure). After the exercise was completed, classroom discussion, often for a long period, ensued. The results are tabulated in Table 4.3:

Table 4.3: Simple set: environmental perceptions of St Helenian students (%)

| | Secondary Selective | | | Other Senior | | |
	Close	Low	High	Close	Low	High
Can locate the Equator	82	18	0	83	16	1
Distances to Cape Town and Southampton	0	40	60	8	10	73*
Travel time to Cape Town and Southampton	10	30	40*	10	20	62*

	Yes	No	Yes	No
Can locate St Helena and Ascension	100	0	92	8
Can roughly convert miles into kilometres	30	70	5	95
Can locate Tristan da Cunha	20	80	5	95

*Figures not totalling 100% are accounted for by 'don't knows'.
Percentages are rounded.

Sample: Secondary Selective N=11 (all girls). Other secondary (Harford and Country Secondary) N=42 (males 24, females, 18).

As one might expect, the Secondary Selective Sample (being a year older and in the elite school) showed a higher level of accuracy in their perceptions and knowledge about the simple set of questions than the group from the other secondary schools. Nearly all the students, however, could locate their own island, Ascension and the two points of regular communication with the island – Cape Town and Southampton. Significantly, where there was error, in terms of distances and times to these points, the errors were *downward*, thus showing a strong tendency to 'compress' communication points towards the island. This was done by shortening the distance, shortening the travel time or in several cases conveniently moving the location of Cape Town up the African coastline. Most pupils were unable to convert the distances they provided in miles into kilometres, while overwhelmingly they could not locate Tristan da Cunha, despite the fact that Tristan is governed in association with St Helena and indeed, like Ascension, is legally a 'dependency' of St Helena. The fact that the children showed little familiarity with a measurement like 'a kilometre' did not auger well for their adequate 'preparation for the world outside'. This 'failing' was, however, minor compared to the wild distortion and fantastic errors that were revealed by the more complex set of questions asked (Table 4.4):

Each of these responses bears brief discussion. In most cases the northern border of South Africa was massively exaggerated, in several cases reaching the northern side of the Sahara. The links with South Africa are, of course, very strong. Six thousand Boer prisoners-of-war were sent to the island during the Boer War (1899–1902), there is easy reception of Radio South Africa, there are continuing family links with St Helenians in the Republic, while finally, South African history (of a white variety) is

Table 4.4: Complex set: environmental perceptions of St Helenian students (%)

	Secondary Selective			Other Senior		
	Yes	High	Very High	Yes	High	Very High
Can roughly draw northern border of South Africa	20	40	40	6	42	52
Can locate five African countries/cities (Nigeria, Lagos, Sierra Leone, Freetown, Cape Verde)	*All 5* 0	*1–4* 30	*None* 70	*All 5* 0	*1–4* 10	*None* 90
Can locate USA, Canada, Texas	*2–3* 70	*1* 10	*None* 20	*2–3* 43	*1* 21	*None* 36
Can locate islands (Cuba, West Indies, Falklands, Madeira, Madagascar, New Guinea)	*All 8* 0	*2–7* 41	*None* 58	*All 8* 0	*2–7* 25	*None* 75
	Yes	No		Yes	No	
Can locate Namibia (South West Africa) and Angola	20	80		6	94	
Can locate USSR and China	30	70		18	82	
Can provide rough population estimates for USSR and China	10	90		0	100	
Can locate Hong Kong and draw its borders	40	60		14	86	
Can locate Brazil and Rio de Janeiro	20	80		12	88	

Sample: Secondary Selective N=11 (all girls). Other secondary (Harford and Country Secondary) N=42 (males 24, females, 18).

taught in the schools. This response might be linked with the abysmal ignorance shown of the countries of independent black Africa, ex-Portuguese Africa and Namibia. In each case I tried to identify a place on the continent meaningful to St Helenians. For example, Angola is the nearest land mass and there is a historical connection via the expansion of Portuguese mercantilism. Many ancestors of the St Helenian population came from Angola or further north along coastal Africa. Lagos, Cape Verde and Freetown were connected via Cable and Wireless activities and a number of 'Saints' had worked in these places while laying the cable, or during the Second World War. In addition, with the movement of African liberation there were virtually daily radio bulletins by the BBC and Radio South Africa about the situation in Namibia and Angola. In spite of this Angola was 'shrunk' or wrongly located in nearly all cases. Only one (out of 53 students) had heard the designation 'Namibia', despite the fact that this is the UN-recognized term and even when designated 'South West Africa', few could hazard a guess as to its location. Lagos, Freetown, Cape Verde, Nigeria and Sierra Leone were predominantly wildly placed all over the continent of Africa (and outside it) with countries shown as cities and vice versa. In discussion, the contours emerged more clearly.

'Africa' was, overwhelmingly, South Africa, which was seen in a positive, pro-white, and more powerful and larger profile than was indicated even in the geographical misconception, shared by a number of students, that it occupied three quarters of the continent. The harsher aspects of apartheid and the racial definition accorded to St Helenians by the South African authorities were concealed from the students. On the other hand, black Africa was Africa of tribal wars, cannibalism and the drum; these, the crudest of stereotypes, remaining unchallenged by the educational system. Indeed it would be difficult to transcend such ignorance by the written word. The official and only weekly newssheet, the

St Helena News Review (known by the islanders as the 'Two Minute Silence') contains no African news, while the Public Library in Jamestown stocked only one novel by an African writer (Ekwensi's *People of the City*). The psychological ambiguities of being a darker-complexioned people with this combination of images of black and white Africa, are probed later in the section on identity.

With regard to other countries, Canada was 'enlarged' (possibly because the Chief Education Officer was Canadian, an important person whose country must therefore be important), the USA was often correctly placed, while Texas was nearly always shown as in California. The association of 'the Western movies' and Texas occasioned this error, as was apparent in discussion. An interesting 'shrinkage' (and frequent misplacing) of the USSR and China was evident despite the fact that several hundred Chinese had built the roads and the number of Chinese names showed that they were a significant element in the making of the population. In discussion, despite urgings, it was impossible to elicit from the students a population estimate of China in excess of 10 million people, many respondents seeing the Chinese population as fewer than the 5,000 St Helenians. By contrast, the size and population of Hong Kong was massively exaggerated (and also misplaced), largely because among one group the researcher reminded the students that no less a person than the Superintendent of Police had his last posting there. The question asking the location of Brazil and Rio de Janeiro was put mainly because many slaves were sent from Angola to Brazil via St Helena and a number of Portuguese slavers were after 1832 apprehended on the high seas by the British Navy, with St Helena acting as an Admiralty Court and a place of refuge and hospitalization. This wholly creditable part of St Helenian history is unknown. In addition to this historical connection, the government radio station was, at the time of research, running a serial on Brazil, which as is shown in the results of the question (over 80 per cent not knowing Brazil's location) must have been wholly meaningless for much of the population of the island. Finally, the sense of isolation and uniqueness that was already evident might have been relieved by providing information about other small island communities. But again, the education system provided simply a shroud of ignorance and mystery, leaving pupils in St Helena unable to compare themselves or their fate with people in the Caribbean, the Seychelles, Mauritius or the Falklands.

The overall impression left, both from the tests and related discussion, was that St Helenians were unprepared for life outside the island and indeed operated with such severe and fantastic distortions of that world, that they were inadequately prepared to understand the raison d'être and workings of their own society. The shrinking of geographical horizons has, of course, important effects in buttressing the status quo, in that it limits the capacity of the islanders either to conceptualize alternative economic possibilities or to imagine a different political order. What expectations and aspirations do St Helenian students, however, share? It is to this that we turn next.

Aspirations and expectations

To measure aspirations and expectations amongst St Helenian students, a somewhat different methodology was employed. Short essay assignments were given to the students from which the principal findings were derived. Though some support for this method as an independent line of enquiry can be given,[14] in this

---

14 See B. Berelson, *Content Analysis in Communication Research* (Glencoe: The Free Press, 1952) and B. Unterhalter 'A content analysis of the essays of Black and White South African high school pupils', *Race*, 14(3), January 1973, pp. 311–29.

case although our conclusions were drawn largely from contents analysis, some feedback discussions with teachers and students also influenced the interpretation of results. The sample comprised 16 students from the Secondary Selective School, 30 from the Country Secondary and 25 from Harford Senior School. The students were asked to provide accounts, answering two queries: 'What would you *like* to do after you leave school?', 'What do you *expect* you will do?' In the first essay the students were encouraged to give free play to their imaginations and fantasies, to write without inhibition or the fear of their views being individually discussed (the answers were all anonymous). Certain definite themes emerged from a contents analysis of the essays i.e. the themes of [a] 'Peace and Quiet', [b] 'Desire for a simple career', [c] 'Excitement and adventure', [d] 'Travel, Speed, Escape', [e] 'Prodigal son', [f] 'Helping others', [g] 'Going to Ascension', [h] 'Emigrating and life abroad'. How these categories were derived, is perhaps best typified by a few examples (I've retained the original spelling and grammar).

> *Example of [b]*: 'I would like to work on the land and in case sheeps go on a beach, go find them. I would like to plant the garden corn for cows'.
> (Male, Country Secondary School, Age 15).

> Examples of [c] and [d]: 'First of all I would like to explore all the continents, such as Africa, America, Asia but mainly Europe, than swim the largest river of lake … take a route from Ascension, Tristan da Cunha and down to the Southampton take a good look there than go India. … I would like to go in a rocket go up and take a well look at all the planets. … Also swim the Atlantic, climb the largest tower in the world and also the biggest mountain.'
> (Female, Harford School, Age 15).

Example of [h]: 'If I find America interesting, stay for a while, get a husband, a nice one. Start singing, getting in the movies. Go to Utah and get hold of one of the Osmonds and marry him. Go to the moon with him. Stay until he'd like to come back when he thinks our honeymoon is over. Start a family and go back to his hometown, Utah and settle there.'

(Female, Secondary Selective, Age 16).

Often categories crossed, or there were contradictory statements in each essay. For example, students stated both that they wanted to settle abroad permanently and that they wished to return to St Helena. To cover these and other ambiguities a scoring system was evolved as follows: '3' for strongly stated theme or special emphasis, '2' for definite statement of theme, '1' for subsidiary statement of theme. The score was totalled then expressed as a percentage of the total response within each school. The results are tabulated in Table 4.5, below.

What appeared significant in these findings is that even in terms of their aspirations, the students at the non-elite schools, Harford and Country Secondary, had lower horizons, hoping *more* for a simple career, peace and quiet and working on Ascension and hoping *less* for excitement and adventure, travel and escape, emigration and fame and fortune, than the students at the Secondary Selective School. It is also interesting to note that despite the stated aims of the education department to produce students who would 'rise above more selfish concerns and organize co-operative enterprises to achieve socially-desirable goals' only a tiny minority of the students aspired to 'help others'. Indeed, given how small and isolated the community is, and the sociologists' expectation that such communities are normally characterized by '*gemeinschaft*', the degree of individuation (with almost no mention of friends, parents and relatives let alone

Table 4.5: Aspirations of St Helenian students (%)

		SS	HSS	CS
[a]	Peace and Quiet	4	14	12
[b]	A Simple Career	0	9	6
[c]	Excitement and Adventure	21	15	18
[c]	Travel, Speed and Escape	43	35	32
[e]	To be a Prodigal son	11	8	7
[f]	To help others	4	0	2
[g]	To work on Ascension	3	12	17
[h]	Emigration and Life Abroad	14	7	6
Total		**100**	**100**	**100**

Key and numbers

SS=Secondary Selective   N=16, Males=2, Females=14
HSS=Harford Senior School   N=25, Males=16, Females=9
CS=Country Secondary   N=35, Males=19, Females=16

others 'less fortunate') was quite striking. Despite the difference between the schools, however, the most common responses were those of getting off the island, speeding up life and escaping the drab monotony of the environment.

'I would like to be a fish that swims the Atlantic in a seconds', 'I would like to be a ship that goes round the world in nine days', 'I would like to have spaceship go to space', 'I would like to going for a good ride round and round the world and stop at different places in the world and keep going all the time. Get on an aeroplane but still keep going'. These insistent and typical responses suggest that it is not too fanciful to argue that many St Helenians perceive the island as a place from which to escape, a prison from which one needs to 'keep going'. Indeed, given the present difficulties of travel and emigration, the analogy of society as a prison, which informs a book written by two sociologists,[15] gains a much more literal meaning in the context of St Helena.

Many sociologists of Africa, Asia and Latin America have glibly talked of 'the revolution of rising expectations' in the context of discussing how the weak and partial efforts to industrialize have failed to provide the jobs that school-leavers have 'demanded' in the 'modern' sector. Too often, however, as a sociologist of West Africa has pointed out, there is a failure to distinguish between the aspirations and expectations of school-leavers, the last often being surprisingly 'realistic' and closely geared to the employment market.[16] This insight was strongly confirmed by asking St Helenian students to write an account of 'What do you expect you will do' or 'think will happen to you' after school. The characteristic contrast in levels of abstraction and between aspirations and expectations expressed by the students can again be illustrated by quoting directly, this time from a 14-year-old boy at Country Secondary School.

> Aspirations: 'When I leave school I would like to be a captain of a ship belongest to the Bristis Navey where I can see many other countries. ... And able to speak different kinds of langue which other nations speak, for instant, Franchs and USSR.'

> Expectations: 'I think I will be an ordernary labour on the A & F (Agriculture and Forestry) Department and do farming and tent to animals.'

---

15 Stanley Cohen and Laurie Taylor, *Escape Attempts: The Theory and Practice of Resistance to Everyday Life* (London: Allen Lane, 1976).

16 Margaret Peil, 'Aspirations and Social Structure: A West African Example', *Africa*, 38(1) 1968, pp. 71–8.

The generalized responses to the expectations are listed in Table 4.6. Where more than one job was identified both were tabulated, the results being converted into percentages within each column.

Table 4.6: Expectations of St Helenian students (%)

	SS	HSS	CS
Clerk, other white collar	52	0	0
Teacher	16	3	0
Navy, Police, Sailor Nurse	0	6	6
Shop Assistant	12	3	7
Job or Live Abroad	12	4	15
Labouring (Ascension)	0	12	7
Labouring (St Helena)	0	12	8
Work on Ascension	0	9	8
Domestic Work	0	8	13
Fishing	0	13	14
Pastoral activities (farming, 'collect wood and stone', etc.)	0	17	18
Other	4	0	0
Not known or unusual (e.g. a 'lover' [prostitute?], 'a black frog', 'starvation')	0	8	10
Total	**100**	**100**	**100**

Key and numbers

SS=Secondary Selective   N=16, Males=2, Females=14
HSS=Harford Senior School   N=25, Males=16, Females=9
CS=Country Secondary   N=35, Males=19, Females=16

When Table 4.6 (Expectations) is compared with Table 4.1 (Actual Occupations) some fairly close comparisons are evident. In the Secondary Selective School, the expectation of being a Clerk, Teacher, Nurse or Shop Assistant (in that order) is stated in a similar order to the proportions of graduates from that school who actually entered those occupations during the previous three years. As the students in their final year at this school were usually a year older than their counterparts at other Secondary Schools and had the benefit of careful career guidance by their teachers, it is perhaps not surprising that they had their sights set realistically at the available opportunities. What they and other students seemed unwilling to accept is the almost certain reality of unemployment, at least for the first few years after leaving school. Perhaps naturally enough, the students tended to look beyond that first period of unemployment (15–18 years usually) to their first 'proper job'. Somewhat more of the Secondary Selective students proclaimed their expectation of living or working abroad than was likely to be their lot (as measured by the data set out in Table 4.1).

With respect to the students in Harford and Country Secondary, the spread of job expectations was much greater, though with minor exceptions, not including any white collar work. What was surprising in view of the small number of independent farmers and fishermen on the island, were the numbers of students who opted for these occupations. On closer examination, however, it seems as if many of the activities suggested were part-time and ancillary work rather than full-time farming or fishing. A few examples must suffice to illustrate this point: 'When I leave school I kind to get wood and ston and like to go fish', said one, 'I will be getting wood in from the forests for my mum' said another. 'I think I will get a job in the farm work. Set a little business up of poultry. Sell alot of the farm's eggs. Work for A & F', said a third.

In effect, some of the group who would be categorized officially (namely in school records) as unemployed, see themselves as performing jobs in the forests, on the farms or at sea, though often these would fall far short of a full-time, let alone self-sufficient, occupation. For the rest, the students at Harford and Country Secondary, have a generally realistic appreciation of their position in the job market and the different occupations open to them. In the light of the new consciousness about domestic work that the women's movement has aroused in Western industrial countries, it is notable that there is little self-consciousness about housework among the young women of St Helena. 'I would like to be a housemaid along with someone else cleaning the house and also I would like to help in the kitchen so that I would like to do', wrote one fifteen year old. 'If I don't get any work on this island, I would like to work in England for a person. I would cook, clean windows, sweep the rooms out, polish the furture [furniture] and so many other work than she expect me to do', wrote another.

To sum up. While the aspirations of St Helenian schoolchildren varied widely, and were of a higher order of imagination and possibility among the students of the Secondary Selective School, all the students exhibited a desire for escape and adventure to break the monotony of everyday life on the island. Expectations, by contrast, did not show a high level of fantasy, as many students seemed to have adjusted their life expectations to the likely possibilities for employment and self fulfilment in the island. Only in respect of the massive likelihood of unemployment were expectations still more optimistic, though it is probable that some activities perceived by teachers as unemployment were not so conceived by the adolescents concerned.

A St Helenian identity

The definition and creation of a 'social identity' is of course, a complex and problematic area of discussion, and we can advance no profound theoretical insights here.[17] There are, however, normally two major elements to the formation of a group's identity: (a) a self-conscious attempt by members of the group to characterize its own origins, culture and relationship to other groups, and (b), the definition by other significant actors of a group's identity and characteristics. In the latter case, the group is a recipient, not an initiator, of the definition. In so far as an outsider's definition (or label or stereotype) becomes internalized by the defined group, it acknowledges the power of outsiders to establish the group's own sense of reality and corporate nature. In the context of St Helena the significant outsiders are the British Government, its colonial officials on the ground, some of the small group of white settlers (usually from Southern Africa) on the island and more intermittent contacts from travellers, development 'experts', Americans and Europeans on Ascension.

Here I want to concentrate the discussion on three constituent 'strands' of a group's identity – religion, nationality and race – examining the interaction between outside and internal definitions of these constituents. We may start by looking at the official data on religion and nationality derived from the last census:

---

17 See, however, Erving Goffman, *Stigma: Notes on the Management of Spoiled Identity* (Harmondsworth: Penguin, 1968) and, for a discussion of the particular character of the colonized people's identity, Frantz Fanon, *The Wretched of the Earth* (London: MacGibben & Kee, 1965) and *Black Skins, White Masks* (London: Paladin, 1970).

Table 4.7: Religion and Nationality in St Helena

Nationality		Birthplace		Religion	
British Born	4627	St Helena	4465	Church of England	4182
British by Marriage	8	Ascension	5	Baptist	139
Naturalized British	4	UK	116	Salvationist	122
Canadian	3	South Africa	33	Jehovah's Witness	92
South African	5	Canada	3	Seventh Day Adventist	62
US National	2	Others	27	Others/Refused	49
Total	**4649**		**4649**		**4649**

Source: Government of St Helena, Census of the Population of St Helena Island and Ascension Island, 1966, Table VII, VIII and XI.

The picture that emerges from these statistics is apparent. Most islanders are overwhelmingly St Helenian born, of British nationality and belong to the Church of England. What the statistics miss in respect of nationality is that the British Government arrogates to itself the right to change the benefits that British nationality confers, at will. Thus, St Helenians have to carry a distinctive passport and have no rights of entry and settlement to the United Kingdom (except for the minor provisions regarding dependents allowed for in the Commonwealth Immigrants Act of 1968). Again, whereas many St Helenians would be able to qualify under the 'patrial' rule for 'full' British nationality, equivalent to the metropolitan citizen, (a father or grandfather on the male side born in Britain or of British nationality), no St Helenian on the island has, as far as the researcher is aware, ever invoked this right. Patriality may, of course, be more difficult to demonstrate in an island where the great majority of islanders are born 'out of wedlock'. The change in the status for St Helenians, i.e. the stripping over the last ten years of their ancient rights to full British citizenship and nationality, again as far as this researcher is aware, has not been the subject of a debate in the Legislative Council, has not been debated in the *St Helena News Review*, nor again has it ever merited an official announcement by the Governor or his officials. In short, the British Government and its local minions have, by unspoken agreement, chosen to define the rights of St Helenians in a manner which they see fit, without serious input from the islanders.

What representation the islanders can make is severely limited by the backward state of constitutional development. The right to vote for a twelve-member Legislative Council has only been established since January 1967, while the St Helenians on Ascension have been denied the right to vote. When one adds to this, the fact that employees of the Government (which is virtually the only employer on the island) are not permitted to stand in elections it is perhaps not surprising that the Legislative Council is dominated by white settlers of independent means. A few hesitant protests began to surface about this concentration of power in a limited number of hands in the late sixties. For example, a letter to the Editor of the Newsletter of the St Helena Workers' Union about the poor state of the educational system, had this to say:

> As far back as 1847, the Bishop of Cape Town found the state of education in St Helena unsatisfactory. ... Yet, so far no one has got down to concrete terms with the problem. The colonials come out here with preconceived ideas and, even after years of holding positions which were hitherto as unfamiliar as the sea is to non-swimmers, are unwilling to change their ideas, lose their prejudices, and come down off their high horses. They simply do not

understand the natives and are unwilling to reach some understanding. It is high time we were given the opportunity of telling them what we consider best for us.[18]

This letter is interesting in counterpoising the terms 'colonials' and 'natives', thus defining the relationship more accurately than the official blandishments about being 'of British nationality', which conceal the fact that no attendant rights of holding that nationality have, in practice, been accorded to the islanders. Protests have, however, normally remained dormant until the recent arrival of G. A. D. Thornton on the island, who purchased 62 per cent of the shares of the remaining mercantile company on the island, Solomon & Co., a firm first established in 1790. While many islanders could identify with his entrepreneurial flair, his attacks on the incompetence of the colonial officials and the reactionary character of the settlers who dominated the Legislative Council, the fact that he is an outsider, based in South Africa, and an employer himself, means that he can hardly be regarded as representing the authentic voice of the islanders. But whatever protest emanated from that quarter has also now been silenced by the Government's purchase of the controlling shares of Solomon and the banning order, still in force, served on Thornton.[19]

The impotence and ignorance of the islanders regarding their status is, to a large degree confirmed by the results of an essay

---

18 St Helena Workers' Union, *The Voice of the Union* No.48, 8 July, 1967, pp. 1–2.

19 Thornton's position has been stated in numerous memoranda and letters, many of which he has kindly provided to the author. His programme for the development of the island is crystallized in *The St Helena Manifesto*. Government's views are partially represented in the news items referred to in Note 13 above, and in Legislative Council debates in 1974/5.

assignment given to fifteen students at the Secondary Selective School. The students were asked to write on the topic 'Who am I?' and, in separate sessions, the answers were followed by intensive discussion. With respect of nationality, the following definitions were provided: 'I am of St Helenian descent', 'I am of British nationality and was born in St Helena which I feel very proud of:', 'I am half English and half St Helenian', 'I was born on this tiny island of St Helena. I am a St Helenian girl', 'I have been living on this forgotten island. Therefore I have obtained St Helenian nationality'. While the schoolchildren can hardly be expected to have followed the legislative moves in Britain which were passed due to the influence of the anti-immigrant lobby, in discussion a deep sense of disquiet and unease was revealed about how their nationality was tinkered with without consultation. Only one sixteen-year-old girl (above) pronounced herself 'proud of being born in St Helena; other students tended to emphasize either uncertainty as to their status, or over-emphasized their 'Britishness' – either in terms of their ancestry or their nationality.

With respect to religion, nearly all students ritually identified themselves as members of the Church of England. This formal adherence does represent a deeply held religious conviction by many islanders, but it also signifies a strong aspirant identification with 'things British'. The Church's teaching notably conflicts, however, with island custom and social practice in respect of marriage and sexual liaisons. Most of the islanders are born from unions not sanctified by the Church which can be more accurately compared to the 'friending relationships' practised on many West Indian islands.[20] The reconciliation with the Church comes in frequent formal marriages at a much later stage of a couple's

---

20 H. Rodman, *Lower Class Families: The Culture of Poverty in Negro Trinidad* (New York: Oxford University Press, 1972).

relationship, which, it should be added, is frequently very stable. Often, the couple is in a better position at a later stage in life to throw a large and expensive party – a 'blow-out' occasion akin to the redistributive mechanisms noted by anthropologists in egalitarian communities. The author was a guest at a wedding party reputedly costing £450, approximately the annual income of the bridegroom. The teenage daughters of the couple were the bridesmaids. Formal adherence to the Anglican faith does not exclude, as Shine reports, a humorous justification for the practice of father–daughter incest ('I wouldn't trust a man with a tom cat, much less a she cat'), nor the fairly common incidence of first cousin marriage, despite the fact that the church has preached against it.[21] Nor again does Anglicanism preclude a widespread belief in the power of the 'evil eye'. As Shine observed, 'The idea that certain people with the evil eye can bewitch, injure or even kill with a glance, is extremely common'. The two medical practitioners on the island are supplemented by a number of witch doctors whose skills include the power of inserting objects like pumpkins, rabbits, snails, goats or motorcars into various parts of the body.[22] In this case, the reconciliation with the Church of England is achieved by quoting a passage from Deuteronomy: 'If you will not hearken unto the voice of the Lord thy God, then all the following curses will fall upon you – the man that is tender among you and very delicate, his eye shall be evil toward his brother.'

While, as Shine notes, the belief in the evil eye was common among many societies, in St Helena the practice has been associated historically with the relatively small numbers of African slaves on the island whose beliefs, particularly where they were thought

---

21 Ian Shine, *Serendipity in St Helena*, p.39.
22 Ian Shine, *Serendipity in St Helena*, pp. 35, 36.

capable of mobilizing a slave revolt, were firmly suppressed, often with great cruelty. In the eighteenth century, blacks were, for example, castrated for assaulting a white person, severely whipped for 'giving saucy language' and branded, mutilated and whipped for 'resisting'.[23] This leads us to our last, and most problematic constituent strand of a St Helenian identity, the question of race. The different racial elements that go into the making of the St Helenian population are very diverse and include Europeans (English, Portuguese and Dutch principally), Malays, Malagasies, East Indians, Chinese and Africans. Because there exists a particular sensitivity and negative stereotype to the African inheritance, it perhaps is worth indicating, as closely as is possible, the African element in the population. We can conveniently divide population history between pre- and post-1832. From 1650–1792, the European settlers imported slaves from Malabar, Bombay, the Maldive islands, Bengal, Calabar, the Guinea Coast and Madagascar. The last was a particularly important element, as each of the passing ships, several hundred a year at the peak, from 1679 onwards was 'taxed' one Madagascar slave. After 1792 the importation of slaves was forbidden. In 1806, however, the need for labour was such that the East India Company, which governed the island under Royal Charter, imported 650 Chinese from Canton as gardeners, mechanics and builders. By 1832, when slavery was abolished, these diverse elements had a sufficient degree of corporate identity to describe themselves as 'yam stalks', referring to the crop that had taken root on the island. After 1832 (and in particular over the period 1840–47) many Africans in other nations' slave ships, captured on the high seas by the British Naval Squadron, were hospitalized,

---

23 E. L. Jackson, *St Helena: the Historic Island* (London: Ward, Lock & Co., 1903) pp. 64–6.

and released on the island. Of the 9,155 who landed, many were returned to Africa or chose to emigrate to the West Indies (5,744), quite a number died from the privation they had suffered, and about 500 stayed on the island.[24] Technically, the liberated Africans of the 1840–47 phase were 'recaptives', slaves only in the sense that they had been caught, but not slaves in that they had never worked in plantations or the like. Nonetheless, as J. C. Mellis recorded with some asperity (1875), the 'Yam stalks' (St Helenians) practised discrimination against the Africans: He wrote:

> The 'Yam stalks' must not be confounded with Africans or Negroes, as the greatest insult they can hurl at one another is the epithet 'nigger' … [they] consider themselves as occupying a much higher step on the ladder of social position than the African, who certainly had the disadvantage of arriving at the island just eight years after the 'natives' became free men.[25]

If one considers slaves from Madagascar as Africans in the pre-1832 period, takes account of the gradual assimilation of the post-1840 African population, minus the fair number of departures, a rough guess (which should be compared with Shine's views)[26] is that about half of the population derived from African stock, a quarter from China and the Indian Ocean (excluding Madagascar) and a quarter were of European ancestry.

In the 1970s, however, the only distinct racial groups are the European colonial officials and the white settlers, the others

---

24 E. L. Jackson, *St Helena*, p. 261.

25 J. C. Mellis, *St Helena: A Physical, Historical and Topographical Description of the Island* (Ashford, Kent: L Reeve & Co., 1875) pp. 79, 80.

26 Ian Shine, *Serendipity in St Helena*, p. 16.

being blended together in what one islander described to the researcher as a 'liquorice all sorts, which is all mixed up'. What is clear, however, is that most islanders determinedly reject, or are kept in ignorance of their African past. Of the fourteen students who mentioned their racial origins in their assigned essays, none made any reference to Africa and several doggedly found European ancestors: 'I am a girl of Irish descent on the father's side and English on my mothers', 'I am of Irish descent on my mother's side, but I don't know my father', 'We are the only family of (English surname) on the island', 'My great grandfather on my father's side is Irish', 'My grandmother was born in Kent. My mother was born on St Helena. In other words some people would class me as a half-breed', 'I am of Chinese descent', are examples of the responses by the schoolchildren at the Selective School.

Perhaps the most interesting attempt by an islander to peer through this sad veil of delusion and self-hatred was made by Keith Yon in a dramatic performance of a concert, entitled Slave Song, staged at the Paramount Cinema on 14th August 1974. Quotes are from the programme notes or texts[27] assigned to the schoolchildren who were under Yon's charge as drama teacher on the island. For Yon black and white are 'potential building forces within everybody. Balance the instinct of one and the intellect of the other, we become whole and survive'. The message of Slave Song is to 'exercise this unhappy, uncertain, unnecessary blockage'. For the first time ever on the island, Yon sought to dramatize the issue of racial origins and force his audience to confront what they felt they had to hide. In so doing (in this

---

27 Slave Song (Text 12 pp.) A concert of Slave Song (programme), both 1974. I am grateful to Keith Yon for providing these also a typescript of Fashia Gestation (1974).

writer's view) he was in danger of accepting the identification of sensuality with blackness that forms part of another racial stereotype. Nonetheless, Yon's lyrical poetry is of an unusually high standard and recalls the work of Senghor. In his 'five poems', Black is Beautiful, recited by the boys of Harford School, he dared speak the previously unspeakable:

1. Your EYES shine brown leaf suns sunk in night pools dripping pearl tears under crescent silk lashes.

2. Your NOSE is a little mountain of perfumed everlastings a cluster of nutmegs.

3. Your LIPS are thick and luscious deep purple kissing fishes swimming in sweet wine.

4. Your HANDS are deft, sponge palms sepia inside sunburnt outside your smooth fingers are jointed like bamboo flutes

5. Your BREASTS are pawpaw cool as dusky arum on a swaying ebony trunk like twin moons in eclipse.

(Keith Yon, August 1974)

This startling and beautiful poem articulated what needed to be said, that is, that a St Helenian identity could not, and cannot exist without at least a recognition, preferably an acceptance and possibly a celebration of all the racial elements that go into the making of the island's population. Deny one, cling onto the increasing figment of 'Britishness', and the purpose and meaning of existence on the island evaporates and creates instead resentment, helplessness and the desperate loneliness borne of isolation and rejection. A characteristic St Helenian postscript to Yon's performance must be written. The Governor, who was in the audience, reportedly was in tears of rage at the racial imagery. Many islanders were embarrassed. Keith Yon left the island a year later to settle in England.

Only one further assault on the precariousness of a St Helenian identity needs final mention. St Helena was 'created' as an outpost of the mercantile trade, a prized outpost for some periods, but one which lost its strategic and economic purpose, once the island could be bypassed by the ships carrying the East Indian trade. Thereafter the island's isolation had the sole virtue (in the minds of its overseers) of being a convenient prison – for Dinizula in 1890 (the Zulu King who dared defy the British armies), for 5,000 Boer prisoners of war in 1899–1902, for three members of the Bahraini opposition from 1959–62, and, above all, for Napoleon who was sent to the island in 1815 and died there in 1821. That the island is only known to foreigners and visitors as the last place of imprisonment for a deposed French emperor, does not, of course, help the self-esteem of the islanders. As Charles Darwin perceptively observed in his *A Naturalist's Voyage*: 'A modern traveller … burdens the poor little island with the following titles: it is grave, tomb, pyramid, cemetery, sepulchre, catacomb, sarcophagus, minaret and mausoleum'.[28]

Conclusion

The education system has been seen not to be performing its stated idealistic role and self-declared aims. Instead, through the use of various indices concerning the environmental perceptions, aspirations and expectations of a group of St Helenian school-children, it has been seen as providing an education for depend-ence. But it is important to understand the thrust of our wider

---

28 Cited in S. P. Oliver, *On Board a Union Steamer* (London: W. H. Allen and Co., 1881), p. 58.

argument. The teachers and educationalists might be naive in their belief that education can transform, rather than (as is more evidently the case) simply reflect the prevailing economic and political circumstances. But they are as much the victims as the perpetrators of the situation: many indeed are dedicated and idealistic, but working against extremely stiff odds. These odds are determined by the hopeless trading situation, the poor level of self-sustaining productive activities and by the dulling effects of British colonialism itself. This is a society which lacks binding self-definitions, a people without a nationalism. The Governor and his officials cannot inspire, galvanise or transform anything (including the educational system); first, because the raison d'être for the original existence of the island has disappeared; second, because British colonialism cannot provide a legitimating ideology for its existence and instead engages in shoddy manipu-lations of its subjects' rights, and finally, because St Helenians have failed, so far, to come to grips with their own history and what is being done in their name. The impoverishment of St Helena is not only of the body, but of the intellect. Neither form of impoverishment can be overcome until St Helenians start to make history themselves rather than being made by it.

Addendum

I undertook an extended research trip to St Helena in 1975. I wish to thank the Board of the Faculty of Social Sciences, University of Birmingham, Patricia Thomas (Nuffield Foundation), Judy Lewis (Dependent Territories Economist Unit, Foreign and Common-wealth Office) and Basil George (Headmaster, Secondary Selective School, St Helena) who, in different ways, made this research possible. I had met 'Tony' Thornton (G. A. D. Thornton) at a cocktail party in Cape Town and he lobbied me furiously to take his side in a dispute with the St Helenian government. As my comments indicate, I refused to do so, but I had developed a strong independent critique of official policy. I discussed my findings at length in the Foreign Office in London, but to no avail. I was persuaded to delay publication to allow time for response and change, but I finally published this chapter, under the present title, in *Manchester Papers on Development*, 8, 1983, 1–30. I add that I had met Keith Yon, the author of the quoted poem, once or twice in the UK and enjoyed his company. He had a successful career at the innovative Dartington College of Arts as a musician and drama teacher, specializing notably in the therapeutic value of drama for those who struggling with mental illness.

Chapter 5
African islands and enclaves:
an introduction

Robin Cohen

This chapter appeared as the introduction to an edited book (Robin Cohen ed. *African islands and enclaves*, Beverly Hills, CA: Sage, 1983). References to authors in the book appear as 'Ch. X in *African islands*'.

Even President Reagan's staunchest political opponent must have felt some sympathy for his expression of bewilderment at Britain going to war for an 'ice-cold bunch of land' in the South Atlantic during the early months of 1982. But however irrational this outburst of British militarism appeared, the dispute over the Falklands/Malvinas islands simply drew to the public's attention what had been apparent to specialist scholars and strategists for a number of years: that small territories and islands are significant flashpoints in the contemporary world order. They are both exposed to the vicissitudes of international power rivalries and find it difficult to sustain a stable internal political and economic order. The contours of this dual exposure are derived in some respects from the very fact of their size, their characteristic economic weakness, and their historical dependence on larger countries for budgetary support and political protection.

It is true that size alone is not an absolute index of economic unviability. Witness the case of Hong Kong, which ranked fifteenth in the world in the value of manufactured exports in 1978 (World

Bank 1981: 156–7). The per capita incomes of the United Arab Emirates, Luxembourg, and Kuwait also show that small populations and territories can occasionally take advantage of a bonanza (like oil) or a special status in the financial markets. But the general association between smallness and weakness is clear. Of the 45 territories listed in United Nations statistics as having GDPs under US$ 500 million (1977), no less than 26 are island countries. Even the smallest continental economy (the enclave of Djibouti, with a GDP of US$ 90 million) has an economy larger than sixteen independent island economies. The smallest independent state in the world in terms of GDP is the Maldives, with no more than US$ 11 million (Dommen 1981: 1). An equally salient measurement is that of the 31 members of the United Nations and the World Bank with populations under 1 million, 24 countries have GNPs per capita of under US$ 3,000, 19 of them being islands or small enclaves surrounded by other territories (World Bank 1981: 185).

Economic and political realities

The reasons for this demoralizing economic performance are not hard to find. Islands (and, to a lesser degree, enclaves) are rarely able to take advantage of economies of scale. They are frequently remote from major markets; they face adverse factor constraints (like limited fresh water supplies and inadequate person-power); their markets are wide open to market fluctuations; they often record high rates of emigration while the cost of their administrations is disproportionate to the populations they serve. Ed Dommen has also shown that hurricanes are more frequent on islands (affecting some two-thirds of island countries); fewer animal species are able to survive; and island countries are more densely populated than are their continental counterparts, while their populations are growing at a lower rate – the effect of lower crude birth-rates and high emigration (Dommen 1980: 931–43).

By the standards of the development agencies, then, small island countries and enclaves are being left behind in the race to 'development'. As the globalization of production and distribution reaches out toward the periphery, micro states remain in or are pushed further toward the margins of the world system. Paradoxically, however, smallness and weakness have not been important constraints on the attainment of self-determination and the international recognition of sovereignty. Many islands, of course, remain dependencies or parts of larger political units – including St Helena, the Canaries, and Diego Garcia. But many more have achieved formal independence, an extraordinary triumph – considering the size of some of the territories concerned – of nineteenth-century notions of national self-determination. The proliferation of micro states has led to the anomalous situation in which the Maldives and Comoros islands have a combined voting strength in the UN General Assembly equivalent to that of China and the USSR. Naturally, this equality is merely a nicety of international law and in no way mirrors the strengths of the countries concerned. Nevertheless, the recognition of national status is not without significance. States, however small, have the right to levy tariffs, customs, and import duties; to print currency; to raise taxes; to be eligible for all kinds of international grants and assistance; to operate free ports; to be a home for international bankers and investors; down to the right to print postage stamps. It is a formidable set of advantages and (this is the point) a feature that permits small sovereign islands to evince a degree of power totally disproportionate to their size or their factor endowments. It is for access to the possibilities conferred by international recognition that so many nationalist and independence movements have been started in island countries, normally by the wealthy and dominant elements. The attainment of political independence has provided numerous opportunities for the more unscrupulous individuals in island societies to enrich themselves, an intriguing example being the case of James Mancham, formerly president of the Seychelles and the subject of a fawning biography (Lee 1976).

But with these opportunities for some, come dangers for the islands' populations. Casinos, hotel chains, and hot money often held by criminal elements in metropolitan societies seize the advantages conferred by international law. The massive seesaws in the currency market experienced over the last few years owe not a little to the protective haven that small islands confer on currency speculators. Local governments are often hopelessly weak, ill-organized, or incapable of resisting the gifts and onslaughts of international finance. Where micro states are independent, the ruling parties tend to be precarious alliances of a local comprador bourgeoisie and its administrative supporters. The result tends to be a sharp polarization of wealth and opportunities within the island. Older notions of equality and harmony are rapidly transformed as the effects of the penetration of international capital are differentially spread among the populace. In some cases, the local leadership is able to maintain the sharp inequalities only by resort to terror. Sundiata's chapter on Equatorial Guinea [Ch. 3 in *African islands*] provides a detailed account of one such regime, which has unfortunately escaped much public attention. Other independent island states discussed in African islands (the Seychelles, the Comoros) have witnessed a successful revolt against the ruling groups and a precarious attempt to move to a more egalitarian path of development.

Dissent does not, however, always stem from internal forces. Island and micro states are also increasingly prone to secessionist tendencies characteristically resulting when a fraction of foreign capital can find a local leader – for them a pliant client – to use the rights conferred by independence in the interests of his paymasters. The tone of this new form of domination was perhaps best captured by an article in *Esquire* called 'The amazing new-country caper.' This article describes how a group of businesspersons, including a firearms manufacturer, sought to subvert and ultimately seize by military force, the Abaco Islands in the Bahamas. The islanders, leading lives that were described as 'ranging from quiet stagnation to mute poverty', were enjoined to fight for the status of a self-governing community in order better to further the conspirators' plans (St. George 1975). Though the Abaco scheme soon floundered, in June 1980 the attempt to foment a rebellion in Espiritu Santo, part of the New Hebrides in the Pacific, very nearly succeeded. The rebel leader, Jimmy Stevens, was able to take advantage of the multiple confusions wrought by the joint British and French condominium of the islands with the help of his sponsors, the Phoenix Foundation of America which, according to one source, has 'right-wing views and a good deal of money' (*Guardian Weekly* 1980). As far as newspaper reporters were able to discern, Mr Stevens enjoyed a minimal level of popular support.

The historical legacy

The foregoing examples concern islands that were to be 'decolon-ized' in the interests of private enterprise. In some cases, like those of the Canary Islands and St Helena, decolonization is barely on the agenda. The Canaries are an integral part of Spain, though the pressures for autonomy, as Sanchez-Padron [Ch. 1 *African islands*] shows, increased with the prospect of the islands losing their favoured trading status when Spain was to join the Common Market. Historically, the forms of dependence the island has on the mainland have conditioned the ways local powerful interests can dominate the island. In a sustained theoretical analysis, Sanchez-Padron argues that 'rent' and 'profit' have intertwined to support the local oligarchy/bourgeoisie, but that this form of domination now depends on the continuing reconciliation of local and national interests. It is this protective relationship that is challenged by the autonomy movement which, I add, is unlikely ever to succeed. Intra-European Union tourism to the Canaries has served to bind the islands ever more firmly to Span.

Even though it is also under direct metropolitan control, the case of St Helena offers a strong contrast to the Canaries, since there is no basis for local accumulation. The British rule of the island is hinged, rather, on that country's inability to escape an administrative burden acquired first during a period of relative prosperity and strategic significance of the island. Many islands had their basic economies established during the mercantile period of capitalism's expansion. Some, like St Helena, were settled and populated precisely to service the ships carrying the expanded trade of the European economy. Historically, the island was in effect a vegetable garden, a ship's chandlery, and a refreshment station for sailing ships going to the East via the Cape route. Once the steamship was invented and the Suez Canal opened, there was simply no reason to call there anymore. The island drifted into a debilitating decay, one that has not been arrested to this day.

Other islands, equally structured and conditioned by mercantile trade, have managed to achieve a precarious independence. Mauritius, the Cape Verdes, Equatorial Guinea, the Seychelles, and the Comoros (discussed in other chapters in *African islands*) all have independent administrations, yet the burden of the past weighs heavily on them. Whatever level of internal reproduction existed, this was typically dependent on a monoculture, a plantation economy worked by imported slave labour. A number of the islands described in *African islands* share with their Caribbean counterparts the heritage of a plantation-based economy. Of the islands surveyed, only in Cape Verde, Mauritius, and in the Seychelles [Kaplinsky Ch. 8 *African islands*] does there appear to be some basis for local accumulation.

The general pattern, however, seems to follow that proposed by Geoff Kay (1975), who argued in opposition to André Gunder Frank that dependence does not arise automatically from capitalist expansion; rather, the underdeveloping effects of capitalism are seen when merchant capital predominates and where therefore there is little basis for indigenous capital accumulation (the profits of trade being realized in the metropoles) and no growth of the local means of production beyond a small range of simple commodities or a single crop. Many island communities are still living with the underdeveloping effect of merchant capital. Fluctuation in the world demand for their products – commodities like sugar, coffee, bananas and copra – leave them totally at risk. Even when prices are historically high, they are insufficient to wipe out previous troughs in world demand. Competitive advantage is difficult to exploit where the shipping lines are in control of their dominant trading partners, there are no regional markets, and the islands are located far from their principal markets.

While many islands have barely escaped and still show many signs of their mercantilist character, one recent development has been the attempt to start export-oriented manufacturing industries on a number of islands. The trend is not wholly new, though it has been rapidly accelerated in recent years. Such a strategy was pioneered by Hong Kong, Taiwan, and Puerto Rico, but now there is scarcely an island in the world that does not have plans for at least a modest export manufacturing sector, often encouraged by agencies like the United Nations Industrial Development Organization (UNIDO) and the World Bank. What prospects of success do the attempts at peripheral industrialization have? The case of Puerto Rico (a state in 'free association' with the US) does not auger well for subsequent imitators of this development. Some 55 per cent of the population take advantage of the food stamp scheme, costing the federal government $1 billion. Some 2 million islanders and their descendants live on the mainland, as opposed to 3.2 million on the island. Between 30 and 40 per cent are unemployed or have given up seeking work, one-third of the work force works for the government or its agencies, the govern-ment of Puerto Rico owes $7 million to the mainland banks. This is on an island where the undoubted growth in GDP consequent on the US-sponsored Operation Bootstrap has been deemed a great success, even an economic miracle, by its defenders.

The collapse of the 'state of nature'

All this evidence of economic stagnation and political weakness – the implosion of the effects of world economic forces on remote islanders – is in marked contrast to a romantic view of island societies that is deeply embedded in Western cultures. David Pitt has pointed out that the interest in islands goes back at least to the Mediterranean odysseys. The European Age of Discovery (so-called, for of course the islanders themselves had already dis-covered their own islands) provided a good deal of new imagery for poetry and fiction and for scientific and social comment. As Pitt goes on to argue, the published work of explorers, missiona-ries, castaways, and traders had a great appeal to the Western consciousness and led to the publication of some of the most enduring works of fiction: *Robinson Crusoe*, *Treasure Island*, and a host of lesser imitations. The imagery of the South Sea Islands, in particular, contrasted with the drab, back-to-back, urban landscapes of the industrial revolution. Islands also held out a prospect that was both exotic and erotic – Rousseau's 'state of nature' gained its artistic expression, for example, in the paintings of Gauguin. Again, the assumed permissiveness of many island cultures contrasted with the repressive social norms of the eighteenth- and nineteenth-century bourgeoisie and the asceticism that accompanied the growth of capitalism in Western Europe and North America. Even in the twentieth century, this imagery was hard to dispel, with the work of leading anthropologists like Bronislaw Malinowski (*Argonauts of the Western Pacific*, 1922) and Margaret Mead (*Coming of age in Samoa*, 1928) undoubtedly gaining more attention precisely because of their exotic settings (Pitt 1980: 1051).

In many ways, then, islands represent an alternative vision to Western industrial culture – one that is marked by an exchange economy, naturalness, a simple division of labour – an image often of the preindustrial age. Seen more at the level of individual psychology rather than at the social level, to participate in island culture has become an expression of another side of the human personality – a form of escape into fantasy, warmth, and romance. It is this side of the appeal of islands that has now been transmuted through international travel and tourism into a consumer good, to be purchased through the local travel agent [and, now, on the internet]. Here escape is packaged into neat two-week periods, with any element of threat removed by the provision of the identikit hotels, similar cuisine (spiced occasionally by some local recipe), and guaranteed sea, sun, and sand. One of the dominant characteristics in the modern economies of small islands has thus become the fulfilment of an ersatz, temporary, plastic version of the adventures of the early explorers.

While the package tourist cannot easily reach St Helena, would be excluded from the joys of observing the military manoeuvres of the US fleet on Diego Garcia, or would be terrified by the macabre and random violence Sundiata depicts in Equatorial Guinea, of the cases covered in *African islands*, the tourist impact in the Seychelles, The Gambia, Mauritius, and the Canary Islands is especially evident. While it is difficult to generalize across all islands in this respect, the growth of tourism presents an increasingly sharp choice between the economic benefits to islands in terms of the growth of the service industries and the acquisition of foreign exchange on the one hand and, on the other hand, the damaging environmental and social costs incurred. Sometimes even the economic benefits of tourism have been challenged by some who show that the infrastructure of island economies can be easily distorted by a too-dominant tourist industry. The food-and-luxury-item import bill goes up to serve both the visitors and the locals who have acquired their consumer tastes, while foreign tour operators, hotel chains, and airline companies are able to extract a lion's share of the profits, to the detriment of the local economy. The environmental costs of tourism are increasingly evident in many places, as pollution, unsightly development, and overdevelopment imposing strains on the local ecology – in particular, in the need to provide new sources of fresh water, sewage disposal systems, and agricultural land for airport and road development. The social costs of tourism can also be extremely heavy, and the gross disproportion of wealth between the islanders and the visitors then leads to a loss of confidence in the local culture, an imitative style of behaviour and conduct, and, in some cases, the turning of the local population into waiters, pimps, and prostitutes. Only recently have we become aware of another possible cost of tourism: the political one. In The Gambia, the locals (some of them Muslim and fundamentalist, others simply trying to retain some of their own cultural norms) were long resentful of the tourist invasion of their country. School attendance rolls dropped as children left to beg money, while the tourists' standards of dress, or rather undress, offended the locals.

Strategic factors

If tourism, an apparently innocent twentieth-century fulfilment of a nineteenth-century dream, has shown such a capacity for producing destructive social, political, and environmental effects, we are clearly dealing with societies that are highly brittle, highly exposed, and highly vulnerable to outside forces. But even if sophisticated tourist operators are able to insulate the romantic dreams of their clients from the harsher realities of island life, the final collapse of romanticism must follow the newly rediscovered strategic importance of islands. This importance derives from three principal factors. First, many islands sit astride important sea lanes. This mattered little to the imperialist powers when Britain, and later the United States, monopolized naval power on a worldwide scale. It matters a great deal more when Soviet naval power is expanding so dramatically and a host of medium-sized powers (including India, Argentina and Brazil) have substantial merchant and naval fleets. The incoming conservative prime minister of Jamaica, for example, was not slow to point out to his potential US backers that 61 per cent of US oil is routed through the Caribbean. Again, following the Suez crisis of 1956 and the oil cartel crisis of 1973, Western nations have become acutely conscious of their need to move strategic materials through waters not fully controlled by them. As Britain once used Gibraltar to police the sea lanes to the Mediterranean, so now the USA and a number of other countries have constructed military and naval facilities on islands.[1]

This leads to the second factor enhancing the strategic

---

1 To bring this story up to date, the dumping of sand on reefs in the South China Sea by the Chinese government is clearly designed to allow military installations. The extent of these developments is likely to cause increasing tension with the USA, especially in the wake of Trump's election. See: https://goo.gl/yIwzDv.

attractiveness of islands. The stationing of dangerous warheads, missiles, and bomb stores, plus security-tight operations like space satellites and radio and other electronic transmission stations, can conveniently be sited on islands. The populations can be expelled (as in Diego Garcia), and many governments are easily coerced into compliance by the dominant power. Moreover, with the growth of antinuclear sentiment in Europe and the attempts by the peace movement to have Europe declared as a nuclear free zone, the temptation to take over an island solely for military purposes must be great.

Although there is already a storm of protest building up in the Canary Islands over the proposed siting of NATO facilities there, perhaps the most brutal reminder of big-power realities is the case of Diego Garcia, now entirely given over to US military use. Jooneed Khan [Ch. 7 *African islands*] has employed his skills in investigative journalism to expose the dubious moral standards of the departing colonial power, Britain, made all the more visible by its supposed principled stance in the analogous case of the Falklands. The election in Mauritius of a socialist government with historical claims on Diego Garcia and a program calling for the demilitarization of the Indian Ocean ushers in what could be a period of considerable instability.

Both Kaplinsky's chapter on the Seychelles and Selwyn's analysis of the Mauritian economy and social structure [Chs. 8 and 10 *African islands*] provide information integral to an evaluation of the strategic significance of the Indian Ocean. The region as a whole is indeed fraught with uncertain geopolitical considerations. Are we to regard the US facilities on Diego Garcia as a surrogate for its loss of influence in Iran?[2] Will the Soviet Union

---

2   In the event, the island was used to launch strikes during the Gulf War, the invasion of Iraq (2003), the war in Afghanistan, and the

expand its naval presence in the area? Will the Indian or East African governments support the Mauritian call for the neutralization of the region?

The final factor influencing the strategic salience of islands and enclaves is that they happen sometimes to be located either where important mineral resources exist or where they can serve as gateways to hitherto unexploited resources. In the case of Cabinda, analysed by dos Santos [Ch. 4 *African islands*], the oil reserves operated by Gulf Oil in the enclave triggered a series of contradictory positions taken by the US State Department. On the one hand, the intervention by Cuba and the accession to power in Angola by what was seen as a Marxist government impelled some sections of the State Department to lend covert support to South Africa's sustained attempts to destabilize the Angolan regime. On the other hand, Gulf's need to evolve a working relationship with the Angolan government eventually forced a modus vivendi. Nonetheless, as dos Santos shows, any attempts to develop Cabinda socially and economically are severely constrained by the security situation. Where strategic materials are not located in enclaves or islands, they nonetheless might provide bases for the expanded development of fishing resources, mining of the sea beds, and aquaculture, particularly since successive Law of the Sea conferences have expanded the territorial limits surrounding a coast line. While some of these developments are still somewhat speculative (U.S. Council on Environmental Quality, 1982: 105–16), at least some commentators on Britain's military expedition to the Falklands pointed to the possible exploitation of oil and mineral resources in the South

---

bombing campaign against the Islamic State in Syria and Iraq, http://www.globalresearch.ca/the-truth-about-diego-garcia-50-years-of-fiction-about-an-american-military-base/5455763.

Atlantic and Antarctica as an explanation for the action supplementary to that provided by the British prime minister.[3]

Some final comments

Most of the chapters in *African islands* speak for themselves. It would be misleading to try to impose an artificial unity of theme on all the contributors. But it may be helpful to readers if I make a few comments on the criteria I employed for the selection of chapters in *African islands*. There are, by one estimate, some 77 micro states with populations of less than half a million people out of a total of 224 identifiable inhabited regions in the world (Caldwell et al. 1980: 953). In and around Africa alone, there are about two dozen islands and enclaves that could qualify for our attention. What I sought to achieve here was a reasonable balance between enclaves and islands, between Indian and Atlantic Ocean territories, and between territories that were self-governing and those that were still integrated into metropolitan political units.

What the authors share is a close familiarity with the territories they surveyed, one that goes beyond the tourist brochure or a traditional anthropological fiction into a direct and sometimes brutal appreciation of the difficulties and realities of constructing a modern life in such limiting contexts. The contributors, in short, transcend the view of islands as self-sustaining utopias fostered

---

3 It has taken many years to admit to the extensive oil reserves (about 1bn barrels of oil within the 200 nautical miles around the two islands). This would represent potentially the largest single hydrocarbons find within British territory anywhere outside the North Sea, and a valuable addition to global energy supplies. In September 2016, the governments of the UK and Argentina finally accepted that the exploitation of these resources is unlikely to occur without peaceful co-operation between the two countries.

during the Age of Discovery. The possibilities of autarky, if they ever existed, passed with the underdevelopment occasioned by mercantile neglect and mono-production in the eighteenth and nineteenth centuries. This heritage remains an indelible legacy of many islands and small territories today. The twentieth century has seen the emergence of new opportunities for islands, possibilities essentially of using their sovereignty to foster tourism, protect shady operators, and promote industrial development. These possibilities, as I have argued, have their own dangers and problems. But perhaps the real crisis, the crisis born of the increased recognition of the strategic significance of islands, is yet to come. Islanders have traditionally responded to such threats to their survival by migration, as Meintel [Ch. 6 *African islands*] shows in her contribution on the Cape Verdes. But with the avenues of international mobility increasingly closed off to them, islanders are going to have to evolve autonomous solutions to the challenges that confront them. I cannot but help express some pessimism as to their eventual capacity to resist the powerful extraneous forces I have described.

References

Caldwell, J. C. et al. 1980. 'The demography of micro-states', *World Development*, 8: 953–67.

Dommen, E. 1980. 'Some distinguishing characteristics of island states', *World Development*, 8: 931–43.

Dommen, E. 1981. Invisible exports from islands. Paper presented at the Conference on Small Island Economies, Universidad de La Laguna, Canary Islands, September.

Financial Times 1981. November 27.

Guardian Weekly 1980. June 6.

Kay, G. 1975. *Development and underdevelopment: a Marxist analysis*, London: Macmillan.

Lee, C. 1976. *Seychelles: political castaways*, London: Hamish Hamilton.

Malinowski, B. 1922. *Argonauts of the Western Pacific*, London: Routledge & Kegan Paul.

Mead, M. 1928. *Coming of age in Samoa*, New York: Morrow.

Pitt, D. 1980. 'Sociology, islands and boundaries', *World Development*, 8: 1051–9.

St. George, A. 1975. 'The amazing new-country caper', *Esquire* (February).

US Council on Environmental Quality 1982. *The Global 2000 Report to the President*. Harmondsworth: Penguin.

Vine, David. 2011. *Island of shame: the secret history of the US military base on Diego Garcia*, Princeton; Princeton University Press.

World Bank. 1981. *World Development Report*, 1981. Washington DC: International Bank for Reconstruction and Development.

Addendum

As mentioned at the beginning, this chapter appeared as the introduction to an edited book (Robin Cohen ed. *African islands and enclaves*, Beverly Hills, CA: Sage 1983). It was the first attempt at a comparative analysis of African islands and enclaves and, of course, had some flaws. However, the movement away from a romantic view of individual islands to a comparative political economy approach, yielded important insights, as did the enhanced emphasis on their strategic importance. We really needed a separate and complete analysis of Diego Garcia, which appears here fleetingly, but nobody at the time had researched the issue in any depth. I can now recommend David Vine's *Island of shame: the secret history of the US military base on Diego Garcia*, Princeton; Princeton University Press, 2011 to offset this deficiency.

Chapter 6
St Helena: welfare colonialism in practice

Robin Cohen

The small island of St Helena is located in the South Atlantic Ocean at latitude 16°S and longitude 5°45W. It is somewhat over 1600 km west of its nearest mainland, Angola, but this is of little significance as no regular lines of communication or travel exist between Angola and the island. As St Helena had no airport until 2016, the only regular means of reaching the island was to undertake the two-week journey from Britain (7240 km.), which normally called at Ascension St Helena's 'dependency' (1131 km NW of the island). Alternatively one can travel by sea from Cape Town (2726 km.). Though an airport was finally opened in 2016, commercial flights have been delayed for months due to 'wind shear' and, even using a smaller aircraft, are unlikely to commence until 2017. One would have imagined that wind data would have been collected before building the airport. The geographical isolation of the island, the airport debacle and the continuing difficulties of traveling there signify its collapse into obscurity.

This was not always the case. During the sixteenth and seventeenth century, the Portuguese, Dutch, and British occupied the island, the Dutch abandoning their claims when they settled the Cape of Good Hope. With the exception of Ireland, St Helena is Britain's oldest colony and looks very likely as if it will be its last. The English East India Company effectively administered the island for 182 years after the granting of a charter to the company in 1659. St Helena was used to repair and provision the many ships that called on the way to and from the East. The large garrison stationed on the island during the period of Napoleon's captivity (1815–21) also produced great prosperity for the island. So vital was the island to the sea routes that until 1869, when the Suez Canal was opened, the island was sometimes considered the most important of all the colonies.[1]

Though the depredations of goats introduced by the settlers and the casual treatment of the land by colonists soon took their toll, when the island was discovered in 1502 Mellis noted that 'rich vegetation clothed its surface, the interior being described as an entire forest, with gumwood and other indigenous trees overhanging some of the sea precipices'.[2] The contrast with St Helena in the mid-1970s, when I undertook fieldwork on the island, could not be starker. The island survives virtually entirely on budgetary support and development aid provided by the British government. Since the collapse of their flax industry in the mid-1960s, due to competition from artificial fibres, the islanders have been unable to develop any form of export. Large areas of the arable land (only about one-third of the total surface area of forty-seven square miles) are still covered with the carefully planted, but now useless, crop. A promising attempt to use the green bark of flax for cattle fodder was abandoned, while clearing the flax for pasturage or cultivation was undertaken fitfully.

What land remains comprises, for the most part, precipitous slopes and thinly covered pastures incapable of supporting

1   C. Hughes, *Report of an enquiry into conditions on the island of St Helena*, St Helena Government Printer, 1958, p. 3.
2   J. C Melliss, *St Helena: a physical, historical and topographical description of the island*, Kent: L. Reeve & Co., 1875, p. 1.

sufficient stock to meet the local demand for animal protein. Frozen meat and even poultry are imported in large quantities. Fresh vegetables and fruit are grown on a private basis on small acreages or in backyard plots, but of the score or so full-time farmers, only a handful operate at a profit and without a supplement from a wage income. The difficulties in sustaining independent primary production are threefold: the rainfall has been unreliable, particularly in the early 1970s; the use of irrigation has been minimal; and finally, farmers have to compete with the heavily subsidized Agricultural and Forestry (A&F) department. In April 1975 a new Agricultural Development Authority (ADA) was created, replacing the A & F's combined functions of research and the production of at least some vegetables and meat for the local market. As many islanders comment, it is remarkable that an island that once produced enough to provision 800 sailing ships calling annually in the eighteenth century can now produce only a small fraction of the food consumed by the 5000 members of the local population.

Other than agriculture, the major natural resource is fishing. Here too the picture is dismal. Only nine boats go out regularly and these are small rowing boats usually fitted with low-powered and (as I found to his cost one day) unreliable outboard motors. Fishermen cannot fish the untried deeper grounds and have to huddle in the leeward side of the island. Despite the vagaries of this precarious form of fishing, substantial catches of tunny and edible small fish are brought in, if on a rather sporadic basis. The major problem in using fish as part of the regular protein diet of the islanders lies in questions of storage and distribution.

The economy of the island can be simply summarized. No exports, minimal production for local needs, a low level of savings, and an overwhelming dependence on imports for consumption – the level of which is determined by the quantity of

British aid. The roots of this appalling economic record lie deep in St Helena's history. The opening of the Suez Canal, the invention of the steamship, which allowed ships to bypass the island, and the recall of the garrison for Napoleon all knocked the props from under the island's economy. But this common interpretation of the island's history – as a series of unfortunate accidents of fate – is analytically superficial. The island's decline was conditioned by the dominant form of capital found there, namely merchant capital. In Kay's words, 'The conditions which merchant capital had created throughout the underdeveloped world by the middle of the nineteenth century, were absolutely unconducive to the full development of capitalism.'[3] In the case of St Helena, the land was stripped bare and the major mercantile firm, Solomons & Company, left almost no basis for local capital accumulation and investment. Instead, the profits of trade were invested in gold and diamond mines in South Africa where the Solomons family became prominent magnates, politicians, and judges. The English East India Company also abandoned its no longer useful colony, dumping it back into the hands of Whitehall and a local colonial administration, who, since the mid-nineteenth century, have administered it in a patient, but far from munificent, spirit.

The timing of my research on the island happened to coincide with two major attempts to revitalize the island's development. The first was an attempt – which ultimately was to be officially stopped – led by an outside entrepreneur who saw the development of the island in terms of the classical prescriptions of stimulating local initiative through the injection of capital and the development of the productive forces. The second was the introduction of St Helena's first integrated development plan by the

---

3   G. Kay, *Development and underdevelopment: A Marxist analysis*, London: Macmillan, 1975, p. 103.

colonial government, which is characterized here as a new phase of 'welfare colonialism'. But before examining these two alternative strategies it is necessary to describe in greater detail the social and political conditions presently existing on the island.

Social conditions on St Helena

By the mid-1970s the island had made only limited progress in terms of constitutional development. The governor, together with the executive council (appointed officials plus some representatives from the legislative council, effectively took local decisions within the framework of policy and aid established by the Foreign & Commonwealth Office. Direct representation was limited to a 12-member legislative council, established in 1968. The exercising of a democratic voice was thus a recent phenomenon, but participation in elections was sufficiently high to belie the views of those who have berated the St Helenians for their passivity.

This assumed passivity has often been generalized and remarked upon by outside observers. Cledwyn Hughes, a British parliamentarian who visited the island in 1958 commented that 'several factors have combined to produce a subservience and shyness in their nature and tardiness to complain or appeal for help. The great majority suffer distress in silence and really outspoken St Helenians can be numbered on the fingers of one hand.' Hughes goes on to speculate that memories of slavery, fear of victimization at work, the monopoly of business by one company, and 'the aloof and often unimaginative rule of the Colonial Administration over the years' have combined to produce the attitudes he observed.[4]

My own findings based on a period of residence and a sample

---

4   C. Hughes, *Report of an enquiry*, 1958, p. 2.

survey conducted in 1975 (N = 110, see below) suggest a more complex reading of the island 'character', attitudes being conditioned by a compound of affection and loyalty for Britain (many islanders are partly descended from British stock, while nearly all expressed sentiments of patriotism and identification), cynicism and hostility directed to colonial officials, acute suspicion of certain visitors and 'experts', and a sense of resentment and helplessness in the face of the adverse circumstances that confront them. What then are these circumstances? It is difficult to obtain an accurate gauge of living standards, or one that would provide a meaningful point of comparison with the standards of, say, a Western industrial society. Private housing is modest, though far from squalid. Public housing in Jamestown, the capital, is functional, but badly sited and aesthetically uninviting. Tenants complained of noise, lack of space, and expensive fuel costs. Many homes on the island are fitted with 'chip boilers' burning virtually free wood or shavings, but, as for some reason this was not considered appropriate for new public housing, the tenants have to burn expensively generated electricity or (imported) bottled gas. Outside Jamestown, whose Main Street boasts Georgian frontages but rather less prepossessing interiors, houses comprise simple breeze block rectangular constructions, with asbestos or tin roofing. A few more affluent country properties occupied by settlers or well-established families hark back to the days of the East India Company.

Other indices of living standards, like family income, must also be treated with care. At the time of the survey, wages were low (£10 a week was the common remuneration for unskilled government employees) especially in relation to the cost of imported foodstuffs: at a rough estimation 8 to 12 per cent above 1975 British prices. However, rents on government-owned properties are minimal, electricity is subsidized, and education and medical care are provided by the state at a nominal cost. Welfare payments included such items as food vouchers to the needy and outdoor relief work. Since September 1973 supplementary benefits, at the rate of £3.50 per couple per week plus 50p for each additional dependent, generally replaced these forms of welfare. Some private charitable work is also undertaken, particularly by the Salvation Army, which provides meals-on-wheels to 400 islanders. Remittances from relatives abroad, however, constitute the most important supplement to the income of families remaining on St Helena. Such income is not revealed to the authorities (it may jeopardize welfare entitlements), but interview data suggest that it sometimes constitutes from 30 to 50 per cent of a household's total income. The social welfare and health departments are also responsible for the running of an old people's home, a children's home, and a Dickensian mental hostel, which was undergoing some physical improvements to its blackened and fly-blown kitchen. The education system comprises eight primary, three secondary and one senior selective school, and though the buildings are generally adequate, the system has failed to achieve even a modest success in examinations and has been unsuccessful too in living up to the department's own stated goals of ensuring that children are 'less-dependent minded' and more adequately prepared for life on the island and abroad. Instead, in a separate study I carried out, the educational system has been described as 'education for dependence' (see Chapter 4 in this book). The general impression is one of a down-at-heel welfare state.

The traditional solution by the islanders to their lack of economic opportunity has been emigration, overwhelmingly to South Africa and to the United Kingdom. The rate of emigration slowed considerably with the passing of discriminatory legislation in those two countries. In the case of South Africa, most St

Helenians are classified as 'Coloured', since 1948 hardly the most comfortable of denotations. In the United Kingdom the Commonwealth Immigrants Act was enforced, probably in violation of an ancient Royal Charter that promised St Helenians full rights of citizenship 'as if they had been abiding and borne within this our realm of England'.[5] After 1981, with the passing of the Nationality Act, St Helenians were classified as citizens of the 'dependent territories' and their historic rights to full British citizenship were ignored. The application of immigration controls has adversely affected a common form of mobility, particularly among girls – domestic service for a couple of years, followed by permanent settlement in the United Kingdom. In addition to such restrictions on mobility, passages are expensive and scarce – until 1978 the only regular means of communication were two cargo ships, spaced three to four weeks apart, running between the South African ports and Southampton. The ships carried only twelve cabin passengers, and many of the passages were taken up by government officials. Since 1978, a 78-passenger ship, the RMS St Helena was purchased, partly by the St Helena Government. Though the ship only undertook the journey from Avonmouth (Bristol) to Cape Town once every two months, this service was undoubtedly a boon to the island. However, the continuing immigration restrictions mean that employment opportunities abroad are very limited.

Considerable numbers of young men do, nonetheless, travel to the island of Ascension to work as contract labourers for Pan Am, Cable & Wireless, the BBC, and a few smaller concerns, which have bases on the island. The comparatively high wages earned on Ascension are an attractive bait to the 'Saints', as the islanders

---

5 E. L. Jackson, *St Helena: the historic island*, London: Ward, Lock & Co, 1903, p. 22.

abroad are called, but employment in Ascension provides only a partial and diminishing solution to unemployment in St Helena. Short of discovering a new El Dorado on St Helena, the possibilities for self-sustaining economic development appear in the to be negligible. The island was too far off the beaten track to sustain a large tourist trade and technical difficulties, as well as the low volume of anticipated traffic, mitigated against the construction of an airfield.[6] In the early 1970s, the prospects for a shift in the island's trajectory of development became possible with the injection of some external capital, while the colonial government, for its part, embarked on a five-year development plan. These two strategies, while not intrinsically incompatible, soon showed themselves to be pulling the island in divergent directions.

The failure of capitalist development

The injection of foreign capital into the island was first heralded in 1968 when a majority shareholding in the island's major private enterprise, the old mercantile company of Solomons & Company, was purchased by the South Atlantic Trading and Investment Company (SATIC), which was headed by a British-born, but South African-based, businessman, Tony Thornton. When news of this reached the island, fears of a South African government takeover, even the introduction of apartheid, were generated on the island. Such a scenario was inherently absurd. Even the most hardened member of South Africa's Race Classification Board would despair at trying to construct a racial typology of St Helena's citizens. The islanders are blended together from people of European, Chinese, African and even Polynesian origins in exemplary display

---

6 These difficulties were said to be overcome in May 2016, when an airport was due to open, but the first commercial flight only landed in October 2017.

of racial tolerance (as one urbane islander remarked, 'We are a selection of liquorice all sorts'). Moreover, the South African government could hardly have found a more inappropriate Trojan horse. Thornton has liberal political views; his wife was banned in South Africa for her anti-apartheid activities.

In an island where no independent news medium exists, rumour is the only effective means of communication, and the colonial government was sufficiently alarmed to intervene. It bought 32 per cent of the shares, leaving SATIC with 30 per cent and the rest divided among small shareholders. An agreement signed in London in 1968 also allowed the government to purchase, in the national interest, SATIC's share – anytime it chose to do so. In April 1974, this is what it did.

By this time other issues obtruded. Thornton proved to be an energetic director. He revitalized Solomons' multifarious activities: the company was the major importer and owned stores, pubs, a hotel, and the biggest slice of nongovernment farming land. His dynamism attracted a fierce loyalty from his own staff and many islanders who saw in him the epitome of innovativeness and resolution that, so they suggested, was sadly lacking in the government's own conduct of its affairs. One typical response to a questionnaire (see later) on the development plan included the comment, 'This island is far behind the times. We did had a good start, by Mr. Thornton; it would have developed the island and [given] a good improvement to many. Maybe you don't know, but the little that is done is built on Mr. Thornton foundation, but it won't carry on ... because all the development money [will] be down the drain.' Another islander pointed out that while there was little accountability in government-supported schemes, private investors at least had their own money to lose. In a clear reference to the Thornton affair, one respondent commented:

> A private Company was taken over by the Government
> against the wishes of the people. If the man come to
> the island with a grant-in-aid if he don't produce any
> food no-one say anything about it, but if that same
> chap had his own money, he would make a better show
> because it would be his money he would be wasting. If
> anyone who comes to the island makes an improve-
> ment he is soon sent off.

Such pro-Thornton responses were found among a number of islanders in government or Solomons' employ, young and old, in Jamestown, other settlements, or the country. There was a slight tendency for pro-Thornton supporters to be younger and better educated and with working experience overseas.

By contrast, the strength of the opposition to Mr Thornton was considerable. The opposition stemmed from three quarters. The government itself, the legislative council (in the critical debate eleven out of twelve opposed Thornton), and some island opinion – organized essentially around the St Helena General Workers' Union (GWU). The GWU attitude is perhaps most difficult to understand as Thornton initially paid better wages than the government. As in much else on the island, the answer lay in the particularities of island politics. The previous GWU secretary was an adherent, indeed one of the inspirations, of the Thorntons-as-South African-neo-Imperialist-agents theory. His successor, also incidentally a Legco member, was one of a group that saw a danger to the island in Thornton's manner of financing company expansion – running one company, Solomons, into debt to SATIC. The legislative council's attitude also partly reflected the fear that the arrival of the new management of Solomons would disrupt the traditionally stable relations between the islanders and the two dozen white settlers, who held five of the twelve seats in the Legislative Council. Mr and Mrs Thornton were themselves convinced that this was at the root of the moves against them. In an interview with a British newspaper Mrs Thornton maintained:

> The local establishment have been upset because my husband has promoted the islanders to positions of authority in the company and has doubled the wages of the workers. This cuts the settlers' standard of living. The settlers have come for a tax haven and the low cost of living. They are not a group of socialists who want to take over a company on behalf of the people. These are a most reactionary people, some of whom have come to St Helena from Zambia and Rhodesia. They are Smith supporters.[7]

As to the government itself, there is little doubt that they resented Thornton's steamrolling tactics and his practice of not sharing major decisions with the government-appointed director on the Solomons board. In their arguments advocating the purchase of SATIC's share, government officials also pointed out that the company had not paid dividends since Thornton's control and that its cash difficulties could only be resolved by further indebtedness to SATIC.

Political and social life on the island became organized on factional lines, pro- and anti-Thornton. Few on the island succeeded in maintaining an indifferent or neutral stance. The battle was joined with petition and counter-petition, public meetings, demonstrations, and court cases that were ostensibly about something else. Among the British officials and some of the small settler element, Mr Thornton and his family were subject to a degree of social ostracism that in a community of St Helena's

---

7   *The Guardian*, 15 April 1974.

size and isolation can only be described as ludicrous. The critical decision – to buy out SATIC's remaining shares – went to the anti-Thornton group, whose position was ultimately approved by James Callaghan, then minister at the Foreign Office. Despite the fact that Thornton was successfully able to rally 1139 islanders who demanded a referendum on the issue (a number, incidentally, well in excess of the 826 people who voted in the legislative council elections), the Foreign & Commonwealth Office supported the advice of the governor that the government should exercise its option to buy out Thornton's share in Solomons. There is little doubt that the ground for the politicians' acquiescence was well prepared by the prevailing views of the responsible civil servants in Britain. One official from the West Indian & Atlantic Department of the Foreign & Commonwealth Office, for example, made some highly damaging remarks about Thornton's alleged conduct in an internal memorandum:

> His most notorious trait is to regard local institutions – particularly the Legco – with contempt, and to look upon Government's proper insistence that he, as well as everybody else, should conform to local legislation, as parish-pump meddling. This is particularly noticeable in regard to planning permission and the ownership of property, where he appears to see normal legal and administrative requirements as applicable only to lesser mortals. When he is reminded of his obligations in this respect he is prone to regard this as unreasonable interference by interfering busy-bodies.

Once his major commercial interest was subjected to compulsory purchase, Thornton left the island, but attempted to rally support for his position by helping to found a new political party, the St Helena Labour Party in 1974. The manifesto of the party is a sustained attack on the colonial government's neglect of the island and a critique of the new development plan it proposed to implement. The next election for the legislative council was not due until 1976, and the party was ultimately to command little support at the polls. But by this time the government had moved more decisively against Thornton. The launch of the party in 1974 and a statement that Thornton intended to start an independent newspaper appeared to be the events that triggered the governor's decision to issue an exclusion order in September 1975 formally banishing Thornton from the island. Thornton's interests, other than Solomons, included his fishing company, fell into disuse. A fifty-ton freezer plant, which would have helped in the important area of fish storage, lay rusting in an open shed. The government now held in its possession all the major assets on the island and, according to the Labour Party manifesto, controlled 95 per cent of the land and 95 per cent of the employment on the island.[8] As there were no other contenders in the field, development had perforce to rest with the government's own efforts.

Depending on one's interpretation of the events described, the people have been protected from a malign foreign enterprise, or outside capital has been prevented from contributing to the development of the island. Whatever the rights and wrongs, the already adverse commercial opportunities for external capital have been damaged by the Thornton case. Potential foreign investors can hardly read the government's attitude sympathetically, while the government, for its part, is afraid of 'another Thornton'. That the government's attitude to foreign enterprise was less than encouraging is argued forcibly by one islander who claimed:

---

8   St Helena Labour Party, *The St Helena Manifesto*, Jamestown, 1975, p. 29.

> The St Helena Government must encourage private enterprise and not drive it away from St Helena such as they have been doing. In the last year I've seen an Englishman come here and wanted to start a poultry farm, another wanted to re-establish coffee, another a civil engineer, was going to buy a private piece of land and employ some islanders. All was turned away.

Although this author was not able to verify the cases of the civil engineer and proposed coffee grower, that these charges were not without foundation can be seen in the case of Robin Castells of Middlesex, who did indeed make a detailed proposal for a deep-litter poultry to make the island self-sufficient in table poultry and eggs (the island imported 5,937 chickens and 59,400 eggs annually). The proposal involved growing sorghum locally on 60 acres and Castells was prepared to invest £12,000 of his own money. Though the proposal to use so much scarce land would have been difficult to concede, Castells complained bitterly that his proposal was not even given serious consideration. In a private letter to the government secretary, shown to the present author, Mr Castells remonstrated: 'I'm offering my own money and I can't even get on a boat. ... You will no doubt need a few assistants in the archives as it seems to me that everything will end up there – perhaps before being read.'

How then do we summarize the reasons for the failure of private entrepreneurship on the island? As has been argued, the structural constraints on the domestic productive forces were deeply embedded in the underdeveloping effects of mercantile capital. This left very little room for domestic savings. The savings/income ratio is extremely low, and there is little incentive for the islanders to accumulate wealth. Indeed in the absence of a banking system, the only institutional form of savings was in the Post Office which, in 1975, paid 3 per cent interest. So if private investment were to form a part of the island's economic development, it would have to come from outside. In this respect, the rejection of Thornton's initiatives and the coolness shown to other potential investors suggests that the government, despite some public protestations to the contrary, was extremely wary of permitting the importation of outside capital. Part of their caution is to be explained by the particular experience of dealing with one persistent and challenging entrepreneur, who had little inhibition in politicizing his case in London or on the island. But, as will be argued in greater detail later, part of the answer lay in the static nature of colonial government itself. The absence of any significant nationalist opinion, the fact that the islanders were faced with government monopoly of their employment prospects, and the tendency of the small but powerful settler community to social stasis all reinforced the caution exhibited by colonial officers on the ground. Their position was generally reinforced in the Foreign & Common-wealth Office in Whitehall, which was committed to the shedding of all remaining colonial responsibilities, seen as burdensome and irrelevant anachronisms. St Helena was, however, a special case in that it was self-evidently unable to govern itself or maintain an even marginally viable economy, even by the minimal standards established, for example, for the micro states of the Caribbean. At least one senior official in the Overseas Development Ministry was prepared to contemplate mass emigration as a solution. Others in the Foreign and Commonwealth Office caught up in the new rhetoric of 'development', alarmed by the turn of events in St Helena, concerned at the fate of their colonial charges, or, less generally, apprehensive of international disapprobation (the UN decolonization committee maintained an interest in the island) decided to press for an integrated development plan for the island. It is to an analysis of this development plan that I next turn.

Welfare colonialism: the development plan

The St Helena Development Plan was based on a series of reports by visiting experts and advisers commissioned by the Foreign and Commonwealth Office and the Overseas Development Administration in 1973. The major report was divided into a General Survey (Part One) and a set of specialized reports on employment, agriculture, fisheries and the prospects for civil aviation (Part Two). It was presented to the governor in February 1974 and to the secretary of state for Foreign and Commonwealth affairs at the same time. The latter approved the recommendations in principle in June 1974. From the beginning, the plan was conceived as statement of principles and a set of policies to be directed from the top downward. This can be seen, for example, by the fact that the plan was presented to the legislative council only in July 1974, after the secretary of state had approved its recommendations. Even then, no debate was expected, the council having simply been asked to approve a notion that it 'welcomes and supports the Development Plan for St Helena and requests that an expression of its appreciation be conveyed to Her Majesty's Government'. This motion was passed with desultory discussion. Though a public document, the plan itself was not published in Jamestown until eight months after its commencement. Only 100 copies were produced and no attempts were made at the time to ensure public discussion of the document. The major capital expenditure involved approximately £1.5 million over the plan period from 1974 to 1979. The distribution between sectors is listed in Table 6.1.

With the grant-in-aid added, the British taxpayer was committed to provide some £5.5 million to support the administration of the island over the plan period, making St Helenians, at £220 per capita per year, one of the largest beneficiaries per head

Table 6.1: Capital expenditure, 1974–79 (000's)

Natural resources	£329
Economic infrastructure	£450
Social services	£243
Loans and grants	£100
Unidentified	£358
Total	£1480

Source: *St Helena Development Plan 1974 to 1979*. Part One.
St Helena Government Printer, 1975.

of British aid. Of course, the distribution of this revenue is heavily skewed toward the costs of the administration itself, while the per capita measure gives a poor idea of the real incomes of the islanders themselves. Nonetheless, with such a relatively large per capita expenditure, it is instructive to examine what the guiding principles of the planners were. These are clearly enunciated in a number of key statements in Part One of the plan.

- There can be no alternative to grant-in-aid unless and until fresh industry is able to revive the economy. The aim must therefore be to direct capital expenditure towards those sectors which serve to reduce the island's present dependence on imports of even the most essential foodstuffs, and which will increase the island's attraction for outside investors.

- The main strategy for investment is therefore to develop those sectors of the economy which support the objective of greater self-reliance, as fast as possible, and to give lower priority to the development of sectors which do not meet this objective.

- The two extreme alternatives would be to decide the island would never regain a measure of importance, strategic or otherwise, and to initiate a policy of active depopulation, or else to accept that the island will ever remain a perpetual and ever more costly pensioner tied to the UK standard of living. Neither of these positions is likely to be acceptable to Britain or to the majority of St Helenians. A compromise must be found whereby the islanders may be led out of the low productivity trap into which they have fallen and to provide the community with objectives for an exciting challenge and a sense of purpose. The basic strategy of development therefore must be to enable the islanders as far as possible to determine their welfare and their future by their own efforts.[9]

Let us examine these objectives in turn to see what likelihood the development plan has of shifting the pattern of St Helena's dependence. With respect to the overwhelming dependence of the island on imports, the planners did indeed confront a formidable challenge. The pattern of exports and imports in the financial year before the plan was commissioned can be seen in Table 6.2.

The list of imports includes many goods for which, on the surface, islanders may reasonably be expected to produce local substitutes or at least reduce their needs for the imported items concerned. These goods included, with their values indicated, Canned Meats (£13,758), Beer and Stout (£17,815), Confectionary (£8,607), Milk and Milk Powder (£11,129), Margarine (£4,658), Tobacco and Cigarettes (£11,164), Biscuits (£4,869), Lard (£4,796), Cheese (£3,872), Butter (£2,651), Spirits and Liqueurs (£1,043), Wines (£2,651), Soaps (£1,769), and Fruit and Vegetable Juices (£2,254). What evidence Is there, then, that the planners were able to suggest areas where the island might develop

---

9   St Helena Government, *Development Plan 1974 to 1979*. Parts One and Two. St Helena Government Printer, Part One (ii), pp. 1, 2–3.

Table 6.2: Imports and exports, 1971–72 (in £s)

Exports	
Frozen fish (40 tons)	4,000
Hides and fleeces	400
Total	**4,400**
Imports	
Food, drink and tobacco	185,587
Raw materials and largely unmanufactured articles	8,743
Manufactured or mainly manufactured articles	209,594
Miscellaneous and unclassified	8
Total	**403,832**

Source: United Kingdom Government, Information transmitted to the Secretary-General of the United Nations by Her Majesty's Government in the United Kingdom in accordance with the provisions of Article 73(c) of the UN Charter concerning the territory of St Helena and the dependency of Ascension for the period 1st April 1972 to 31st March 1973, 1973 Transcript copy, pp. 13–14.

a reduced dependence on such imports? At a total level, the achievement of greater self-reliance does not in fact appear to have guided the allocation of the projected expenditure. A stark illustration of this is provided not in the sectoral breakdowns, but in the estimates one can calculate for the ratio of revenue to aid (defined as all income coming from Whitehall). Here an already adverse ratio of 1:2.3 (1974–75) was projected to increase to 1:1.9 in 1978–79. Seen in purely economic terms, the notion of 'development' acquired a rather curious meaning for what was acknowledged to be a planned form of increased dependency.

Turning to the more specific area of food production, where the import bill amounted to £155,000 in 1971, the plan argued that many foodstuffs 'could be substituted by island production' and acknowledged that the main problem in persuading islanders to engage in agriculture was that, since the 1960s, the government agricultural department had driven out independent production by 'keeping down the cost of its products to below the cost of production'.[10] As the agricultural adviser himself noted: 'There is little enthusiasm among the islanders for agriculture as an occupation. This no doubt arises from the fact that it has not been, and is still not, a very profitable occupation. None of the three large landowners claim to make a profit from their farming activities and indeed the government, which farms more than half the arable land on the island, shows a substantial loss on its production enterprises'.[11] Yet despite this gloomy account of the government's own record in agricultural production, the take-over of Solomons & Company placed 90 per cent of the pastures (as opposed to 80 per cent previously) directly under government control. Moreover, the section of the development plan concerned with agriculture devoted much attention to organizational matters – in particular to the creation of the Agricultural Development Authority – yet had no satisfactory account of how, where, and by what amount agricultural, livestock, and dairy production was meant to change over the plan period.

There was, in short, no reason to assume that the levels of agricultural production under state control were likely to increase at all. The one area where denationalization was suggested was

10 St Helena Government, *Development Plan 1974 to 1979*. Parts One and Two. St Helena Government Printer, 1975, Part One, p. 3.

11 St Helena Government, *Development Plan 1974 to 1979*, Part Two, p. 17.

in the 'eventual' creation of 'farming units which could be handed over to medium scale tenant farmers' (St Helena, 1975, Part Two, 27). Yet despite the adviser's argument that these rented units should provide a comparable income potential to other occupations, the Labour Party's manifesto justly points out that the smallholders would, in essence be asked to pay off the ADA's development costs, pay a commercial rental to the authority, and then try to compete with ADA's production subsidy of £150,000 (St Helena Labour Party, 1975: 16). That this sceptical view is not merely advanced for political ends can be seen in the response of one 31-year-old islander who had worked as a merchant seaman and was keen to start an agricultural enterprise on the island:

> The Development Plan states under ADA, farm units will be lease to the people. Do Government expect a man who gets a regular income to take over a farm unit where he has watch the same land been own by Government for years and they cannot produce anything with their tractor, and men and thousands of pounds – and the man in the street don't make enough to keep his family let alone save enough to gamble on taking over a farm unit.

The increasingly adverse ratio of aid to income, together with the doubtful benefits of agricultural reorganization, in short, suggest that the planners are unlikely to achieve their goal of reducing the level of imports. Nor does the government have any clear idea of which imports it wishes to identify as capable of being replaced or reduced by local production. As this author pointed out in a lengthy letter to the acting governor in March 1975, the plan in fact encouraged the consumption of imported goods and built in no effective protection or positive policy to stimulate local production:

Initially one can see this on a trivial level. Canned fruit is a preferred item, even though equivalent quantities of locally grown fruit are readily available, approximately one quarter of the price and certainly healthier, given the already high levels of sugar intake. Though trivial, such an example can be magnified throughout the economic system. By raising living standards without an increase in productive capacity, an aid programme simply feeds consumer tastes alien to the community, raises demand for imported 'sophisticated' items and further accentuates a sense of relative deprivation amongst those who have been exposed to consumer fads but have no means of satisfying their new demands. Where there exists an island substitute, efforts should be made to encourage the consumption of local goods. ... There seems to be little reason why locally-produced fruit, preserved and bottled jams and fruit, and eventually a full range of garden vegetables shouldn't be produced locally for local consumption.

The letter continued by arguing that selected import duties should be imposed, that the government needed to promote local produce by other measures, and that the symbolic value in producing something locally would have an important effect in stimulating other efforts at self-reliance. Though the author's views on this question have often been echoed by island opinion, nothing credible has been done to selectively reduce food imports. As to increasing the island's 'attraction for outside investors', we have already seen that such a prospect appears to present as much of a threat as an opportunity to those who administer the island's affairs.

If we consider the final quoted aim of the planners – namely, to provide the community with a sense of purpose, to build self-reliance and allow them to determine their own future – one can perhaps see these remarks as a rhetorical moral flourish, not meant to be taken at their face value. But there are some virtues in so doing, because the dynamics of the administration of colonial St Helena and the way in which the plan was implemented are thereby revealed. But let us start first with a logical objection to the planners' aim. If the community is to be involved in its own development there is also no clear distinction or hierarchy drawn between the roles of government, the role of foreign capital, and the role of the community – all three of which are equally and undiscriminatingly applauded. There is also a rather revealing inconsistency in on the one hand invoking the islanders' involvement and participation in their own future 'by their own efforts' and, on the other hand, suggesting that they will have to 'be led out of the low productivity trap into which they have fallen'. Have they fallen, or were they pushed? Who are they to be led by? If the islanders are to be the decisive actors in the determination of their own fates, how are they to be involved and what do they think of the plans drawn up on their behalf? It is to the discussion of these issues, that the next section of this chapter is addressed.

Responses to the Development Plan

It has already been shown that the plan was drawn up entirely by visiting experts and advisers. No public meetings were held by these advisers, and consultation took place virtually entirely with government officials on the ground and in Whitehall. The plan was to be implemented entirely from the top downwards, little publicity was given to it, and no attempt made to build in participatory groups in the implementation of monitoring of the plan. The legislative council members were, in effect, notified after the event and made a ritual obeisance to Her Majesty's government for its kind endeavours.

It was in these circumstances that the author decided to undertake three tests of opinion. First, he contacted in person, or by letter, all twelve Legco members. Second, he conducted selective in-depth interviews with a cross-section of islanders and officials, supplemented by visits to community projects, the schools, government departments, and the mental asylum. Finally, he surveyed 200 members of the electorate by means of a mailed questionnaire (the response rate was 55 per cent).

The Legco questionnaire elicited only a written response from three members, though others talked to the author informally. Only one councillor had contacted his constituents by letter concerning the development plan, though he was not able to organize a constituency meeting. Two other councillors had organized meetings, though attendance had been disappointingly small, at 15 to 20 people and 40 people, respectively. Another councillor organized a meeting subsequently to being contacted and perhaps as a response to the interest shown in whether any consultation with his constituents had taken place. When asked 'what features of the plan do you approve of', one councillor argued in vague terms that 'it is necessary to the growth and maturity of the island'; another approved of the broad agricultural strategy, the loans policy for house building, and the proposals for water storage and sewage; a third argued that the committees of Legco 'decide the projects to be undertaken, thus giving the people a direct say in expenditure'. The last comment is of some interest as the budget heads and major projects had all been tightly allocated prior to the plan reaching the Legco. It also clearly indicated that the councillor concerned conceived the democratic will in representative, rather than participatory or mandatory, terms.

When asked whether 'there are any features of the Plan that you personally disapprove of', it is interesting that the same councillor who saw direct democracy at work commented that he thought it a waste of time that all project plans had to be submitted to the United Kingdom for approval. Perhaps the most startling response, however, came from one councillor who thought that 'the priorities of the plan are questionable'. He also strongly attacked the lack of an economist's report in the specialized reports of Part Two of the Plan (this had been excised from the printed version as some recommendations did not square with the overall arguments of the planners). 'We have no guidance whether a project would be economical over a reasonable period, or not', he complained. Yet this fairly fundamental disagreement with the plan by an elected member was never, to this author's knowledge, referred to in official memoranda by those in the administration responsible for the plan's implementation.

When asked 'What role, if any, can a councillor play in activating public support for the development plan', the answers were generally evasive or vague. Only one councillor had a strong position to proclaim. She insisted that councillors could improve relations between the government and people, seeing the former as 'amazingly divorced from the day-to-day needs of the people'. Councillors should also prevent blunders, keep up faith and morale, investigate grievances, and 'can break their hearts, their backs and their spirit trying to achieve a more productive attitude on the one hand and some concrete proof of development on the other'. Despite this one idealistic statement, most councillors seemed to reflect a patrician, paternal view and represented their constituents as having negative, indifferent, or cynical views toward the plan.

This author was, by contrast, surprised at the level of interest generated by his own inquiries. The sample survey was constructed by taking approximately every fifth name from the 1972 Register of Electors, which listed 1073 names (St Helena,

1972). To ensure geographical representativeness, the sample was slightly biased in favour of the small constituencies of Levelwood, Longwood East, and Longwood West and corrected also for sexual bias. Using the cheap local post with a stamped addressed reply envelope proved an effective means of reaching the respondents, who despite St Helena's small size are widely scattered, sometimes in settlements that are difficult to reach. The response rate was unusually high, respondents often thanking the author effusively for his interest and returning the questionnaire in person, by slipping it under the door of his residence or by covert means. The fact that so large a number of responses were elicited and the manner of their return suggest both that such a level of consultation was a novel experience and that the islanders are less indifferent to their fate than has sometimes been adduced.

Findings

As can be seen from Table 6.3, the returns were particularly good from those in the 30–40 age group, those with working or travel experience abroad, while slightly more returns were made from men rather than women. The last bias is, however, somewhat misleading as the women tended to respond more fully and frankly. A somewhat disproportionate number of replies came from outside Jamestown, the capital, perhaps suggesting that people in the outlying areas were more attracted by the novelty of having their views sought. The basic attitudes to, and knowledge of, the plan by the respondents are summarized in Table 6.4.

The responses listed in Table 6.4 are somewhat difficult to interpret. It's clear, first, that with a sample drawn from the electorate and respondents who might be expected to be better informed, the government has been unsuccessful in providing even

Table 6.3: Profile of respondents

Demographic Variable	Percentage
Sex (N = 110)	
Male	68
Female	42
Age (N = 101)	
20–30	25
30–40	50
40–50	12
50+	13
Travel Experience (N = 95)	
Left for period over 2 years	23
Left for short periods	43
Never left island	34
Employment Abroad (N = 58)	
Contract worker (Ascension)	65
Employment abroad elsewhere	27
Merchant seamen	8
Residence (N = 110)	
Jamestown (capital)	34
Rural	66

the most basic knowledge of the plan, 76 per cent claiming, sometimes indignantly, that they knew little or nothing of its contents. This finding confirms the basically elitist character of the plan, awareness of which seems to have hardly filtered down to the Population. The poor level of governmental initiative in this respect is compounded by the lack of any independent medium of communication, other than an occasional Parish News, issued by an Anglican minister. The radio station (controlled by the government) did apparently broadcast some discussions of the plan, but

Table 6.4: Knowledge of Development Plan

QUESTION: What do you know of the Development Plan? What are its good points? And its bad points?	Percentage
A. (N = 110)	
Knows nothing/little	76
Knows basic provisions	13
Provides informed comment	11
B. (N = 32)	
Those finding 'good points'	12
Those finding 'bad points'	88
C. 'Good points' identified (by rank) (N = 4)	
General improvement	75
Loans for private housing	50
More frequent ships to island	50
Better education	25
More employment	25
Better communications	25
D. 'Bad points' identified (by rank) (N = 28)	
The government will do little/nothing	79
Not enough done to provide water	61
Not enough done to provide housing	39
Specific projects are 'waste of money'	32
Not enough done to provide help for poor	25
Communications not improved	25
Miscellaneous	29

its main output comprises a constant diet of popular music, interspersed with the odd sports commentary. The *St Helena News Review*, the official government weekly, carried some bald announcements of the plan's provisions, but these apparently were not widely read. It is not without justice that some islanders have nicknamed this slim publication 'The Two Minute Silence.' The fact that the overwhelming majority of respondents claimed little or no knowledge of the plan did not, however, prevent some of this group from commenting on its good and bad points. This explains the discrepancy between the smaller number who answered Part A affirmatively and those who were prepared to comment in Parts B, C, and D of Table 6.4.

Of those who expressed their views on the plan, the majority were clearly unimpressed with the work of the development adviser and his team of experts. Several, indeed, were hostile to the advisers. Respondents described episodes when the visitors had revealed their ignorance and complained that they were not asked for their views. Other epithets directed to the planners included 'frauds' and 'idiots'. Those who saw some good in the exercise nonetheless engaged in some wish-fulfilment. The plan is, at best, ambiguous on the questions of improving shipping, communications, and employment prospects, and only the promise of improved loans to those who wanted to build houses seems both to have gained unqualified approval and conformed to the planners' intentions. Two respondents provided detailed evidence of the slow pace of government house construction in support of their views that this endeavour was best left to private initiative. Perhaps more significant is that none of the people who held a positive view of the plan actually identified the major areas of investment promoted by the planners, namely, agriculture and fisheries.

Those who were sceptical of, or hostile to, the government's plans were far more articulate and often impressive in their command of the possibilities for alternative improvements other than those mentioned in the plan. The prevailing mood of the responses was, however, that the government, its advisers, and agencies were incompetent or stingy or indifferent to the islanders' fate.

Only a few islanders expressed their indignation in what could be recognized as a proto-nationalist response. One 31-year-old male with a lengthy working experience abroad, for example, stated:

> It's my opinion that the people who come to St Helena wants it to be the poor place it is, because for the islanders it's hell to live with, but to the Englishmen who come it's 'A White Man's Paradise.' For years we saw the same thing happening. ... Don't think the St Helenian people are happy with the set up here. ... What point is there in being a voter if our suggestions is just pushed aside? If St Helenians was violent people blood would flow here many a time, but maybe it would be the only answer.

The majority of respondents with negative views of the plan were far more muted. Many comments reflected a disbelief that the development plan represented anything but 'talk' with little chance of practical success. Other criticisms concerned the government's record in housing and water supplies and the provision of aid to the needy, themes that reoccurred strongly in an open question asking for what improvements the islanders themselves wanted (see below). Finally, a number of respondents attacked specific provisions of the plan. Several were directed to the lease proposals for farm units, some of the proposals on communication, while one islander argued that levelling Francis Plain for a cost of £5,000 was a 'waste of money'.

The last set of responses were directed to the question, 'What do you think should be done to improve life for yourself and your family?' This question triggered a vigorous set of responses covering a wide field, the variety of the responses not easily reduced to tabular data. A number of islanders used the opportunity to complain about life in general 'being hard', but the specific suggestions for improvement can be grouped into four categories – improvement of water supplies, improvement of houses, improvement of roads, and additional financial assistance. In nearly all cases the proposals were modest, reasonable, and not unduly costly – yet these grassroots demands gained little attention in the planners' proposals. The flavour of these responses is best conveyed by direct quotation. On the question of water supplies, one 33-year-old male living in a country area stated:

> We have a spring which never been run dry. We would be very grateful if they would prompt water to our houses which would help me a lot, as I work in a garden, and if we have water actually we would have something growing in the dry weather, which would help as I say.

Two respondents were more concerned with having to carry water over long distances that then became stale. Though the man advocated the simple provision of 'jerrycans', the woman felt they would be too heavy. The male respondent wrote:

> This man all now one by himself with a weekly small wage of £3 a week. And this is another problem concerning water business. I am living up on a hill and have to fetch this water a very long distance. ... Hard to fetch this water in lard tins. Then some poor people haven't a donkey and no cans and some people have in less than a week the drums gone bad and cannot make of the water only use for garden use. Why not help these poor people with some jerrycans with no payment?

On the question of housing, a number of islanders seemed to be more interested in having access to small loans to improve their own houses than in some of the more grandiose schemes of the planners. One 73-year-old woman who had never left the island commented:

> As for my home, it is not in a good condition. One room has no window, the weather beats in through the curtain and my bedroom window has no boards nail to it, so that shows the room is very dark. I have written to the Government for a loan, but it seems they not appreciating me and the wind has blown my verandah away. It's not a Government place; it is my own home and it is not [within] my means to buy materials.

The state of the local roads also attracted many suggestions for improvement, despite the planners' comment that 'there is little that urgently needs to be done at this stage on road development on the island' (St Helena 1975, Part One: 9). Here the contrasting views of just two islanders can be quoted:

> Also the road is not completed. When it rains its mud and water. It's [possible] to walk in only one small bay near the finish end. Only small cars can turn. Large vehicles have to keep reversing, reversing. For the want of an under land drain, the dirt settle in the road and make a lot of mud. This is my complaint in life.

Another islander was more concerned that he and his neighbours were unable to get to the main road easily:

> Really plenty can be done to help my neighbours and myself like we haven't got any sensible road, how if we got sick, we would have a hard time to get them on to the main road where a car can get. We take half an hour in walk to get there, and carrying only one it's a hard job.

Lastly, a group of respondents had various complaints about the meagreness of the social benefits paid to them. One woman wrote:

> I have seen the form that you wrote to someone, so now I am writing to you. My walk of life is this. I am 68 years of age. I have no father no mother no husband and no children. I am living with my sister who is in the same circumstances as I am. I applied to the social welfare twice for help. All they can afford to give me is £1.8 per week. It is not enough to give me the food that I require. A person of my age should have an income and to retire from worries.

The islanders' responses to the development plan seem, in short, to have little to do with the expectations and intentions of the planners. Most of those surveyed knew little about the plan; those who did were often hostile to, or critical of, the proposals in the plan. Even the small number of islanders who approved of the plan did not show a close identification with the planners' priorities. The islanders wanted different, more modest, more piecemeal improvements, which had little to do with the assumed needs to which the planners gave priority. Under these circumstances, it is perhaps not surprising that the islanders' representatives in the Legco found little enthusiasm for the development aims of the government and, with one exception, showed little inclination to activate their constituents in helping to implement the stated objectives of the government.

Conclusion

It is perhaps not too grand a generalization to suggest that colonial governments tend to encourage inertia and the preservation of the status quo and, by their very nature, are incapable of galvanizing the social changes necessary to transform a society.

However, this generalization is lent particular force in St Helena for three reasons. First, the administration comprises virtually the last cohort of British colonial officers. Unlike a minority of their predecessors who, in a remote district, might have experimented with a more bottom-up style of administration, the officers in St Helena are anxious not to blot their copybooks and are clearly conscious of Whitehall looking over their shoulders. Second, the civil servants in Whitehall are, for their part, primarily concerned with shedding Britain's remaining colonial responsibilities with the minimum of diplomatic and political fuss. Third, the social situation on the island itself encourages stasis. This stems partly from the conservatism of the small settler element, but also from the difficulties islanders have experienced in forming themselves into effective political lobbies. This stems in turn not from some inherent passivity or apathy, but partly from the all-too-recent experience of exercising a democratic choice and the small number of islanders who are self-employed and therefore immune from their felt obligations as government employees. The educational system and the narrow basis of consultation, representation, and participation permitted by the government also allows little room for the expression of opinions and grievances.

The St Helenian government is, on the whole, successful in maintaining the traditional goals of colonial state – just govern-ment, the maintenance of law and order, the preservation of legal and constitutional formalities, and the more paternal goal of trusteeship and protection for the inhabitants of the island. But these characteristics of colonial rule proved wholly inadequate to the challenges confronting St Helena in the 1970s. The colonial government was unable to harness private entrepreneurship to its stated task of reducing St Helena's dependence on the United Kingdom and, in the face of a challenge from this quarter, retreated to its prior position of trusteeship. It was also unable, despite formally adopting the modern goals of community development and self-reliance, to build in or activate the structures of consultation and participation that would have made the realization of these goals possible. Instead 'development' remained an abstraction, far removed from the needs and wishes of the people in whose name it was propagated.

References

Cohen, Robin. 1983. 'Education for dependence: aspirations, expectations and identity on the island of St Helena', *Manchester Papers on Development*, 8, 1983, 1–30, and Chapter 4 in this volume.

The Guardian 15 April 1974.

Jackson, E. L. 1903. *St Helena: the historic island*, London: Ward, Lock & Co.

Kay, G. 1975. *Development and underdevelopment: A Marxist analysis*, London: Macmillan.

Melliss, J. C. 1875. *St Helena: a physical, historical and topographical description of the island*, Kent: L. Reeve & Co.

St Helena Government. 1972. *The St Helena Government Gazette* Registers of Electors X, 12, St Helena Government Printer.

St Helena Government. 1975. *Development Plan 1974 to 1979*. Parts One and Two. St Helena Government Printer.

St Helena Labour Party. 1975. *The St Helena Manifesto*, Jamestown: St Helena Labour Party.

United Kingdom Government. 1973. Information transmitted to the Secretary-General of the United Nations by Her Majesty's Government in the United Kingdom in accordance with the provisions of Article 73(c) of the United Nations Charter concerning the territory of St Helena and the dependency of Ascension for the period 1st April 1972 to 31st March 1973. Transcript copy.

Chapter 7
Living with dependence: a Caribbean lament

Robin Cohen

This is a review article of three books, namely:

Payne, Anthony and Paul Sutton (eds.) 1984. *Dependency under challenge: the political economy of the Commonwealth Caribbean*. Manchester: Manchester University Press. Pp. xii+294.

Payne, Anthony. 1984. *The international crisis in the Caribbean*. London: Croom Helm. Pp. iii+177.

Payne, Anthony, Paul Sutton and Tony Thorndike. 1984. *Grenada: revolution and invasion*. London: Croom Helm. Pp. x+233.

The three books under review all have as principal authors and editors the dynamic Northern trio of Payne, Sutton and Thorndike (Huddersfield, Hull and North Staffs respectively). Payne and Sutton gained their Caribbean experience in the days when there was a thriving exchange of students and staff between the Departments of Government at Manchester and the University of the West Indies. All three are (by the standards of the sudden emergence of Caribbean Studies in the UK) old Caribbean hands, not given to rash enthusiasms or sudden political conversions. Even though the last book on Grenada is somewhat breathless in tone given its hasty production, the general impression created by all three books is that the political economy of the region will continue to be indelibly marked by the smallness, weakness and limited range of manoeuvre of the Caribbean states within the international polity and economy.

The Commonwealth Caribbean

This low-key realism is so pronounced in Payne and Sutton's *Dependency under Challenge* that their publishers feel constrained to apologize for their taking Commonwealth Caribbean as a major site for investigation. The Caribbean is used as 'a forum to explore the prospects of challenging dependence in the Third World' while the book reaches 'general conclusions of some importance about the character of development and under-development'. Such a defensive statement could not be written after the invasion of Grenada propelled the region into political and strategic prominence. Although published in 1984 (and indeed subsequently to *The international crisis)* it is clear from internal evidence that the Manchester book was the longest in preparation. As a result it has a more scholarly feel to it, but somewhat antedates in tone and substance the exciting debates and events of the last years and months.

In the opening essay, Payne shows how the New World Group, based in the economics departments of the University of the West Indies, had developed by the 1960s a fairly coherent statement of the region's dependence on the core economies for markets and supplies, for transfers of income and capital, for banking, technical, financial and business services and even for 'ideas about themselves' (p. 1). The Group mounted an effective critique directed at Lewis's model of 'industrialisation by invitation', but as Payne argues, they were unable to transform a radical critique into a 'radical practice. Virtually all the leading personalities were co-opted by state or international agencies, or (in the case of Best) moved into reformist politics. As Payne hints, but does not fully explore, New World or 'pure plantation' theory, like other pristine dependency theories, are at their core radical trade theories, and by that very fact cannot be extended to a significant analysis of the state or of class politics. Co-optation was thus the only possible political posture for the New World Group if any one subordinate state appeared to be trying to gain a more favoured place in the international market-place. Payne opposes to this form of accommodation with international capitalism, those who sought to contest this external structure by developing the theory and practice of the 'non-capitalist path' (of which more anon).

The remaining ten essays in this book are of mixed quality, but all deserve at least a brief mention. Payne has a substantial essay on the Manley period in Jamaica which argues that 'The pattern was one of endless vacillation in which [Manley] danced uncomfortably in turn with the domestic left and the international right' (p. 37). This is clearly a correct characterization, but Payne is unwilling to admit a structural logic to Manley's dilemma. The collapse of the regime was attributable in his view to a number of political errors. The alliance with Cuba and Manley's adoption of a 'democratic socialist' label made him appear to be more threatening to the established order than he really was. Manley (Payne does not make much reference to the interests, movement or ideas he represented) failed at the end of the day 'because he got himself into a muddle' (p. 40). This rather easy attribution of failure or success to the level of the individual human agent is continued in Sutton's review of the politics of Trinidad. This perhaps has greater justification in view of the effective dominance of the executive by Williams over the period 1955–81, which was such that he reduced his bureaucrats, fellow ministers and opposition politicians to playing the 'politics of a Renaissance court' (p. 57). Yet again one wonders if politics can be reduced to personality in view of the remarkable continuities observable in the post-1981 period under the Prime Ministership of the decidedly less Machiavellian and indeed lacklustre figure of George Chambers.

In Thomas's account of Guyana we begin to get a more definite analysis of the post-colonial state, which he sees as going through a process of 'fascistisation'. This is not an easy word to use in a lecture hall but is meant to signify the increasing use of military power to suppress internal dissent, the movement from politics to bureaucracy and the increasing state control over the ideological apparatus. In showing how 'co-operative socialism' has become a mask for the construction of a deadening state socialism, Thomas produces one telling statistic – one in every 35 Guyanese is a member of one or other branch of the state security services (p. 99). The remaining essay in the national case studies section of the book is one by Thorndike on the first years of the Grenada revolution. Although it contains 'some useful information, the analysis is superseded in his part-authored book on Grenada, which I will consider later.

Among the regional and international studies in *Dependency under challenge* I found little to set the pulse racing. I always thought of Caricom as one of those empty – regional organizations that provide employment for international civil servants and a dissertation topic for PhD candidates. There is nothing here to disabuse me of this belief. The provisions for movements of capital, skilled labour-power, management and plant under the Caricom Treaty are so weak that Payne describes them as 'meaningless' (p. 147). Axline is a little more hopeful regarding the Food and Nutrition Strategy (pp. 153–70), but as agricultural production is collapsing all over the Caribbean, this seems a rather limited advance. Ramsaran's essay on US–Commonwealth Caribbean relations is of greater import, but he has a tendency (with the exception of a few passages) to assume a monolithic and unchanging US interest in the area. This is of course a true picture at one level, but there were salient shifts in policy between the early and later Carter periods and between the Carter and Reagan presidencies. These shifts and the rise of the 'new right' in the USA had a direct bearing on internal Jamaican politics and on the decision to invade Grenada. If we are to understand such effects, the 'US interest' must be more finely differentiated and explored. The remaining essays include Sutton on the EEC, Vaughan Lewis on what he elaborately calls the 'hemispheric middle powers' (Brazil, Mexico, Venezuela and Cuba) and Benn's appraisal of the New International Economic Order – a display of excessive caution by an international bureaucrat so anxious not to say anything controversial that he ends up saying not very much at all. Although the book is titled *Dependency under challenge*, it is clear from the observations of the authors and from Sutton's concluding remarks that 'the most case argument' would lead to a continuation of dependency, not to its alleviation, let alone its challenge. Only in the case of Grenada, as Sutton points out, is (was) there a possibility of 'reversing visions of permanent mendicancy by posing radical solutions to development problems which had hitherto been thought incompatible with the fact of US hegemony in the region' (p. 282).

The international crisis in the Caribbean

We all know by now that this glimmer of hope was a chimera. The invasion of Grenada, which is considered in the postscript to Payne's *The international crisis*, ended all illusions that Reagan and his advisors might tolerate the brave little experiment that Grenada represented. In *The international crisis* Payne is clearly alert to the new sensitivity of the region. As he argues, in the past 'the rest of the world was indifferent to Caribbean politics, sometimes it was curious, sometimes amused, but hardly ever concerned' (p. ii). Now the instability of the region has forced a recognition that rival ideologies and strategies have found a new battleground. As is its wont, the British government responded with vigour to the changed situation by setting up an enquiry on the Caribbean and Central America under the aegis of the House of Commons Foreign Affairs Committee (HMSO, 1982) to which Payne acted as a specialist advisor. The fact that the report was unusually intelligent and well-informed did not of course mean that it was read or acted on. When the Grenada crisis erupted, the characteristic mixture of confusion, double-dealing and ineffectual expressions of goodwill, further eroded Britain's position in the Caribbean.

At least, however, Payne was able to rescue a decent book from his involvement. *The international crisis* is neither profound nor original; but it does provide a respectable and nearly up-to-date introduction to the politics of the region (it would provide a more accessible one if the publishers could be persuaded to issue a cheaper paperback edition). Payne has ventured outside his traditional area of interest, the Commonwealth Caribbean islands, to include pithy updates on Puerto Rico, Suriname, Haiti, Belize and the Dominican Republic (although the book predates the most recent 'IMF riots' in the DR). His account of US foreign policy in the region amply testifies to the weakness of the parallel chapter in *Dependency under challenge*, for it includes a good discussion of the shifts in policy over the Carter and Reagan periods and an account of the purposes of the Caribbean Basin Initiative, the so-called mini-Marshall Plan meant to buttress the collapsing economies of the region.

Payne also includes workmanlike discussions of the other international powers active in the Caribbean basin. Cuba, the Old European Powers (Britain, France and the Netherlands) and the New Latin American Powers (Venezuela, Mexico, Colombia and

Brazil) are all in turn allowed to make their entry and rehearse their lines on the Caribbean stage. Of all this material, perhaps the most interesting comments are those on Cuba. Again Payne exhibits his preference for hard-headed realism. The 'bottom-line' of the USSR–Cuba relationship is the military alliance and the exercise of Soviet power in the Western hemisphere (p. 71). But Payne is not so foolish as to believe that Cuban influence in the Caribbean is predicated on the crude exercise of political and military muscle. He is clear that the attractiveness of the Cuban model reflects 'the unquestionable success of the Castro regime in reducing inequality, eliminating open unemployment, virtually eradicating illiteracy, improving public health and building up the housing stock' (p. 82). The contrast with the decrepit condition of the post-colonial, or metropolitan-ruled, Caribbean, is sufficiently great for Cuba to be 'more wooed than wooing' (p. 82). As to Cuban ambitions in the area, Payne comments thus: 'As in the rest of Latin America, Cuba has lately been much more concerned to establish good relations with the existing governments of the Caribbean than it has been to promote revolutionary change' (p.79). I shall refer to this statement, with which I concur, a little later. Payne's book concludes with a lugubrious six-page epilogue on the US invasion of Grenada. His views on this are best summarized in the final book I review, but it is worth citing Payne's own overarching resume of the current crisis in the Caribbean. As he puts it in current newspeak, the crisis 'emerged out of the problem of development and underdevelopment (the North–South dimension) but has been transmuted into a sub-plot of the new Cold War (the East–West dimension)' (p. 154).

Revolution in Grenada

Such a process was all too evident in the events leading up to the invasion of Grenada in October 1983, described by Payne, Sutton and Thorndike in *Grenada: revolution and invasion*. Given the haste of its production, there are bound to be some rather light-weight passages and sections, but the authors' long experience of this area has permitted them to avoid a number of the worst pitfalls of the instant potboiler. In documenting the background to the revolution, they characterize the early New Jewel Movement (which was to form the core of the People's Revolutionary Government, the PRG) as uneasily combining 'elements of racial and national pride, Rastafarianism, "popular power" and participatory democracy with social reformist zeal' (p. 11). They argue that it was only in 1976–77 that any Marxist and socialist theory emerged. What appeared, of course, was nothing else but the 'non-capitalist path' to socialism, this time dressed in a Grenadian guise.

While giving credit for the regime's economic and social achievements, the authors are clearly concerned that it failed to safeguard liberal democratic rights. 'Power lay unambiguously with the Central Committee. Party policy was at best only margin-ally amended by [nascent institutions of mass participation] whose main purpose was more to mobilize support for develop-ment objectives, educate the masses politically, disseminate information mid help defend the revolution' (pp. 38, 39). In short, the participatory structures set in place by the PRG were there to support the regime, not to represent 'the masses'. Those whose criticism went too far were questioned (perhaps 3,000 people), although only one-tenth of that number were imprisoned, normally for hours and days, not for weeks or months (p. 39). The PRG was not running a tea party, but neither was Grenada a large Gulag, as Reagan's propaganda machine suggested.

In addition to some useful chapters on the US, Cuba and the Commonwealth Caribbean's attitude to Grenada, which are unexceptionable, the authors attempt a first reading of the four and a half years of PRG rule. At the core of their assessment they point to a 'paradox' – namely, that the economic and social advances made by the regime were made within a reformist, idealist and social democratic framework. At the same time the New Jewel Movement seemed hell-bent on constructing a strict Marxist–Leninist political organization (p. 105). Despite sifting through the minutes of the Central Committee (thankfully rescued for analysts by Richard Hart, the former Attorney General), Payne, Thorndike and Sutton never quite seem to explain the roots of the paradox they discern. They are forced back into explaining the internal struggles for power in the immediate period preceding the invasion in terms of personality differences. Fortunately, they reject any crude versions of this and have a much more sympathetic view of Coard's position than surfaced either from the right ('a man who would sell his mother for a nickel and country for a dime of Red money', according to the *New York Post*) or from many sections of the left who needed a convenient scapegoat to demonize as soon as Bishop entered the ranks of the martyrs. Payne and his co-authors argue a modified personality thesis – that the internal crisis was 'a struggle for the control and direction of the revolution in a deteriorating economic situation which, because of the specific circumstances of Grenada, inevitably involved personality clashes' (p. 143).

But neither the level of economic deterioration nor the perception of economic crisis is convincingly shown. The failure of the regime, as they acknowledge elsewhere, was a political failure (p. 217) and rested ultimately on the inadequacies of the theory that informed the regime's political practice. I return, then, to the 'non-capitalist path'. The authors upbraid the present reviewer and his co-author for their 'familiar' argument that the theory of the non-capitalist path was hijacked by Stalin in the 1920s. They also criticize our view that the Soviet Union and 'even' Cuba acted as a restraining influence on radical developments in the Caribbean (p. 220). This is no place to abuse a reviewer's privilege, but a brief reply is necessary to advance the argument.

The point about the Comintern's tactics was made not in pursuit of an old polemic but to show how the theory was twisted for totally instrumental ends so that, then and now, the definition of which states are on a non-capitalist path is determined by foreign policy interests, primarily those of the Soviet Union, rather than any deep appreciation of the balance of class forces within any one state. For Grenada, the result, at the international level, was that an alliance of largely rhetorical supporters of the Grenadian revolution was stitched together from North Korea, Vietnam, Ethiopia, Mongolia, Libya, Iraq, Syria, some Eastern European countries and the Soviet Union. These relations triggered the anti-communist reflexes of the Reaganites, but were, in effect, useless to defend the revolution at the moment of its greatest need. The Cuban involvement was of course a different matter, but it is odd to find Payne concurring in the view that our argument regarding Cuba's restraining role was 'scarcely credible' (p. 220) when he himself argued that Cuba's recent role in the Caribbean has been conciliatory rather than revolutionary (see passage cited earlier). The Cuban airport workers did put a brave and dignified fight against overwhelming odds, but as Castro made clear in his post-invasion statement, Cuba had made a number of friendly gestures to the US, was in no position to defend the Grenadian revolution physically, and had no inclination to do so once Bishop had been killed.

In short, at the external level, all the theory of the non-capitalist path provided was a thin linking skein providing diplomatic and limited economic support, but crucially exposing the regime to the reactionary elements in control of a powerful hegemonic power. At the level of internal politics, the theory masked the inability of the regime to combine economic and social advances with the protection of democratic rights. It also served to subordinate the working class and the peasantry to other sections of the class alliance – in practice, in Grenada, to the leading party officials and ultimately to sections of the military. Thus the so-called 'paradox'. Both these points have been forcibly addressed by C. Y. Thomas in a passage cited by Payne, Sutton and Thorndike (p. 217). Too little recognition has been given in the theory, he argues, to 'bourgeois freedoms' such as 'freedom of speech, association and publication, the independence of the judiciary and the insistence on the establishment of institutions representative of the popular will.' These rights, he continues, were won by mass struggle and should be expanded *as a pre-condition* of socialist construction' (emphasis added).

Although the PRG did attempt to establish alternative organs of popular will, the mass organizations and village assemblies remained peripheral to the main decision-making organs. Further, the dismantling and derision of bourgeois democratic rights (including elections and *habeas corpus*) was a costly, and unnecessary, error. In the face of such an indictment of the experience and practice of the non-capitalist path, it is difficult to see quite why Payne and his colleagues still want to cling to the residue of such a discredited notion. They admit the theory needs 'redevelopment rather than mere reformulation and refinement' but think it is the bathwater 'not the baby' that needs pouring away (p. 220). To change the metaphor, such a baby would be more like the proverbial fish out of water. The 'water' surrounding the Grenadian revolution meant that it had to take account of the hegemonic claims of the USA and also respect and surpass the legal and bourgeois democratic traditions of the Westminster model (even if these were widely violated under Gairy). Such an agenda implied a necessary parallelism and mutual relationship between socialism *and* democracy internally, and a subtlety ('socialism by stealth') in external relations. Neither of these elements could possibly have been found by running some more bathwater for the same 'non-capitalist' baby. Indeed, the pessimists among us might argue that it is impossible to envisage such an alternative theory at this stage of Caribbean development. The strains of an old Caribbean lament still linger. Should the tune composed by the Grenadian revolutionaries be retitled 'false optimism' not 'new dawn'?

Addendum

This review article was published in the *Journal of Development Studies*, 21(3), April 1985, pp. 458–63. I did not get to know Tony Thorndike very well, but saw something of Anthony Payne when he moved to, and helped to fashion, the excellent politics department at Sheffield. Paul Sutton and I worked closely together as trustees on the David Nichols Trust (which supported, inter alia, educational opportunities for Caribbean students). They were all gracious about this review, which was mostly positive but also made some critical remarks. Perhaps I need to explain that, at that time, serious intellectual engagement was important to all of us, and getting the theory and praxis right was part of taking political writing seriously. I should add, on the question of the 'non-capitalist path' to development, that I was somewhat scarred by the cynical manipulations of the expression by the South African Communist Party. As I explained in Chapter 2 of this book, I was all too familiar with this debate because of my South African background and I was probably more combative on this issue than I needed to be in the Caribbean setting.

Chapter 8
Decolonization and small states:
too weak or too strong?

Robin Cohen

In the period of decolonization, when many new small states were created, politicians and administrators were pre-occupied primarily with the theoretical minima of economic and political viability. Now the focus has shifted somewhat to the problems of integrated or autarkic development and the threat posed to international security by the political instability of many small states. The security threat is, in turn, derived both from internal political and economic factors and by regional or great-power rivalry for effective control over small countries.

However valid the earlier considerations of the minima for economic and political viability were, the fact is that, for better or for worse, the nineteenth century doctrine of self-determination has triumphed more frequently than any reasonable application of such criteria would have dictated or the most ardent advocates of self-determination could have anticipated. What I want first to establish in this short chapter is why practical considerations were often discounted as small states were established in the post-war world. Second, I want to probe the implication of two contrasting characterizations of the problems facing small states. Finally, given the *de facto* existence of small states which would historically have been considered 'unviable', I ask 'how does one measure success?'

The triumph of self-determination or the weakness of empire?

When John Stuart Mill wrote that 'it is in general a necessary condition of free institutions that the boundaries of government should coincide in the main with those of nationalities' (cited in Kohn 1961: 39), it is clear that he considered 'nationality' widely, as a social bond of common sympathy and association that could transcend the bonds of race, language, religion, or ethnicity. Adherents to some of these narrower affinities in the post-war world have none the less sought to clothe themselves in the more ample robes of 'nationality' in their quest for a separate political identity. This attempt to use 'nationality' as a substitute for narrower loyalties means that the accession to statehood by so many small states in the period after the Second World War is neither a vindication of classical liberal notions of representative government nor a guarantee of 'free institutions'. Nor again, as I shall argue, can the proliferation of new 'nations' automatically be assumed to have enhanced the sphere of individual or collective freedom against illiberal or alien tyrannies.

Lest this statement seems like a reactionary response or even an unqualified defence of colonial empire, let me specify more exactly what I mean by suggesting that nationhood is by no means simply a synonym for freedom or liberalism, as nineteenth century political liberalism assumed. Virtually every empire, even those that we remember for their despotic or militarist character, had some universalizing principle which regulated the relations between the core society and its peripheral outposts. Long-term conquest, settlement, and trade within an empire would otherwise have been impossible. The Roman system of international law, *jus gentium*, made dialogue and transactions between Roman and foreigner, and between provincial and provincial, possible and profitable for the first time. The *Code Napoléon* extended these principles and introduced other universal concepts inherited from the Revolutionary Jacobin tradition.

Many of the small states that emerged in the period of decolonization were territorially formerly part of the French, British, Spanish, and Dutch empires. These empires *also* advanced universalizing principles. The *pax Britannica*, the French notion of the civilisable colonial subject, and the equivalent Spanish notion of the *asimilativo 'indiano'*, however patronizing, nonetheless did presage the possibility of a wider association, on more equal terms, with the core society. This possibility survived, residually, in the notion of a 'British' (the adjective was later tactfully dropped) Commonwealth, and more vigorously in the 1954 Charter of the Kingdom of the Netherlands (which gave theoretically equal status to the Dutch Antilles, Suriname and Holland). Equality was also theoretically on offer in the French *départements d'outre mer* – Réunion, Guyane, Martinique, and Guadeloupe – whose inhabitants enjoy the same political rights and social security benefits as metropolitan residents. It would, of course, be absurd to deny that Holland is the dominant power in Aruba, Curaçao, or Bonaire or that the 'assimilationist path' has not caused bitter controversy in the *départements d'outre mer* (Blerald 1983).

Yet, however vigorously one espouses the right to self-determination, it is difficult to argue that the inhabitants of such territories are notably less free, or enjoy less extensive political expression (or indeed are materially worse off) than their 'independent' small state neighbours. It is perhaps easier to see the dead hand of colonialism or the denial of open democratic debate in British dependencies such as the British Virgins, the Turks and Caicos, Hong Kong or St Helena. Yet, none of these territories exhibits an even moderately convincing nationalist movement and most of the residents seem accepting, if not enthusiastic, beneficiaries of reasonably efficient, normally honest, colonial administrations committed to equality before the law. What follows from this apparent (if qualified) defence of the colonial order? Essentially, the proliferation of small states dismembered from the twentieth-century empires represented a failure of these empires' universalizing ideals. Here and there, as in the *départements* and dependencies, the founding ideals survived, but more as faded notes on worn-out gramophone records than as a triumphal Elgarian fanfare.

What is often assumed to have taken the place of these ideals is a vigorous alternative nationalism, fuelled by powerful anti-colonial sentiment and commanded by leaders determined to allow their enthusiastic followers to walk tall in the comity of nations. Of course there were, and are, many national liberation struggles having precisely that character. Those with a taste for such events might have cheered on the Vietnamese peasantry who demolished the French Empire at Dien Bien Phu, then proceeded to defeat the massive forces of the US, both militarily and ideologically.

But if the armed national liberation struggle mobilizing the bulk of the population in defence of self-determination represents one end of the spectrum, there are many intermediate cases of constitutional decolonization, with a powerful leader at the head of a popular national campaign, which fall far short of violent and sustained struggle (Nehru, Nyerere or Nkrumah are cases in point) and many more, in the small states, where the sanctions and pressures mounted by the nationalist movement were extremely weak. In a number of cases an anti-independence, pro-metropolitan party even developed. In short, the empires cut many of their peripheral outposts free; when judged in strict military or political terms they need not have done so. In probing for the reasons why empires were abandoned one also finds a first approximation of the problems of development, political instability, and security that were bound to follow.

The collapse of ideological legitimacy

The simple fact is that the ideological justification for empires had collapsed in the wake of the Second World War. This was partly because of a serious erosion in morale and pride on the part of the two principal European powers with extensive empires – Britain and France. Whatever the ultimate outcome of the war, French military prowess had tumbled like a house of cards, and the British, subjectively perhaps even more humiliatingly, had been driven from their Asian territories by a non-white power, Japan. The fact that some Indian nationalists and Malaysian insurgents were happy to co-operate with the Japanese in order to displace their colonial masters was a further disheartening factor. There seemed little point in proclaiming the glories of empire when the 'jewels in the crown' wished to glitter on some other head, preferably their own. The founding statement of the United Nations, the San Francisco Charter of 1945, drove the ideological point home, demanding that all colonial powers devolve greater autonomy to the territories they administered.

In Britain, the ideological defence of empire was virtually impossible, despite Churchill's blustering, except in the weak Fabian terms characteristic of the Attlee government and the period of welfare colonialism. In this, the Colonial Office harked back to pre-war days when the notion of a temporary 'trusteeship' underpinned the expansion of the colonial administration. Only this time the beneficiaries felt they had escaped their statuses as minors and demanded that the trust be dissolved. Some longer-sighted administrators sought to make the best of their situation and committed themselves to an imaginative programme of devolution and welfare, hoping thereby to retain the loyalty of former colonial subjects. Other British administrators went through the motions of delivering welfare institutions and installing systems of representative government in their colonial territories without very much belief in their long-term efficacy. For all, sceptics and enthusiasts of British decolonization alike, the question was not whether, but when, 'self-government' would take place.

For the French, the ideological justification for empire was somewhat more tenacious in that their war experience had revealed colonial subjects (in Central Africa and the Caribbean especially) to be more loyal to the founding ideals of the French Republic (as represented by the Gaullist cause) than the metropolitan French citizenry itself. The French notion of civilisation also extended to a small, but significant, section of colonial subjects who were tied psychologically, intellectually and culturally, to metropolitan ideals.

But these differing circumstances between the French and British resulted in largely the same outcome. The French were rebuffed militarily in Vietnam and Algeria and politically in Guinea, where Sekou Touré organized a 'no' vote to the idea of a French West African 'community'. The last was so galling to the French administrators that they are said to have removed everything to the last sheaf of stationery and the last toilet roll as they stomped from their former colony. 'Now manage without us', was the message. But it was a fit of pique that did little to delay the extensive dismemberment (at least at a formal level) of the French Empire in West Africa, Central Africa, and most of the Pacific. Ignoring some dependencies and *départements* alluded to earlier, what remains of the empires is a commitment to a multiracial Commonwealth supported by 30–40 specialized agencies in the case of the British and a somewhat more vigorous set of cultural associations and security arrangements in the case of the French. However, at the ideological level, in the space of less than one generation, the universalizing ideals of the European empire have disappeared.

The rise of rival powers

Internal misgivings aside, the political demise of the European metropoles was paralleled by the rise of rival powers (both global and regional) which challenged the hegemony of Britain, France, Portugal, and Belgium in their old colonial 'patches'.

Just as the USA had destroyed Spain's imperial projects in the Philippines, Cuba and Puerto Rico in the late nineteenth century by imperiously proclaiming the death of imperialism, so too did the USA in the post-1945 period begin to assume imperial responsibilities through its own military assertiveness and push for economic hegemony. Even the old white Dominions began to fall like ninepins to the juggernaut of US power: in 1950, Australia and New Zealand signed a defence pact with the USA to which Britain was not a party. In the Middle East and the Gulf, US companies began to dominate the oil industry and manipulate the price of oil. The existence of a black population in the USA and the country's former status as a colonized nation enabled State Department officials to express sympathy and understanding with nationalist and anticolonial sentiments, while simultaneously rechannelling the movements of trade, the flow of communications, and the lines of dependency away from London, Paris, Lisbon, or Brussels and in the direction of Washington.

The second great global power, the Soviet Union, also sought to influence emerging nationalists, this time in the direction of combining the anticolonial struggle with a commitment to a strategic alliance with the Eastern bloc and an attack on international capital's interests in each territory where they exercised some influence. Military aid to insurgents in Vietnam, Korea, Laos, Burma, and elsewhere in Asia triggered or sharpened a more contested struggle for nationhood than occurred in most parts of Africa, the Caribbean, and the Pacific.

The third power with 'global reach', namely Japan, abandoned its wartime military–imperial dream expressed in the South East Asia Co-prosperity Sphere in favour of a determined and markedly successful effort to penetrate the world's marketplaces with cheaper, and ultimately better, manufactured goods.

While the US, the Soviet Union and Japan carved great slices off the European colonial cakes, significant portions were also claimed by regional powers. Perhaps the point is best illustrated by reference to the cases of Botswana, Swaziland, and Lesotho in southern Africa. Over each of these territories, Britain had proclaimed a 'protectorate'. But the regional power from whom these territories clearly needed protection was South Africa, into whose hands the British delivered them when 'acceding' to their demands for independence.

Let me conclude this first part of my argument by summarizing some salient points. When examining the practical questions of the security, development, and internal political stability of small states, 'an academic perspective' must start by situating these questions within the historical crucible from which they emerged. The elements contained in the mix were characteristically a weakly articulated nationalism covering a narrower set of loyalties; a declining European empire losing its raison d'être; countervailing global powers undermining what little credibility the old empire still retained; and regional powers ready to trouble the waters and to fish therein as and when the opportunity presented itself.

Characterizing the problems of small states

The foregoing remarks should serve to indicate that I would caution against those characterizations of small states that start only from a morphological classification based on appearances. For example, 'many small states are islands', 'over three dozen have populations under 1 million', 'many rely on a narrow range of exports', 'a number are former plantation economies'. One can go on building a more and more finely graded structure of classification, but such an exercise does have real limitations.

The kinds of generalizations that can be made are unlikely to constitute universal (across all small states) statements, though some striking contrasts can be used as illustrative material. For example, the United Arab Emirates and Oman are (or perhaps were) awash with oil money, and the Sierra Leonean and Jamaican populations are more than twenty times as poor as the top 5 per cent of those with the highest incomes (Kidron and Segal 1981: 43). Some states, even with the same colonial heritage, have managed a reasonably orderly and democratic management of regime change (for example, Mauritius and Barbados); others (for example, Grenada and the Seychelles) have stumbled from rigged election to coup to countercoup to invasion. However, using purely observed characteristics and measurements internal to small states will generate only statistical associations (which will often result in bizarre juxtapositions) or, certainly more positively and usefully, some probabilistic statements about likely trends in carefully grouped or predefined cases.

Another and more plodding route may be necessary to secure a more nuanced understanding of the problems of small states – if only for the reason, already implied, that the phrase 'small states' covers too many diverse cases. Thus a possible way of moving beyond case-by-case empiricism is to insist on setting groups of small states in their historical and regional settings, rather than concentrating on their surface characteristics alone. Let me take two contrasting statements that are often made of small states to demonstrate how this cautious advance in generalization might work:

Proposition A: 'Small states are too strong'

Such a generalization might be drawn from Alavi's (1976) widely quoted article on the overdeveloped postcolonial state. His thesis was so striking precisely because it seemed to fly in the face of the conventional wisdom that many states are too weak – either to suppress dissent or defend themselves internationally. On a closer reading, it is clear what Alavi means. Influenced as he is by Marxism, any state was for him an outcome of the efforts of a successful bourgeoisie to manage its common affairs. In many postcolonial states, the bourgeoisie was small or weak, or perhaps even barely existent. The state inherited at independence was neither therefore an authentic state nor one that grew from the strength of an indigenous bourgeoisie. It had been superimposed as part of the superstructure of another country, the metropole, and reflected the interests of its ruling class. Nonetheless, this did not prevent the state, in the absence of any other major source of accumulation, from being the major focus for primary capital accumulation (for example through corruption or the award of contracts to the aspirant bourgeoisie. Access to state revenues is a fierce bone of contention between different contenders, as they seek to displace incumbents or prevent competition. Such a depiction also, of course, would serve to explain the level of political instability often found in many small states.

Provided one sets this thesis within the framework of a departing colonial power and an appreciation of the emergence of states in modern European history, the overdeveloped post-colonial small state can indeed be seen as too 'strong'. The

European bourgeoisies had to fight their way out of feudalism and aristocratic privilege to create a rational state structure, whereas the colonial power left a ready-made structure (courts, parliaments, civil service) which would not otherwise have emerged spontaneously.

By contrast, exactly the same data could be used to demonstrate the opposite proposition, namely:

Proposition B: 'Small states are too weak'

Such a generalization would flow from the argument that the major problem confronting small states is that they do not have the power or resources to stifle internal dissent or ward off the depredations of regional or global forces. Certainly, if the state of Lesotho, say, is incapable of preventing raids across its border by South African troops or acts of sabotage and subversion from the same source, it is difficult to describe such a state as 'over-developed'. It is indeed too weak, relative to the threat presented to it and relative to the ever-escalating demands of national security posed in a world whose economies are fuelled by rearmament and intense confrontation – a confrontation which falls short of war, but is far from peace.

If, again, we can imagine a modern state too remote or small or insignificant to attract the Japanese importer, the US State Department, the Russian ideologue, or a regional 'protector', such a state would more likely than not be 'sufficiently strong' to manage internal change successfully. Small states may therefore be too strong or too weak, or adequate to their task depending on their historical and regional context.

From nations without states to states without nations

By way of conclusion I want to ask how we might gauge the 'success' of a small state. The shortest and clearest answer is a

223

Darwinian one: survival. To this blunt measure can be added others of a more evaluative kind. How autarkic is the economy of the small state or how dependent? If, as is likely, highly dependent, is there one boss who calls the tune or are there many? In that case some manoeuvrability by a well-disciplined ruling class might well be possible. Is the small state implicitly protected by a 'godfather' (thereby preventing regional adventures) or exposed to a potential takeover? The godfather option for a departing power was well described by one astute observer as 'decolonizing without disengaging' in the case of French territories in the Indian Ocean (Houbert 1986). Is there, finally, evidence of progress either in welfare terms, reduced unemployment, better health and education provision, or in terms of conventional economic indicators?

Such measures of success will differentiate one small state from another and also help to situate the question, posed earlier, as to whether within its context a state is sufficiently strong to manage internal change, undertake meaningful development initiatives (even if this is only managing the rules of the game for private enterprise), or show a defiant face to rapacious outsiders. In such an exercise no doubt some of the 50 or so small states which have emerged since 1945 will be deemed 'successful' and 'viable'. But many might be considered as extremely vulnerable to takeover, internal collapse or civil disorder.

This takes me back to my starting point, which turns on the relationship between 'state' and 'nation'. For John Stuart Mill the major source of injustice and instability was the brutal attempt by old and decaying political entities (like the Ottoman and Austro-Hungarian empires) to hang on to territories inflamed by a passion for self-government and independence. In his view and in his time, we had 'nations without states'. Both liberal doctrine and pragmatic reason dictated that oppressed nations should be permitted to attain statehood.

In the post-war world, I would submit, we have all too many cases of 'states without nations'. In their haste to abandon their outposts in the face of competition from global or regional competitors and with their own collapse in morale, the European empires gave birth to many premature offspring. The sense of purpose deriving from a sense of common historical oppression, common cultural symbols, and common social aspirations was imperfectly developed when many states arrived at the UN to unfurl their new national flags (designed and made in the metropole) or issued their first postage stamps (some of which showed national heroes like Mickey Mouse, Donald Duck, and Goofy). It is ultimately a purposive sense of nationhood that will protect the fledgling new states. Where their historical experience was too fragmentary to forge this purpose, it will have to be developed 'after the event', as a form of post-independence nationalism. Failing this development, we shall see the doctrine of self-determination reach an historical cul-de-sac.

References

Alavi, Hamza. 1976. 'The state in post-colonial societies', *New Left Review*, 74, 59–81.

Blérald, P. A. 1983. 'Guadeloupe–Martinique: a system of colonial domination in crisis' In Fitzroy Ambursley and Robin Cohen (eds.), *Crisis in the Caribbean*, London: Heinemann, 148–65

Houbert, Jean. 1986. 'France in the Indian Ocean: decolonising without disengaging', *The Round Table*, 198, 145–66.

Kidron, Michael and Ronald Segal. 1981. *The state of the world atlas*. London: Pan Books.

Kohn, Hans. 1961. *Prophets and peoples: studies in nineteenth century nationalism*. New York: Collier Books.

Addendum

This chapter was first published under the title 'An academic perspective' in Colin Clarke and Tony Payne (eds.) *Politics, security and development in small states*, London: Allen and Unwin, 1987, 203–13. The focus clearly is on small states rather than island states as such, though clearly there are many small island states and consequent overlaps in argument, so I deemed it appropriate to include this contribution in this collection.

Chapter 9
The diaspora of a diaspora: the Caribbean case

Robin Cohen

The word 'diaspora' has crept into social-scientific and historical vocabulary in an untheorized or, at least undertheorized, way. It seems now loosely to refer to any communities in the world living far from their natal homelands. To that extent a 'diaspora' is simply the outcome of continental and international migration.

However, without being pedantic, it may be necessary to return to the original meaning of the term, even if only because so many migrant communities now appear to qualify as a 'diaspora' that the notion has become diluted beyond recognition. We may instinctively feel it is right to talk of the Indian, Jewish, African, Sikh, Armenian and Lebanese diasporas, but how about the Chinese, Italian, Greek, Polish or Turkish diasporas? And, more pertinently for this article, can the term 'diaspora' be meaningfully applied to migrants of African descent from the Caribbean, themselves a branch of the original African diaspora?

Before addressing this issue, let us return to first base. In its origin in the Bible (Deut. 28: 25), a 'diaspora' implies the forcible scattering of the indigenous people, perhaps as a form of punishment by God or fate for abandoning the old ways. In any event, a collectively traumatic event befalls the native people. In the case of Jews this was the destruction of the temple of Solomon; in the case of Africans, the slave raids. In both cases too, we infer a strong sense of betrayal – biblical kings and priests had fallen into sinful practices, while African chiefs had turned their backs on their people by bringing the slaves to the coastal zones for shipment across the Atlantic.

Once dispersed, the diasporic peoples are deemed by some visionary leaders (in my examples, Herzl or Garvey would be prototypical) to be ultimately unfulfilled, even doomed – unless they can return to their original homelands: hence Zionism amongst Jews, Garveyism amongst Africans, and kindred movements amongst other diasporic peoples.

In the Jewish and African cases it appears necessary to the morale of the return movements to imply that at least some brave souls have maintained the organic historical link with the heroic past – thus, the belief that there have always been Jews praying at the Wailing Wall (i.e. the wall of the key symbol, the temple of Solomon), or the equivalent African belief in the historical continuity provided by the Ethiopian royal family. Finally, exile, loss, loneliness, estrangement – these are assumed to be the very conditions and characteristic psychological states of the 'original' diasporic groups. The heart is and, ultimately, can only ever be where the original home is or was.

What I have provided above is not so much a definition *stricto sensu*, but a suggestion for a minimal set of characteristics and historical experiences, without which (in my judgement) the term 'diaspora' is used either too casually or without serious heuristic intent.

Against a Caribbean diaspora

As is well known, the indigenes of the Caribbean, the Caribs and Arawaks, failed as peoples to survive the glories of western civilization – they died from overwork and disease. None of those who settled in the Caribbean – African slaves mainly from West Africa, European settlers, planters and administrators and Indians arriving as indentured workers after the collapse of slavery, were indigenous to the area.

This may, in and of itself, disqualify any notion of a Caribbean 'diaspora'. Settler and immigrant societies are, by their very nature, points of arrival, not departure, sites of a renewed collectivity, not a traumatic dissolution. One cannot, for example, meaningfully talk of a Canadian, Australian or US 'diaspora'. The best one can stretch to is an expression like an 'expatriate community'.

Next, it would surely be expected that, if they are free to migrate, a significant proportion of any diasporic community should wish to return to their imputed homeland. Yet, with the partial exception of the Europeans, Caribbean people of Indian and African origin have been notably disinterested in returning either to India or Africa.

This is not to say this does not happen at all. But, in general, such migration is not self-propelled. Rather, the colonial powers were centrally involved (in, say, the African case). The British recruited a few dozen West Indian train drivers for Nigeria, the French appointed an Antillean Governor, Felix Éboue, for the Cameroons and a remarkable young psychiatrist, Frantz Fanon (whose thought is surveyed in Hansen 1977), was assigned to the colonial medical service in Algeria.

But these are mere drops in the ocean of Caribbean people who decided to migrate to Panama, the USA and Europe.

For a Caribbean diaspora

If we deal with the people of African descent in the Caribbean (and dispense with the more complex issue of Caribbean people of European and Asian origins), it may none the less be possible to see them as fulfilling the minimum criteria for being a diaspora in the senses that I have explained above.

For a start, the horrific consequences of forcible dispersion through the slave trade are still shared by all people of African descent, despite their subsequent liberation, settlement and citizenship in the various countries of the New World. This is partly because, unlike (say) in the case of Jews, where superficial invisibility is possible in Europe and North America if exogamy occurs, in the case of Africans, skin colour remains, if not an indelible marker, none the less a commonly visible marker for two, three or more generations – despite exogamy.

The deployment of skin colour in many societies as a signifier of status, power and opportunity makes it impossible for any people of African descent to avoid the issue of the external definition of Africanness, i.e. 'how African does the group appear?' This phenotypical labelling firmly links the African-Caribbeans (from now on I use this expression for convenience) to the original African diaspora.

However, being phenotypically African is insufficient in itself to carry the label in a sociological sense, even if it is an adequate marker in the popular consciousness. Thus, in addition to appearance, forms of cultural retention or representative statements of affirmation of and identification with Africa or an African identity are also intrinsic to the definition of an African diaspora and, by extension, to a Caribbean diaspora.

Here the evidence is less conclusive. There are clearly examples of a return to Africanness in the Maroon (runaway slave) communities and in many African religious, cultural and social practices (Herskovitz 1958) in the Caribbean. But there are also considerable countervailing data showing how New World peoples (of whatever origin) took the opportunity to throw off the shackles of their prior social constraints. Thus Toussaint in Haiti was as much Jacobin as African (James 1963); while, arguably, during the Second World War the French Antilles was more loyal to the idea of the French nation than the metropole itself. Equally, many Anglophone Caribbeans displayed a remarkable loyalty to Britain in both World Wars and showed a fierce adherence to British social and political institutions. Thus, for example, it presents no paradox to Trinidadians to boast that Eric Williams's famous exposition (1964) of the link between capitalism in Britain and slavery in the West Indies, was presented as a doctorate to the University of Oxford.

To the issue of phenotypicality and Africanness must be added the crucial issue of the articulation of the idea of a return movement. Here, despite the small number of African-Caribbeans who actually returned to Africa, Caribbean visionaries were at the forefront of the Back-to-Africa movements and in the articulation of the idea of a common fate for African people.

The most flamboyant and popular of these movements was the Universal Negro Improvement Association, founded by the Jamaican, Marcus Garvey. Garveyites were particularly strong in the USA and small, but ill-fated colonies were sent to Liberia and elsewhere on the continent. At the height of his influence, Garvey proclaimed himself Emperor of Africa, but he never visited the continent and died in obscurity in London after his movement was infiltrated, then discredited, by the American authorities.

Other great exponents of the return idea included C.L.R James (more of an internationalist than an African nationalist, though none the less influential in African anti-colonial circles) and George Padmore, who abandoned international communism for Pan Africanism in his famous *mea culpa* (1972). These and other Caribbean leaders were partly responsible for convening the watershed Manchester Conference of 1945, when the basic lines of struggle for African self-determination were articulated.

Other manifestations of a return movement took on a more cultural than political appearance. In the case of the Francophone Caribbean, Aimé Césaire made a spiritual but not physical return to Africa. He and other French Caribbean writers developed a major critique of colonialism (Césaire, 1972), strongly influenced the development of *Negritude* and had a continuing dialogue with Africans and the peoples of African descent more generally in journals such as *Presence Africaine.*

The Anglophone cultural equivalent was less cerebral and took the form of religious movements like Rastafarianism, the cardinal principle of which was the divinity of the Ethiopian emperor. The language of Rastafarianism was also drawn from Old Testament prophets and evoked images of Zion highly analogous to those of the Jewish diaspora. As exile was marked by the defeated Jews being dragged off to Babylon, so 'Babylon' became the Rasta key to signify the alien condition of living outside Africa. Much of the Rasta doctrine (originating at least as early as the 1930s) was popularized in the 1970s by the pop group Bob Marley and the Wailers – and was hummed and whistled by many white western teenagers innocent of its message.

Even if African-Caribbeans undertook the spiritual, intellectual and political passage to Africa, physically they moved elsewhere –to other parts of the Americas and to Europe. It is to these migrations that I now turn.

The Caribbean in the Americas

When Ferdinand de Lesseps, the famous maker of the Suez Canal, floated a new Panama Canal Company to link the Pacific Ocean to the Caribbean Sea, the Bourse went crazy with the prospects of great profits. In fact the venture proved a long drawn-out financial failure. The canal and railway works were dogged by mismanagement and the workers suffered greatly from malaria, snake bites, swamp fever, industrial accidents and bad treat-ment. The hands for this operation were drawn from many countries, but predominantly from Jamaica.

The African-Caribbean minority located in the strip of slums surrounding the Panama Canal Company area is descended from these workers. They have remained largely poor and under-privileged in the Panamanian context, with the key positions of authority and influence being occupied by Hispanics.

Other small enclaves in Central America are drawn from Caribbean peoples brought there to establish banana plantations or to undertake public works. Honduras and some small enclaves in Nicaragua and Guatemala (such as the charming Bay Islands) are inhabited by descendants of archipelago African-Caribbeans, who often still fiercely resist abandoning the English language.

The bulk of migrants, however, went to the USA – and in so many capacities that it would be impossible to describe the Caribbean social structure in the USA fully in this short article. Temporary contract workers cut cane in Florida, Haitians arrive often as illegals, many middle-class and professional people occupy important roles in medicine, teaching and in retail services.

One of the oft-remarked on but little researched characteristics of the Caribbean peoples in the USA is their extraordinary success and prominence, not only in the wider black community, but in American society more generally. Within the black community, Caribbean people are referred to, in a not entirely friendly way, as 'black Jews'. Laundries, travel agents and hairdressing shops are monopolized by the Caribbean community in several New York districts. Moreover, Caribbean people have played a prominent role in political movements – the Garveyite movement as mentioned, but also the civil rights struggles and the Black Power Movement – the last led by a Trinidadian.

One further example must suffice. The burly urbane chairman of the Joint Chiefs of Staff who appeared nightly on our television screens during the Gulf War, Colin Powell, is the son of Jamaican immigrants. His father was a shipping clerk, his mother a seam-stress.

The Caribbean in Europe

In some contrast to the USA, the fortunes of the Caribbean migrants in Europe have been less happy. The explanations for this may be complex: different groups may have gone there, the opportunities on offer may have varied, while some migration (to the UK and the Netherlands) was 'panic' migration – with the networks of friends, relations and openings in business and education not fully prefigured or prepared. Caribbean migrants themselves, particularly in Britain, insist that the high levels of racial discrimination and disadvantage present in that country have also worked seriously to jeopardize their chances of success (Solomos 1988; CCCS 1982; Smith 1977).

United Kingdom

The bulk of Caribbean migration to the UK occurred in the 1950s and came to a rapid halt in the early 1960s with the implemen-tation of the Commonwealth Immigrants Act forbidding further unregulated migration. The movement of migrants to the UK so closely shadowed the ebbs and flows of the job vacancies, that an influential social geographer (Peach, 1968) saw labour-demand explanations as the primary reason for migration. This view is accurate, but within limits. First, there was an active recruitment policy in the islands by both public and private companies which distorted a free labour market. Second, an active official intervention in superintending the migration has been revealed by recent releases of documents from the Public Records Office and may have been underestimated by Peach. Third, as Peach himself argues, towards the end of the period, the neat correlation between job vacancies and migrant flows was disrupted as Jamaicans, in particular, rushed 'to beat the ban'. As Peach convincingly shows, the level of migration to the UK was thus significantly higher as a result of prohibitive legislation than it otherwise would have been.

The broad experience of the Caribbean people in the UK has been a negative one. They felt their wartime loyalty was unacknowledged and that they were treated as an unwelcome problem rather than as valued citizens of the Empire and Commonwealth. One black British writer (Thompson, 1990) quotes a respondent in her thesis as follows: 'We came as if children asking for a kiss; instead we got a slap in the face.' So in this instance at least, the diasporic theme of betrayal is relived. The 'Home Country' – which purported to be the protector of the slaves against their masters, turned out to be the 'home' primarily for those masters, not a 'true' home.

Besides this psychic shock, at a more practical level, mobility to professional occupations is limited for people from the Caribbean (for data see Wrench, 1991). Educational successes are also meagre. But there are some intriguing exceptions to the rule. Black British girls outperform black British boys and their white peers in examination success. As in the USA, black athletes and sports-persons are highly disproportionately represented in the boxing ring, in track and field events and in cricket and football. Blacks are also well represented in literary and artistic pursuits, especially the performing arts. This may signify a first stage in a wider and deeper thrust to social mobility – in the third, if not the second, generation. Another important recent finding (Peach, 1990) is that the population in Britain from the Caribbean or from parents born in the Caribbean has dropped significantly from a high of 548,000 in 1971 to 495,000 in 1988. This is partly accounted for by older persons going back to the islands on retirement (itself an indicator of their lack of integration within the UK) and also possibly by secondary migration by younger certified people to the USA and Canada – disillusioned with the slow pace of occupational mobility in the UK.

The Netherlands

Caribbean immigrants to the Netherlands are about half in number of those coming to the UK – about 250,000 compared with Britain's 500,000. The numbers are, however, much more significant when considered as a proportion of the Dutch population and of the Caribbean source population.

Caribbean migrants arrived from all over the Dutch Antilles, but predominantly from the former Dutch colony, Suriname. So large was the departure that about half the population of Suriname was depleted. The Surinamese in Holland fit into the category of 'panic migrants' mentioned earlier, in that the prospects of independence with diminished Dutch support persuaded many people to leave. The Surinamese in Holland divide, roughly equally, into two ethnic sections – Afro-Surinamese and Indo-Surinamese. The housing situation for many Surinamese is surprisingly favourable – their arrival in Amsterdam coincided with the abandonment of a 'white elephant' set of luxury apartments that the indigenous Dutch did not wish to live in.

In other respects, the ultimate fate of the Afro-Surinamese seems to have moved closer to the situation of Caribbean people in the UK. Cross and Entzinger (1988), in their comparative volume on the Netherlands and Britain, suggest that, despite the differences in origin and destination, ethnic marginalization has taken place in the labour markets of both countries for people from the Caribbean.

France

Caribbean migration to France arises in an apparently different form from the cases just considered. The major source areas are the DOM territories of Martinique and Guadeloupe. Because of the juridical status of the DOM, as organic parts of France, migration to the continent is officially considered as internal migration – simply as if one French citizen moved from one *département* to another. The numbers involved are thought to be about 200,000, urban centres, particularly Paris, being the main destinations.

Of course it is important not to confuse appearance with substance. Again we notice a high predominance of unskilled, manual, public sector jobs being held by people from the French Antilles. However, there is also a significant white-collar salariat (for example, in the banks and PTT) recruited by the quasi-official labour agency in the islands. As certification and formal qualifications are far more important in France than either in the UK or Holland, French Antilleans with the requisite pieces of paper have been able to benefit from the relatively strong emphasis in France on merit (see Butcher and Ogden 1984; Peach 1990).

At a deeper level of the *conscience collective*, French Antilleans of African descent have always shared a Faustian pact with the French state. If you abandon your Africanness, embrace mother France, become French, you can *be* a French person, a citizen, a member of a world culture and civilization. This possibility was simply never open to blacks in the Commonwealth Caribbean. Even now it is difficult for many whites in Britain to accept that there can be such a thing as a black Briton.

But what if the French bargain turns out to be impossible to fulfil in practice? What if, as Herzl (an assimilated middle-class Frenchman himself) concluded, the path of assimilation is an illusion, a trap, ultimately a hoax? This perhaps would be the cruellest option of all – as the French Antilleans on the continent will have become a diasporic people, no longer able to capture their distinctive ethnic identity or recover a sense of 'home'.

Conclusion: are Caribbean migrants a diaspora?

We must start by accepting that, unlike the paradigm diasporas, the Caribbean peoples did not suffer a trauma *in the Caribbean* resulting in their dispersal. The migrations to Panama, the USA and Europe were essentially responses to unemployment and poverty or a positive desire for better opportunities. Such migratory movements do not in themselves constitute a diaspora.

However, the original collective trauma of slavery inherited from the African diaspora is still a powerful part of the collective consciousness of African-Caribbeans. This sense of a common history is powerfully reinforced by racism and colour discrimination in many of the places to which African-Caribbean people have migrated. Again, there is strong evidence of an identification with the natal homeland manifested by return movements and other political, cultural and religious ties with Africa.

I conclude by suggesting that the African-Caribbean people, despite neither migrating to Africa, nor (in general) even back to their second home, the Caribbean itself, do constitute a diaspora, though in a special and qualified sense, as specified above.

References

Butcher, I. J. and Ogden, P. E. 1984. 'West Indians in France: migration and demographic change' in Philip E. Ogden (ed.) *Migrants in Modern France: Four Studies*, Occasional paper 23, Department of Geography and Earth Science, Queen Mary College, University of London.

CCCS (Centre for Contemporary Cultural Studies). 1982. *The empire strikes back*, London: Hutchinson.

Césaire, A. 1972. *Discourse on colonialism*, New York: Monthly Review Press.

Cross, M. and Entzinger, H. (eds.) 1988. *Lost illusions: Caribbean minorities in Britain and the Netherlands*, London: Routledge.

Hansen, E. 1977. *Frantz Fanon: social and political thought*, Columbus, OH: Ohio State University Press.

Herskovitz, M. 1958. *The myth of the Negro past*, Boston, MA: Beacon Press.

James, C. L. R. 1963. *The black Jacobins*, New York: Vintage Books.

Padmore, G. 1972. *Pan-Africanism or Communism*, New York: Doubleday.

Peach, C. 1968. *West Indian migration to Britain: a social geography*, London: Oxford University Press.

Peach, C. 1990. 'The Caribbean in Europe'. Paper presented to the Conference on the Caribbean in the 1990s, Institute of Commonwealth Studies, University of Oxford, 10 January.

Smith, D. 1977. *Racial disadvantage in Britain: The PEP report*, Harmondsworth: Penguin.

Solomos, J. 1988. *Black youth, racism and the state: the politics of ideology and policy*, Cambridge: Cambridge University Press.

Thompson, M. 1990. 'Migrants from the Caribbean to Britain: a case study of the West Midlands', PhD thesis, University of Warwick.

Williams, E. 1964. *Capitalism and slavery*, London: André Deutsch.

Wrench, J. 1991. 'Employment and the Labour Market', *New Community* 17(4): 617–23.

Addendum

This article was first published in *Social Science Information*, 31(1) 1992, 159–69 and subsequently incorporated into my work on global diasporas. It was reproduced in French as 'La diaspora d'une diaspora: Le cas des Antilles' in R. Gallissot (ed.) *Pluralisme cultural en Europe* Paris: L'Harmattan, 1993, 61–77. My good friend and colleague Harry Goulbourne has written with perception and an insider's knowledge on a similar theme, but at this time I had not seen his relevant writings, and have retained this original version rather than extend the discussion to incorporate his views.

Chapter 10
Cultural diasporas:
the Caribbean case

Robin Cohen

Migration scholars – normally a rather conservative breed of sociologists, historians, demographers and geographers – have recently been bemused to find their subject matter assailed by a bevy of postmodernists, novelists and scholars of cultural studies. A reconstitution of the notion of diaspora has been a central concern of these space invaders. For example, the editor of the US journal *Diaspora*, Khachig Tölölyan (1991: 3), a professor of English at Wesleyan University, announced its birth with the following statement:

> The conviction underpinning this manifesto disguised as a 'Preface' is that *Diaspora* must pursue, in texts literary and visual, canonical and vernacular, indeed in all cultural productions and throughout history, the traces of struggles over and contradictions within ideas and practices of collective identity, of homeland and nation. *Diaspora* is concerned with the way in which nations, real yet imagined communities, are fabulated, brought into being, made and unmade, in culture and politics, both on the land people call their own and in exile.

For a number of scholars influenced by cultural studies the collective identity of homeland and nation is a vibrant and

constantly changing set of cultural interactions that funda-
mentally question the very ideas of 'home' and 'host'. It is
demonstrable, for example, that unidirectional – migration to' or
'return from' – forms of movement are being replaced by
asynchronous, transversal flows that involve visiting, studying,
seasonal work, tourism and sojourning, rather than whole-family
migration, permanent settlement and the adoption of exclusive
citizenships. These changing patterns have important sociological
consequences. As Vertovec (private correspondence 1996) puts
it:

> Aesthetic styles, identifications and affinities, disposit-
> ions and behaviours, musical genres, linguistic pat-
> terns, moralities, religious practices and other cultural
> phenomena are more globalized, cosmopolitan and
> creolized or 'hybrid' than ever before. This is especially
> the case among youth of transnational communities,
> whose initial socialization has taken place within the
> cross-currents of more than one cultural field, and
> whose ongoing forms of cultural expression and ident-
> ity are often self-consciously selected, syncretized and
> elaborated from more than one cultural heritage.

One way of conceptualizing the social and cultural outcomes
described is to loosen the historical meanings of the notion of
'diaspora' to encompass the construction of these new identities
and subjectivities. Suppose we adopt the expression 'cultural
diaspora' to encompass the lineaments of many migration
experiences in the late modern world? Can cultures can be
thought of as having lost their territorial moorings, to have
become in effect 'travelling cultures'? Can migrants of African
descent from the Caribbean be considered as one of the
paradigmatic cases of a cultural diaspora? Do we need more than

postcolonial theory to demonstrate that, in practice, a cultural diaspora has emerged? Do we need instead to explore the common experiences, intellectual and political visions and religious movements that cement Afro-Caribbean cultural and migratory experiences? Is Gilroy's (1993a) notion of a 'black Atlantic' adequate to our purposes?

Caribbean peoples as a cultural diaspora

Despite the different destinations and experiences of Caribbean peoples abroad, they remain an exemplary case of a cultural, or deterritorialized, diaspora. This arises first from their common history of forcible dispersion through the slave trade – still shared by virtually all people of African descent, despite their subsequent liberation, settlement and citizenship in the various countries of the New World. Partly, this is a matter of visibility. Unlike (say) in the cases of Jews or Armenians, where superficial disappearance is possible in Europe and North America if exogamy occurs, in the case of those of African descent skin colour normally remains a marker for two, three or more generations – despite exogamy. The deployment of skin colour in many societies as a signifier of status, power and opportunity, make it impossible for any people of African descent to avoid racial stigmatization. As one black British writer puts it, 'our imaginations are conditioned by an enduring proximity to regimes of racial terror' (Gilroy 1993b: 103).

Though important, being phenotypically African and being conscious of racism are, in themselves, insufficient to assign the label 'cultural diaspora' to Afro-Caribbeans. I would suggest that at least four other elements should be present:

- First, there should be evidence of cultural retention or affirmations of an African identity.

- Second, there should be a literal or symbolic interest in 'return'.

- Third, there should be cultural artefacts, products and expressions that show shared concerns and cross influences between Africa, the Caribbean and the destination countries of Caribbean peoples.

- Fourth, and often forgotten by the intensely cerebral versions of diaspora presented by cultural studies theorists, there should be indications that ordinary Caribbean peoples abroad – in their attitudes, migration patterns and social conduct – behave in ways consistent with the idea of a cultural diaspora.

Retention and affirmations of African identity

With respect to the issue of retention, there are clear examples of a return to Africanness in the Maroon (runaway slave) communities of Jamaican and the so-called 'Bush Negroes' of Suriname. Other, less dramatic, examples abound. Everything from Brazilian cults, Caribbean savings clubs, folklore, musical rhythms, popular art, Trinidadian 'shouters' and voodoo practices have been minutely recorded by scores of anthropologists (notably Herskovitz 1937; 1947; 1961). This evidence of retention must, however, not be narrowly understood as freezing African cultures in aspic. As with other migratory groups, New World Africans took the opportunity to throw off the shackles of their prior social constraints. Thus, the famous founding president of a free Haiti, Toussaint L'Ouverture, was as much Jacobin as African; while, arguably, during the Second World War the French Antilles were more loyal to the idea of the French nation than the metropolis itself. Equally, many Anglophone Caribbeans displayed a remarkable loyalty to Britain in both world wars and showed a fierce adherence to British educational, social and political institutions. Using a reinterpretation of the work of W. E. B. Du Bois, Paul Gilroy (1993a; 1993b) supplies an insightful analysis of how African Americans and Afro-Caribbeans live within a 'double consciousness', stemming both from Africa and Europe.

The links between Africa and New World Africans also took the form of literary, ideological and political movements. The African, African-American and Afro-Caribbean intelligentsia has long sought to define some cultural and historical continuities between Africans on the continent and in the diaspora. This movement has flowed in several directions. Kwame Nkrumah, the Ghanaian president, studied in a black university in the USA and articulated the ideas of an African personality and African unity. Léopold Senghor, the president of Senegal, advanced the idea of Négritude. The Trinidadian revolutionary intellectuals George Padmore and C. L. R. James were partly responsible for convening the watershed Manchester Conference of 1945, when the basic lines of struggle for African self-determination were articulated. In the case of the Francophone Caribbean, Aimé Césaire made his spiritual journey to Africa in *Return to my native land* (1956). He and other Caribbean leaders were also an important influence on Négritude and had a continuing dialogue with Africans, and peoples of African descent more generally, in journals such as *Présence Africaine*.

A number of literary figures from Trinidad, whose works are imbricated in the evolution of a Caribbean diasporic conscious-ness, have been ably analysed by Harney (1996). The creation of a postcolonial identity was the project of novelists Earl Lovelace and Michael Anthony. The complexities of creating a new nationalism from Indo-, Sino- and Afro-Caribbean elements was addressed by Valerie Belgrave and Willi Chen, while the dilemmas of Caribbean migrants moving to Canada, Britain and the USA were depicted in the writings of Samuel Selvon, Neil Bissoondath and V. S. Naipaul.

Return movements, literal and symbolic

Despite the small number of Afro-Caribbeans who actually returned to Africa, Caribbean visionaries were at the forefront of the Back-to-Africa movements and in the articulation of the idea of a common fate of African people at home and abroad. The most flamboyant, and immensely popular, of New World return movements was the Universal Negro Improvement Association (UNIA), founded by the Jamaican, Marcus Garvey. Garveyites were particularly strong in the USA, and representatives of small but ill-fated colonies were sent to Liberia and elsewhere on the continent. Garvey was born in Jamaica in 1887 and had travelled widely in the West Indies and Central America before starting the UNIA. He drew his inspiration from two main strands – the Maroon revolts, which showed even in the New World, and even after the experience of the Middle Passage and slavery, that blacks could still recover some of their African traditions. Second, he was very influenced by the strength of the British imperial idea that people could bluff their way to political dominance by style, appearance and a belief in their own superiority.

Garvey was particularly unimpressed by what he found in the USA. He saw poor blacks beating their heads against brick wall, trying futilely to gain access to jobs and social acceptance. This experience provided him with the idea of setting up the Black Star Line, a shipping company owned by blacks with the intention literally of reversing the transatlantic slave trade. Though the line was never a great success, when Kwame Nkrumah came to power in Ghana, he adopted it as the name of Ghana's merchant marine.

Although Garvey had returned to Jamaica, with the exception of one large UNIA rally and a convention in Kingston in 1928, he was largely unsuccessful as a politician. He died in obscurity in London in 1940, but he had succeeded in further promoting the consciousness of Africa that had been well developed in Jamaica since the days of the Maroons. The cultural link with Africa was also enhanced by the deep spirituality that converted Christian Jamaicans acquired. They found in the Bible an identification with the ancient Jews. Like the Jews who were dragged off to Egypt and Babylon to slavery, the Africans had been dragged off to the West Indies as slaves.

This biblical and African consciousness became fused together in November 1930, when a new prince, Ras Tafari, was crowned Emperor of Ethiopia and adopted the name Haile Selassie. Some poor, particularly rural, Jamaicans began to describe themselves as 'Ethiopians', or followers of the crowned prince Ras Tafari, namely Rastafarians. The Emperor claimed descent from Solomon and Sheba. The Ethiopian Orthodox Church dated back to the very foundations of the religion. Again that that Ethiopians had seen off an Italian army in 1898 became their symbol of resistance. An article published in the *National Geographic* magazine in January 1931, in which there was a discussion about modern Ethiopia that covered the coronation, was passed from hand to hand. This was no fiction. Here were pictures and an article in a white man's magazine! That the British had taken the coronation seriously enough to send the Duke of Gloucester, the son of King George V, to the event was regarded as further proof. The Jamaican national daily, the *Daily Gleaner* (February 1931), carried this letter.

> The whole Ethiopian race throughout the world, or at least the leaders of thought, should regard with the

greatest degree of satisfaction the well-considered decision of His Majesty's Government to send a deputation headed by a member of the British Royal Family to represent the great Anglo-Saxon people at the coronation of the only independent state among the millions of Ham's offspring.

The movement itself rapidly spread from its origins in Jamaica, not least because Bob Marley, the celebrated reggae singer, spread the message through the popularity of his music. Indeed there may now be more Rastafari living outside Jamaica than on the island, with many activists in the USA, Canada and Britain, as well as Africa itself. Though the movement has often been dismissed as impractical and chiliastic, as Hall (1995: 14) argues, 'It was not the literal Africa that people wanted to return to, it was the language, the symbolic language for describing what suffering was like, it was a metaphor for where they were ... a language with a double register, a literal and a symbolic register.'

Shared cultural expressions

The idea that there might be complex connections between Africans at home, in the New World and in Africa has been suggested by black writers and intellectuals for over a century. One poignant exploration of 250 years of the African diaspora is provided by the Caribbean-born writer Caryl Phillips (1993), who chronicles the sense of disconnectedness and homelessness of peoples of African descent abroad and how they sought to reconstitute themselves as acting, thinking, emotionally-intact individuals. The title of his novel, *Crossing the river*, evokes the transatlantic slave trade. The author (1993: 235–7) hears the drum beating on the far bank of the natal land and sees the 'many-tongued chorus of the common memory' in West Indian pubs in England, an addicted mother in Brooklyn, a barefoot boy in São Paulo, the reggae rhythms in the hills and valleys of the Caribbean and the carnivals in Trinidad and Rio. Despite the trauma of the middle passage and the human wreckage that resulted, Phillips concludes his novel on an optimistic note. Beloved children arrived on the far bank of the river. They loved and were loved.

Another novelist shows how language and popular expressions are carried by Caribbean migrants to the UK. In this passage the protagonist in Samuel Selvon's most famous novel, *The lonely Londoner* (1985), significantly and ironically called Moses, tries with his friends to recapture life in Trinidad and adjust to their new life, after ten years, in London:

> [They] coming together for oldtalk, to find out the latest gen, what happening, when is the next fête, Bart asking if anybody seen his girl anywhere, Cap recounting an incident he had with a women by the tube station the night before, Big City want to know why the arse he can't win a pool, Galahad recounting a clash with the colour problem in a restaurant in Piccadilly
>
> (cited Harney 1996: 103)

While vernacular language crosses the Atlantic in the way demonstrated by Samuel Selvon, a more popular art form is music. Here, in a persuasive essay, Gilroy (1993b: 37) argues that, 'The contemporary musical forms of the diaspora work within an aesthetic and political framework which demands that they ceaselessly reconstruct their own histories, folding back on themselves time and again to celebrate and validate the simple, unassailable fact of their survival.' The politics of black music are barely beneath the surface in the calypsos of Trinidad, reggae and ska from Jamaica, samba from Brazil, township jazz from South

Africa, Highlife from Nigeria and jazz, hip-hop, soul and rap from the USA. In the expressive title of Gilroy's essay, Africans at home and abroad are 'one nation under a groove'.

The most intellectually ambitious attempt to bring out the cross-currents of cultural expression in Africa and the diaspora is made by Paul Gilroy in *The black Atlantic* (1993a). He strongly resists any attempt to hijack the experience of New World Africans to those particular to African Americans, a tendency he found in some of the 'Afrocentric' positions of American black intellectuals. Rather, he sees the consciousness of the African diaspora as being formed in a complex cultural and social inter-mingling between Africa, Europe and the Americas. However, this does not lead to cultural uniformity, but rather to a recognition of 'transnational and intercultural multiplicity'. Of course, some degree of unity must exist in the Atlantic Africans' diasporic culture for it to be deemed a shared impulse and form of con-sciousness. This emergent culture is characterized as 'the Black Atlantic'. His influential work (which needs much more exegesis that I have space to give it here) is also a comment on the nature of modernity, on the idea of a nationalism without a nation-state (or a territory), and on the idea of a 'double consciousness', prefigured in Hegelian phenomenology and expressed in the New World by the double heritage of Africa and Europe.

Social conduct and popular attitudes

Much of the material on the Caribbean diaspora by writers in the field of cultural studies is both challenging and theoretically sophisticated. But to what extent is a transnational identity a lived experience, demonstrated by migrants' social conduct as well as invented in the minds and emotions of writers, musicians and academics? To this question I do not propose a full reply – for only an extensive research project would yield empirically verifiable answers. However, I thought it might be educative to do what might be called a 'reality check' on the broad thesis.

I did this by carefully examining one issue (1–7 May 1996) of the *Weekly Gleaner*, the self-declared 'top Caribbean newspaper' published in south London and comprising a digest of Jamaica's *Daily Gleaner*, together with local editorial matter and letters. That a newspaper of this type appears and sells is, in a sense, indication enough of the strength of a transnational Caribbean identity. What I thought particularly illustrative of the continuing relationship between the Caribbean communities in the UK and the Caribbean was a letter to the editor from a Mr R. Francis of south London. He complained about the discourtesy he had experienced on his last trip to Jamaica in banks, the customs service and government departments. I add the emphasis on the remaining part of his letter:

> I would like to express my view on the way in which *returnees* to Jamaica are treated *back home*. ... Like other people, I am definitely homesick, I am scared of going back to Jamaica because of the treatment often meted out to returnees and people on holiday. Although *we are away* it should be understood that we have and will always contribute to the finance and development of Jamaica. *It is our country as much as it is those who have never left.*

When one examines the advertisements, the link with 'our country' becomes much more concrete. The pages are stuffed with advertisements for shipping lines, airlines, freight handlers, money transfer services ('Send your cash in a flash', says one), plots for sale in Jamaica, architects, removal companies, vacation accommodation and export houses selling tropicalized refrigerators 'good with the correct voltage and specification *for your country*'.

Readers are offered shares on the Jamaican stock exchange and access via a cable company to 'Black Variety Television'.

Conclusion

Theodor Adorno once remarked that 'it is part of morality not to be at home in one's own home' (cited Sanadjian 1996: 5). Certainly this seems to be a recurrent theme in the story of Caribbean peoples abroad. In this chapter I have sought to discover whether the Caribbean peoples constitute a 'new', 'postcolonial', 'hybrid' diaspora of the type envisaged by scholars of cultural studies.

I found the general arguments highly suggestive. They could of course not be *conclusive*, for the resistance to empirical work or to meta-theory on the part of cultural studies theorists would obviate the possibility of any final argument. However, rather than follow a number of the authors I have cited along an endless roller-coaster of meanings, discourses, representations and narratives, I sought to introduce what I have called 'reality markers' to the argument.

In fact all sorts of cultural and political compromises with a diasporic identity arose, particularly, I would suggest, among the French Antilleans in metropolitan France. For example, if we take the four criteria I suggested for assessing whether a Caribbean cultural diaspora existed, the level of cultural retention and interest in 'return' was lowest among those from the Francophone Caribbean. Not of course that it was absent. For Césaire, as for many in the Anglophone Caribbean, the idea of return was subliminal and symbolic. But there is a significant difference between the two language groups. In the English-speaking Caribbean and in the USA, the idea of return spread beyond the intelligentsia to the masses – through the Garveyite and Rastafarian movements.

In their works previously cited Hall, Gilroy, Harney and others have been able to show that in music, literature, art and language there was considerable cross-pollination of ideas, images and concepts over the waves and the air waves of the black Atlantic. As someone who lived in the Caribbean for two years and maintains ongoing friendships and academic contacts in the area, I recognize many of the nuances proposed by these commentators, who focus on the Caribbean imagination. However, I remain convinced that a more solid and accurate understanding of the nature of the Caribbean cultural diaspora will only be possible by gathering full historical information and sociological data. I cannot provide these here. But I would like to provide something of a preliminary corrective to the 'black Atlantic thesis'.

I submit, with Craig (1992), that it is not without coincidence that 'the enterprise of the Indies' as it was called in Columbus's time, joined the major continents of the globe (Europe, Africa *and* Asia) to the Americas and that with the help of Caribbean labour, the Panama canal added the Pacific. Thus, whatever the sophistication and complexity of the black Atlantic argument, at root it is a historical simplification, which cannot fully explain the process of indigenization and creolization in the Caribbean, despite the lack of indigenees. Nor can it account for the complexities arising from the large Asian presence in the Caribbean and *its* subsequent diasporization.

The social behaviour of Caribbean people in their places of sojourn and settlement provides telling evidence of the creation of a cultural diaspora, but more sustained empirical work needs to be undertaken on this issue. How, to pick up two of Craig's (1992) examples, did the Caribbean carnival evolve into a circuit, linking the archipelago to the metropolitan cities or New York, Toronto, London and elsewhere? By 'how' I mean, who were the principal social actors and social organizations involved? How were the enterprises financed? What was the role of Caribbean governments in cementing these ties? Again, to take another example, the Hindu festival of Phagwa was celebrated by Caribbean people for the first time on the streets of New York in 1991. How was this part of their culture transmitted and borne by migration? How did it become modified? In short, through their roots and branches, or to be precise through their rooting and branching, the people themselves make their diaspora. The frontiers of the region are beyond the Caribbean – in the consciousness of Caribbean people to be sure, but also in their social conduct, migration patterns and achievements in their places of settlement and sojourn.

References

Césaire, Aimé. 1956. *Return to my native land*, London: Penguin.

Craig, Susan. 1992. 'Intertwining roots', *The Journal of Caribbean History*, 26(2), 215–27.

Daily Gleaner, February 1931. Newspaper, Kingston, Jamaica.

Gilroy, Paul. 1993a. *The black Atlantic: modernity and double consciousness*, London: Verso.

Gilroy, Paul. 1993b. *Small acts: thoughts on the politics of black cultures*, London: Serpent's Tail.

Hall, Stuart. 1995. 'Negotiating Caribbean identities', *New Left Review*, No. 209, January–February, 3–14.

Harney, Stefano. 1996. *Nationalism and identity: culture and the imagination in a Caribbean diaspora*, London: Zed Books.

Herskovits, Melville J. 1937. *Life in a Haitian valley*, New York: Alfred A. Knopf.

Herskovits, Melville J. et al. (1947) *Trinidad village*, New York: Alfred Knopf.

Herskovits, Melville J. (1961) *The New World Negro: selected papers in Afro-American studies*, Bloomington, IN: Indiana UP.

Phillips, Caryl (1993) *Crossing the river*, London: Picador.

Sanadjian, Manuchehr (1996) 'An anthology of 'the people', place, space and 'home': (re)constructing the Lur in south-western Iran', *Social Identities*, 2(1), 5–36.

Selvon, Samuel (1985) *The lonely Londoners*, Harlow: Longman.

Tölölyan, Khachig (1991) 'Preface', *Diaspora*, 1(1), 3–7.

Vertovec, Steve (1996) Private correspondence.

Weekly Gleaner, (1–7 May 1996), weekly newspaper, London.

Chapter 11

Preface to Laurent Medea's *Réunion: an island in search of an identity*

Robin Cohen

From Laurent Medea *Réunion: An island in search of an identity*, Pretoria: UNISA Press, 2010.

I am delighted to give this study of social identity on the island of Réunion a warm welcome. In the late 1990s Laurent Medea brought a breath of fresh Indian Ocean air into my rather stale existence in a British university. His discussions took me back to my experiences of creolization in Mauritius and the Caribbean, where I had worked for two years in the late 1970s. But despite the resemblances to Réunion, I knew little about the island. The differences and similarities in creolization in the Indian Ocean islands are, in fact, a subject of continuous debates. Of Mauritius for example, Vaughan (2005: 2) has written: 'Without natives, the island's beginnings were necessarily the product of no one thing or people but of many, more or less foreign, more or less "naturalised". It has always been a Creole island'. This was true too of Bourbon Island, later renamed Réunion, when the delegates to a Revolutionary convention reassembled (in a 'reunion') and the first order of business was to rename the far-off colony with an appellation that did not recall the hated royal family. From that moment in 1789, the history of Réunion was thus torn between the universalizing claims of Republican Jacobinism and the island's own self-propelled development. This tension, in other words, was between the French Republic and the peculiarities of creating a new society in the Indian Ocean.

As Laurent Medea shows, the tight embrace of the Republic took many forms – slavery, enlightened autocracy, colonialism, reformed colonialism, devolution and finally départmentalization i.e. full integration into the metropolitan structure and the European Union. Everywhere there is France – in the official language, in the circulation of the Franc (later the Euro), in the supermarkets, the hotel chains and TV channels. And everywhere there is the subversion of France – in the tropical vegetation, volcanic craters and climate, and in the Creole language, religious expressions, cuisine, architecture, music, dance and the appearance and manner of the islanders. Laurent Medea understands this grip of the metropole and the ways in which it can be stifling. He understands this ambiguity from the inside and the outside – as a cultural activist, a Creole and a scholar.

What do we call such a situation? I can recall earnest discussions with Dr Medea in the university cafes at Warwick and while chopping wood on holiday in the Vendée about the relevance and utility of the literary and cultural ideas of 'post-colonialism'. But how could Réunion be post-colonial when the administrative grip of France had significantly tightened, not weakened, and the economic advantages of being part of the European Union were all too evident to the Réunionese? In the end Laurent Medea settled on a modified notion of 'neo-colonialism', which he uses to good effect. Of course we talked too about identity formation and construction, a dialogue that continued for over a year at the University of Cape Town where Dr Medea and I convened a graduate seminar on historical, sociological and anthropological understandings of creolization.

Perhaps it is a helpful idea to think of creolized social formations as developing in three phases, the first and the last being particularly clearly described by Laurent Medea in the first chapter of this book. He writes:

> The society formed in Réunion was itself an outcome of 'early' or 'proto' globalisation. Explorers, colonists, missionaries, venture capitalists and international migrants often traversed these islands with the creation of seaport cultures and trading stations and entrepôts. There would have been no society in Réunion, Mauritius, Jamaica or Trinidad without some form of globalisation. The current phase of globalisation led by the transnationalism of capital and the further and deeper flow of goods, commodities, images and people have profoundly affected contemporary places. Present-day globalisation presents a challenge both to the emergence of a viable creolised culture and to the 'identity resolution' promoted by their metropoles.

The middle period is characterized by colonialism and imperialism. It is also the *locus classicus* where colonial production systems – notably plantations set up to produce sugar, bananas, coffee and rubber – and colonial languages and cultural norms became prevalent. In that crucible, alternative forms of livelihood and ways of life were difficult to articulate and even harder to institutionalize. Yet people managed. In the interior that created Maroon communities augmented by other marginal migrants. In the sugar fields they created *maloya* which, as Dr Medea says, became the music of resistance and refusal. Above all, they created a distinctive Creole language which affirmed their distinctive Réunionese consciousness, a language that became shared by planters, slaves and those seeking economic autarky.

It is possible that my suggestion that we can see creolization in three phases is too schematic but, at any event, you will find a rich array of examples, descriptions and argument in this book that will greatly contribute to the evolution of comparative studies of creolization.

Reference

Vaughan, Megan. 2005. *Creating the Creole island: slavery in eighteenth-century Mauritius*, Durham, NC: Duke University Press, 2005.

Addendum

I use this addendum to thank our colleagues in Cape Town for their contributions to the Creolization Seminar in 2003. It is also a good moment to thank our partners, Selina and Anaïs, for their forbearance. I doubt that they really were so absorbed in our meandering observations and discussions about creolization in the Caribbean, Africa, the Americas and the Indian Ocean. Nonetheless they maintained a polite interest when all four of us finally met up in Réunion itself in June 2006 for an extensive tour of the island – a wonderful trip when friendships were cemented and theory and praxis shook hands.

Chapter 12

La malaise Créole: creolization in Mauritius

Robin Cohen

This is a review of Rosabelle Boswell's, *Le malaise Créole: ethnic identity in Mauritius*, New York: Berghahn Books, 2006, xx+36 pp.

Scholars of creolization in Mauritius are fortunate in being able to tap into a rich vein of good historical, anthropological and political studies. Older standard works by Benedict and Simmons have now been augmented by excellent research undertaken by Alpers, Teelock, Carpooran, Chan Low, Eriksen, Laville, Srebnik, Warner and Miles. Equally, Vaughan's *Creating the Creole island* (2005) is a commanding history of the island though, to be sure, it ends rather early. So the first point to make is that Boswell had some rather high peaks to climb if she was to produce an innovative, original and scholarly account. With one or two flaws she has succeeded admirably.

Boswell has at least four things going for her. She is of Mauritian Creole origin herself, though she was raised in Malawi and now works in South Africa. She uses a 'multi-sited', 'experience-near' ethnography in assembling her material. She is generally well-informed on comparative studies of creolization and on contemporary theories of ethnicity and identity. Perhaps equally important is that she has a strong thesis – namely that one population group, popularly referred to as Creole, is stigmatized and poverty-stricken. 'Creole' has, in her view, become totally identified with marginality. This thesis provides an excellent debating point.

Boswell spends considerable time on discussing the strengths and disadvantages of her biographical background in undertaking this research. I can see that there are concerns here – one is researching 'home' not 'away', or, as Mafeje (1997) put it, 'who are the makers and who the objects of anthropology?' One can also allude to the problems of being too close to one's subjects (Kenyatta's *Facing Mount Kenya* (1938) might be one example) or of a naïve observer being duped or self-denying (dare I mention Margaret Mead?). A graduate course on research methods could profit from Boswell's reflexive twists and turns about being participant and observer at the same time. I have to admit I got rather fed up with it and thought she could have usefully left much of that material in unpublished PhD form. Unlike many other scholars of Mauritius she was able to penetrate the language and subculture of her subjects and this seemed to me such an unquestionable advantage that she should have just got on with it.

When she does, in her ethnographic account of five sites, Boswell really comes into her own. The idea of multi-sited ethnography is generally credited to Marcus (1995) who not only advocates its virtues in picking up complexity (rather like looking at the different facets of a precious stone), but also insists that it is a way of dealing with more mobile populations – a general problem facing anthropologists who can no longer fix their subjects in space. Boswell's work in Flacq, Karina, Roche Bois/River Camp, Le Morne and nearby Chamarel needs to be read in the original to capture its full flavour. I was particularly impressed by her use of music and religious expressions in situating and explaining the development of a Creole identity. Sega (the main form of Creole music) and seggae (sega mixed with reggae) are good ways of showing how identity is performed.

In a number of songs (she argues) the daily suffering, joy and ordinariness of Creole lives are depicted. Singing is thus an important medium for expressing Creole identity in Mauritius and elsewhere in the Indian Ocean. Sega is also an im portant form of lamentation and the varieties and diverse social meaning of the sega to Creoles indicate the ways in which sega contributes to the diversity of Creole identity in Mauritian society (p. 61).

The stress on diversity in the quoted passage is crucial, though I thought that Boswell rather obscures this complexity by trying to prove her strong thesis. In a way her conclusion was rather unexpected, as she spends considerable time demonstrating that Creoles have been valorized and seen in a more positive light in other parts of the world (the Caribbean, the USA and nearby places in the Indian Ocean). She also makes clear that the history of the island shows that Creoles could come in many shapes and sizes. Boswell notes there were *Créole Madras* (Creoles with a Tamil heritage), *Créole Sinwa* (with a Chinese background) and *Créole l'Ascar* (Creoles with an Arab heritage). Historically, locally born whites of elevated status were known as Creoles and *gens de couleur* (those with a white and black background), not far down the pecking order, were also known as Creoles. Vaughan's view, in her history (inexplicably not cited by Boswell), is that, because there were no indigenes, Mauritius was, by definition, a Creole island. Teelock and others support this idea.

Essentially, Boswell's notion is that, despite this more complex and positive history, Creoles have now been reduced to *Ti Creoles* (*Ti* being the truncated Creole word for '*petit*'). But reduced by whom and for what reason? Having marked many undergraduate essays[1] and read the press in Mauritius, I can concur that she

---

1   I should explain that I was external examiner for some social science degrees in Mauritius for three years, which meant I read student examination papers and long essays.

certainly has a case. The popular mood has shifted from a positive regard, or perhaps a neutral acceptance of the expression 'Creole', to a negative caricature. According to such sources, Creoles cannot get their act together. 'They' live in the south west (true, but in fact 'they' are scattered everywhere), 'they' are feckless even if happy, 'they' are high on drugs and crime and low on educational and material achievement. 'They' are victims, in short, of the *malaise Creole*.

That this shift in labelling has happened is true; why it has happened is less well argued. My sense is that the answer lies in changes among some Indo-Mauritians. They inherited the lion's share of political power at independence and began to accumulate significant wealth – rarely challenging the power of the old Franco-Mauritian families, but at least getting close. At the same time, India abandoned its old hands-off policy and started to reconnect with her diasporic populations. These reconnections were benign (cultural and educational exchanges, investment, trade) as well as malign (right-wing political groups, fundamental versions of Hinduism and hot money looking for an offshore location). The more India connected, the less Indo-Mauritians interacted with their fellow citizens. The retaliatory attempt to reconnect with Africa by some Creoles paradoxically reinforced the negative status of Creoles, given the relative development profiles of Africa and India.

Superficially, it looks as though I am concurring in Boswell's thesis. However, she has exaggerated her point. Nearly everybody on the island speaks a French-based Creole language and this continues to be a unifying factor. Christianity, generally Catholicism, links the wealth Franco-Mauritians with the *gens de couleur* and the *Ti Creoles*. Many people on the island are of mixed heritage and do not easily fit into neat ethnographical labels. Finally, although there is some spatial segregation between those who can be ethnically segmented, the island is small and many villages – and the capital Port Louis – have ethnically hybrid zones. Among the working class, there are reasonably strong cross-ethnic sentiments. I conclude that Boswell has been too ready to recognize populist sentiments and not always willing to trust her own fieldwork. That said, this is a very good book from which I learned a great deal. Even if I dissent from her main finding, the book will be a marker and provide a sounding board for further scholarship on creolization on the island and elsewhere.

References

Kenyatta, Jomo. 1938. *Facing Mount Kenya*, London: Secker and Warburg.

Mafeje, Archie. 1997. 'Who are the makers and objects of anthropology? A critical comment on Sally Falk Moore's "Anthropology and Africa"', *African Sociological Review/Revue Africaine de Sociologie*, 1(1), 1–15.

Marcus, George E. 1995. 'Ethnography in/of the world system: the emergence of multi-sited ethnography', *Annual Review of Anthropology*, 24, 95–117.

Vaughan, Megan. 2005. *Creating the Creole island: slavery in eighteenth-century Mauritius*, Durham, NC: Duke University Press.

Addendum

This review was first published in *Ethnic and Racial Studies*, 31(1) 2008, 197–213. I subsequently co-operated with Professor Boswell in a number of projects, in particular on a conference on Islands, Diaspora and Creolization.

Chapter 13

Philosophy and the 'Redlegs' of Barbados

Robin Cohen

This is a review of Michael J. Monahan's *The creolizing subject: race, reason and the politics of purity*, New York: Fordham University Press, 2011 pp. ix x 247.

This book is written by a philosopher who reworks the well-trodden ground of how we to understand race and racism. It is perhaps not too grand a claim to say that for many years US discussion about race and racism was directly or indirectly derived from Gunnar Myrdal's formative study *An American dilemma: The Negro problem and modern democracy* (1944). It is an indication of how far scholarship in this field has moved on, that Myrdal does not even make an appearance in Monahan's list of references. Instead he draws on three newer well-springs of arguments – cultural studies, whiteness studies and creolization.

One of the great luminaries of cultural studies was Raymond Williams at Cambridge, who became so weary of being hailed as one of the progenitors of the field that he complained, 'I don't know how many times I've wished that I'd never heard the damned word [culture]'. This is because the idea of culture is often so vague and so tantalizingly out of reach. For Monahan, cultural studies is accessed not so much through reactions and interpretations of literature (the British tradition), but through phenomenology. Phenomenology, Monahan avers, is character-ized 'first and foremost by a commitment to placing human consciousness at the forefront of philosophical investigations' (p. 106). This gives him 'the subject' in the principal title of his book.

Trained in a more prosaic sociological tradition, I would have supposed that accessing 'the subject' might be easier if the *dramatis personae* in the research were alive and able to be surveyed or at least interviewed. Monahan does not make it easy for himself by choosing, as the central characters in his research, seventeenth-century Irish servants who were indentured to masters in Barbados. The so-called 'Redlegs' of the Caribbean (they went also to St Vincent and the Grenadines) have rightly attracted considerable scholarly attention by fascinated histor-ians. There were a few who were *stricto sensu* slaves (though Monahan denies this); most were semi-free workers who could not be sold or endowed and had to be freed after their indentures expired. They were often impoverished to the point that their conditions approximated those endured by black slaves brought from Africa. In their social attitudes and behaviour they provide an exemplary case for answering the old social scientific question of whether race trumped class or vice versa.

Monahan addresses this issue not through sifting through the historical evidence, but through 'whiteness studies', a field now sufficiently large to have spawned a subsidiary sub-field, namely 'critical whiteness studies', of which he is an adherent. In this reasoning, there is characteristically a 'gravitational pull towards pure racial categories, such that the status of these groups *had*, ultimately, to be settled in such a way that purged them of their racially ambiguous status' (p. 71, emphasis in original). Inter-estingly, the author argues that in the case of mixed or biracial categories, there is also a gravitational pull to existing 'pure' racial categories (one example, I add, is how President Obama's very complex background was re-inscribed simply as 'black'). In this logic the commonality of conditions that embraced Redlegs and black slaves permitted temporary alliances and crossovers, but no escape from the determinacy of pure categories. Monahan allows no boltholes even the in the case of significant (large/ powerful) mixed groups; in those cases, he argues, if prior pure categories cannot accommodate a new group, a new pure category is invented.

The author's way out of this impasse is through advocating a continuous process of 'creolizing'. To be Creole is not in itself a satisfactory outcome; as before that simply generates another pure group. For him, one can only imagine a liberation from racial thinking through the constant reiteration and affirmation of plasticity and ambiguity across all aspects of language, culture, psychology, identity, politics and biology. I enjoyed the book and agreed with much of the argument, but I was aware at several parts that the pieces of the jigsaw – historical, philosophical and the plea for racial justice – did not always fit together neatly. Nonetheless this is a brave, interesting and challenging book.

Addendum

This is my original manuscript for self-archiving and republication. The review was published in *Ethnic and Racial Studies*, 36(3), 2013.

Chapter 14
Islands and identities:
an introduction

Robin Cohen and Olivia Sheringham

This chapter is derived from the introduction to a special issue on 'Islands, Diaspora and Creolization', published in *Diaspora*, 17(1) 2008, © 2013, pp 1–5.

In convening a conference and producing a special issue on the theme of islands and identities, we sought to assess the extent to which islands represent particularly salient spaces for the emergence of creolized and/or diasporic identities. We also considered some of the social, cultural and spatial factors that give rise to various forms of identity construction and expression, notably creolization and diaspora. We had three starting points:

- First, we had already sketched out the idea that 'creolization' and 'diaspora' could be seen as just two of a number of possible 'identity trajectories', the others being sub-national loyalties (to clan, tribe, ethnicity, region or locality), nationalism, supra-national affinities (to world religion or language groups) or cosmopolitanism (Cohen 2010; Sheringham 2012).

- Second, we were alive to the debate about the universal and particular uses of creolization. A number of scholars had expressed uneasiness or outright opposition to the idea that creolization could be transposed from its supposedly singular moorings in Caribbean plantation contexts and deployed as a way of understanding mixture and cultural intersections elsewhere. Though we were already convinced that confining creolization to the Caribbean was an excessively narrow position, we thought it important to investigate space or context as an enabling or constraining element in the articulation of creolized forms of social behaviour.

- Third, we wanted to address the question of whether diaspora and creolization were contradictory trajectories, the first implying a 'there and then' sensibility, the second a 'here and now' response. All these issues were amply addressed in the articles in our special issue.

The following paragraphs summarize the main arguments of the contributors to our special issue.

Olivia Sheringham and Robin Cohen (2008/2013) centre their argument on the question of space and, more particularly, islands. They identify some of the factors particular to island spaces that make them potentially fertile places for the emergence of certain identity patterns. Drawing on the insights of spatial theorists, they examine the temporal dimensions of both creolization and diaspora (including the special historical factors that give rise to these processes) and the spatial realm within which they emerge. They sustain the theories advanced by social geographers that valorize the salience of space and show how spatial and social relationships are mutually constitutive. Cohen and Sheringham further argue that 'islandness' and creolization have an elective affinity, but that they do not necessarily emerge uniformly across islands (only parts of islands and islands with particular characteristics may be affected). 'Islandness' also influences the particular ways in which diasporic identities are formed and reformed, especially the way islands switch onto, or are insulated from, global circuits of power and influence.[1]

---

1 See Chapter 15 of this book where a version of the article is republished.

Looking more explicitly at the theme of creolization, Christine Chivallon (2008/2013) explores some of the diverse ways in which anthropologists, historians and cultural studies theorists have used the concept over the years. Using a four-box matrix, she illuminates the varying interpretations of the term creolization, drawing attention in particular to the clear distinction that exists between scholars who use it to refer to a process and those who use it to refer to a 'product' or essence. Moreover, she notes how scholars in each camp seem to diverge on whether creolization is a process that began prior to the encounters in the New World, or one that emerged in response to that violent encounter. Parenthetically, but importantly, she demonstrates how various types of diaspora map onto the different understandings of creolization she has demarcated.

In her article on 'Dark Arts and Diaspora', Aisha Khan (2008/2013) brings the theme of diaspora centrally into the debate and, in particular, explores the relationship between creolization and diaspora through the concept of community. She focuses her intervention on the cultural phenomenon of *obeah*, a set of magical cum religious practices deriving from West and Central Africa that emerged during slavery and that continue to be practiced in diverse ways among the diaspora. The main purpose of her paper is to explore the role of *obeah* in the formation of a diasporic identity. To contradict one of our initial hypotheses, Aisha Khan argues that diaspora is not only an identity that looks back to the past; rather (she suggests) it can also be a 'here and now' sensibility, a diasporic present.

While the above authors provide expositions and interpretations of 'islandness', creolization and diaspora, the remaining articles in our special issue demonstrated how these foci play out in three settings – the Mascarenes, Cape Verde and Haiti. Rosabelle Boswell (2008/2013) examines creolization in relation

269

to the Indian Ocean islands of Madagascar and Mauritius. She argues that it is important to re-anchor the concept of creolization and explore the specific historical contexts and ethnographic textures that gave rise to these processes. Essentially, she argues that since creolization does not necessarily give rise to 'Creoles', we need to think of it as a process with distinct features. For example, because the Malagasy in Madagascar do not directly associate the creolization process with slavery or indenture, it took on a number of 'free' cultural expressions. In Mauritius, by contrast, creolization is either moored to the experience of slavery, so connotes oppression, or is tied to social and cultural changes and exchanges associated with globalization.

By contrast, Elizabeth Challinor (2008/2013) delineates different manifestations of identity among Cape Verdeans and the negotiations between African and European heritages. She uses the two-headed figure of Janus to illustrate the ways in which identity among Cape Verdeans often entails complex dialogues between past, present and future. Her contribution thus highlights questions of temporality in the evolution of both creolization and diaspora – in other words, how both diaspora and creolization can at once imply a turn to the past and a look to the future. Another important issue she raises in her article is the distinction between *crioulidade* (creoleness) and creolization, a distinction somewhat echoing Chivallon's plea to recognize the underlying semantic complexity attaching to creole, créolité and creolization.

Finally, Martin Munro (2008/2013) considers the unique model of creolization in Haiti, which, he argues, differs from the rest of the Caribbean because slavery was abolished there and independence declared much earlier than in the majority of other islands. He frames his discussion of creolization around a discussion of the chameleon-like popular leader Dessalines, who (some said) was born in Africa but who, in any event, swung subtly between the celebration of his African and Creole identities in the service of the Haitian revolution. Munro also discusses the more recent figures of the *chimères* – gangs from the shantytowns of Port-au-Prince used in the service of Aristide's government. With reference to two documentary films about the *chimères* and one novel, Munro explores the potentially dystopian, apocalyptic outcomes of creolization processes on the island.

Wider issues

While much of the material in our special issue focused explicitly on creolization and diaspora, if we return to our starting points it became apparent that we cannot separate these from other forms of cultural interaction and social change. World religions, colonial powers, slavery, indentured labour, the warp and woof of mercantile capitalism, the more contemporary patterns of globalization and, in the French case, departmentalization buffeted the island spaces in which creolization and diasporas were played out and profoundly influenced their character.

We also made progress during the conference debates about whether creolization, an increasingly fashionable, can be wrenched from its points of provenance, or assumed provenance. We say 'assumed' because scholars from, or those writing on, the Caribbean often assert a proprietorial right over the term. Yet, as demonstrated (Green 2010: 157–66), creolization was developed in all essential respects much earlier in the Cape Verde archipelago. And indeed, Creole languages and other processes of creolization are equally as apparent to Indian Ocean specialists as they are to scholars of the Caribbean. In short, there is ample room for a better dialogue and systematic comparative study between researchers in different parts of the world looking at indisputably similar phenomena – a dialogue to which this special issue makes a contribution.

Of course, the debate gets more complicated when scholars apply the word 'creolization' to metropolitan contexts to describe intercultural and multicultural relations of all sorts. In this respect, it is necessary to point out to those who are using 'creolization' too loosely that they need to make clear reference to the historical settings in which it emerged – for example on certain islands, in plantation societies and under conditions in which, often with the use of violence and degradation, there was an exercise of superordination. As Françoise Vergès suggested, this does not exclude the possibility that we can 'find echoes of the plantation in the modern world and the geopolitics of inequality' (Vergès 2012). These echoes, she added, might be as diverse as metropolitan cities or refugee camps. It is also important, as Chivallon forcibly reminds us in her contribution to this special issue, that we take cognizance of historical contexts and the fact that creolization is a polysemic notion, carrying a number of meanings, not all of them fully complementary.

Finally, we gained a more complex understanding of the ways in which diaspora and creolization are mutually entangled and perhaps, as Aisha Khan suggests in her contribution, predicated on each other. Yet, there is also a sense in which the notions of diaspora and creolization provide the possibility of mutual critique. Thus Glissant's distinction between 'roots' and 'rhizomes', for example, allows us to use creolization to think beyond origins, roots and authenticity. Or, to flip the coin, consider how new diasporic claims made, for example, by Indo-Mauritians, can rupture nearly fully creolized societies. In terms of our conference theme, these discussions can be connected by Glissant's fertile notion of 'archipelago thinking'. As Bongie (1999: 89) suggests, we can understand this idea by seeing archipelagos as sites where chaotically assembled elements join together hitherto unconnected parts of the world. But archipelagic thought also implies that we need to eschew ways of understanding that are either too insular or too continental if we are to grasp the richness of global processes of creolization and contemporary formations of diaspora.

References

Bongie, Chris. 1999. 'Reading the archipelago', *New West Indian Guide* 73(1/2), 89–95.

Boswell, Rosabelle. 2008/© 2013. 'Challenges to creolization in Mauritius and Madagascar', *Diaspora*, 17(1), 64–83.

Challinor, Elizabeth Pillor. 2008/© 2013. 'Home and overseas: the Janus faces of Cape Verdean identity', *Diaspora*, 17(1), 84–104.

Chivallon, Christine. 2008/© 2013. 'The notion of creolization: an attempt at theoretical clarification', *Diaspora*, 17(1), 19–39.

Cohen, Robin. 2010. 'Social identities, diaspora and creolization' in Kim Knott and Seán McLoughlin (eds.) *Diasporas: Concepts, Identities, Intersections*, London: Zed Books, 69–73.

Cohen, Robin and Olivia Sheringham. 2008/© 2013. 'The salience of islands in the articulation of creolization and diaspora', *Diaspora*, 17(1), 6–17.

Green, Tobias. 2010. 'The Evolution of Creole Identity in Cape Verde', in Robin Cohen and Paola Toninato (eds.) *The Creolization Reader: Studies in Mixed Identities and Cultures*, London: Routledge, 157–66.

Khan, Aisha. 2008/© 2013. 'Dark arts and diaspora', *Diaspora*, 17(1), 40–63.

Munro, Martin. 2008/© 2013. 'The apocalyptic creole: from Dessalines to the Chimères', *Diaspora*, 17(1), 105–20.

Sheringham, Olivia. 2012. 'A Delicate Dance: Creolization, Diaspora, and the Metropolitan 'Pull' in the French Antilles', paper given at the Caribbean Studies Association annual conference, 28 May–1 June, Guadeloupe.

Vergès, Françoise. 2012. 'Is Creolization a Useful Concept Today?' Presentation at the conference on Identities: Creolization and Diaspora in Comparative Perspective, University of Oxford, 6–7 December, Oxford.

Addendum

This chapter provides an introduction to a selection of papers given at a conference on 'Islands and Identities: Creolization and Diaspora in Comparative Perspective' held at the University of Oxford, 6–7 December 2012. Olivia Sheringham and Robin Cohen convened the conference to advance their project entitled, 'Diaspora and Creolization: Diverging, Converging', part of the Oxford Diasporas Programme funded by the Leverhulme Trust. The event involved the participation of international scholars from the islands of Réunion, Mauritius and Guadeloupe, as well as from South Africa, the USA and Europe. With pre-circulated papers leaving ample time for discussion, the event provided an ideal forum for the stimulating exchange of knowledge and ideas on the themes of islands, identities, creolization and diaspora. Robin Cohen would like to take this opportunity to thank Olivia Sheringham for assuming the leading role in organizing the conference. We both want to thank Ann Cowie for her administrative help, Margaret Okole for her copy-editing, and Khachig Tölölyan and Sylvia Hunter for their support in bringing this project to a published conclusion.

Chapter 15
The salience of islands in the articulation of creolization and diaspora

Robin Cohen and Olivia Sheringham

In this chapter, we consider whether there is something about the spatiality of islands which makes them particularly fertile spaces for the emergence of creolized and/or diasporic identities. Drawing on the insights of social geographers, we argue that as well as considering temporal dimensions of creolization and diaspora it could also be fruitful to consider the spatial realm within which they emerge. Following an overview of the ways in which 'islandness' has been conceptualized in social theory, we use the examples of the French Antilles and Mauritius to explore in more depth some of the contexts in which creolized or diasporic identities emerge. Our argument is not that creolization and diaspora emerge only on islands, nor do we suggest that all islands inevitably experience creolization and diaspora in some form. Rather, we explore the extent to which the spatial characteristics of certain islands have meant that one could point to a certain 'elective affinity' between creolization, diaspora and islandness.

The two vectors of relativity are time and space. Historians emphasize the first, geographers the second. In this note we want to concentrate on the question of space in the sense of locale or site, while not ignoring temporal change. That social encounters and interactions take place are prerequisites for any social science, but as emphasized by a number of social geographers, where they take place decisively influences their character. In short, space matters. Drawing on the work of social theorists such as Henri Lefevbre and Michel Foucault, geographers such as Doreen Massey, David Harvey and Edward Soja (among others) have highlighted the complex, dynamic and relational nature of space. Key to their argument is the notion that space is a social construct, and thus, as Massey (1993: 70) contends, 'constituted through social relationships and material social practices'. Yet their argument went even further suggesting that, not only is space socially constructed, but the social is spatially constructed. In other words, the spatial organization of society influences how it works. Accordingly, from far from being the realm of stasis or a passive container of human activity (compared to the dynamic realm of the temporal), space is 'the simultaneous coexistence of social relations that cannot be conceptualised as other than dynamic' (p. 81).

We concur with this valorization of space in general (remembering of course that it is never determinant), but we are asking a more particular question, namely whether there are forms of interaction and types of social practices that are that are particular to islands. Is there, in short, a quality of 'islandness' that helps to explain how islanders relate to one another – how they construct their space and how, in turn, island space shapes their social relationships? An immediate difficulty presents itself: islands are by no means all similar. There are 5675 islands over 10 square km., most inhabited (ISISA 2010). However, these include very big and very small ones. It does not seem likely that we can explain the social and normative order in Australia by virtue of that country being an island. If we are to infer that there is something different about the experience of living on an island we have to think first in terms of a space that is relatively small, allowing continuous and perhaps intense forms of encounter between inhabitants.

There are other commonplace observations and questions that follow. The Île de la Cité is an island certainly, but it is the very centre of Paris, supporting two metro stations, linked by majestic bridges to the rest of the city and containing the famous Notre Dame cathedral, admired by 13 million visitors each year. Merely being an island is insufficient. If we are to demonstrate that islandness is sociologically salient, we also imply some degree of remoteness and inaccessibility. That of course prompts the geographical question of how remote, and the temporal questions for how long and over what periods? Often islands are bypassed, then connected or reconnected to global currents. Is this vacillation between abandonment and insertion/reinsertion one of the most significant feature of islandness? As McCusker and Soares (2011: xii–xiii) argue in their introduction to the edited book entitled *Islanded Identities*, 'the very seas that would appear to act as guarantors of separateness have always been conduits, facilitating movement and exchange between peoples and cultures'. Indeed, such movements inform the nature of islands as spaces of colonization and oppression, laboratories for colonial projects, and exoticized spaces in which to fulfil political ambitions or personal fantasies.

We can propose other questions informing or qualifying the special characteristics of islandness. Was the island under scrutiny ever inhabited? If inhabited, did the long-established populations resist newcomers or easily succumb to imported diseases or superior weapons? Were the newcomers ethnically homogenous or from diverse backgrounds? If from diverse backgrounds, how many cultures were represented and how distinct were they one from another? Islands are more vulnerable than mainlands to hurricanes, volcanoes, tsunamis and, now, rising sea levels. Does this enhanced susceptibility to natural disaster provide another distinguishing condition generating particular forms of social cohesion and co-operation?

Islands in social theory

Pitt (1980) was one of the first scholars to move these rather prosaic observations into the main body of social theory. His comments are suggestive but somewhat fragmentary and under-developed. He notices that in 'folk sociology' islands are seen to have a cohesive social and moral order, akin perhaps (we add) to the notion of community. This is based partly on the idea and reality that islands are periodically isolated, though surrounded by oceanic highways. Insofar as islands experience isolation they can become, Pitt suggests, 'centres of seminal ideas' or havens of 'cultural survival' (p. 1055). The mixing of cultures in out-of-the-way settings, he adds, might generate 'vigorous social actions' (like cargo cults in the Pacific or Voodoo in the Caribbean), a high degree of 'religious intensity', or 'creativity' (p. 1055). Like McCusker and Soares, he insists that islands are never totally isolated. They are linked to the larger context (the sea) and to larger societies (the mainland). The natural boundaries of islands thus act to enclose and delimit social groups, but they also permit boundary crossing. Indeed, 'because boundary crossing is so important, because there are many interlinking institutions and even a kind of hybrid vigour, [islanders] may have the potential for productive co-operation amongst themselves and increased resistance to outside interference' (p. 1056).

Much of this reasoning evokes the idea and possibility of creolization. Though Pitt does not use the concept, one may nonetheless infer from his observations that while islandness does not cause creolization, islands provide apposite settings where creolization might develop. To borrow a famous phrase from Weber, islandness and creolization have an 'elective affinity'.

Another strand of social theory is for scholars to examine the sociological profile of islanders, rather than islands. Vannini (2011) for example, depicts the social characteristics of islanders settled off British Columbia, Canada. Many of his 400 inter-viewees appear to be islanders by choice, having dropped out of what they called the 'rat race' on the mainland and turned their backs on urban and suburban life styles. In this, they are atypical islanders, whose choice of residence echoes those who O'Reilly and Benson (2009) term 'lifestyle migrants'. They resemble not at all those islanders who were dumped there by passing ships or taken by force to work in the coffee, cocoa, banana and sugar plantations located on tropical islands. Despite the atypicality of Vannini's sample, he argues that the very fact of their island location provides islanders with two 'constellations' of island liv-ing that seem to be common to all islands, namely the experience of 'insulation' and 'isolation'. He (2011, 267) writes:

Insulation and isolation are two opposite sides of the same coin, as it were, the coin of islandness. Insulation refers to the more positive (as perceived by locals) dynamics occasioned by dwelling in communities that are one step removed from some of the hegemonic spatial mobilities practiced in large cities. Isola-tion refers instead to the more negative (again, as perceived by locals) dynamics which originate as a result of their peripherality and marginalization. Insulation and isolation are not only charac-teristics of these communities' constellations of (im)mobility but also the outcomes of the unfolding of these constellations.

Much of the discussion of islandness implies that the vectors we have alluded to – of insulation and isolation, remoteness and reconnection, introversion and boundary-crossing – produce a particular social character, a form of sociality that is not found in conventional mainland settings. There are clearly serious dangers in producing these lists of supposed collective island personalities, but such attempts are remarkably persistent in the literature, so they should at least be recorded as self-beliefs that can influence real behaviour. As the 'Thomas theorem' proclaimed: 'If men define situations as real, they are real in their consequences' (Thomas and Thomas (1928: 571–2). Here is one example of this sort of attribution of a distinctive social personality, said to be shared by all islanders at large:

> Independence – small boats and social circles demand it if a personality is to survive. Loyalty – ultimate mutual care and generosity, even between ostensible enemies. A strong sense of honor, easily betrayed. Polydextrous and multifaceted competence, or what islanders call handiness. A belligerent sense of competition, interlaced with vigilant cooperation. Traditional frugality with bursts of spectacular exception. Earthy common sense. Opinionated machismo in both the male and female mode. Live-and-let-live tolerance of eccentricity. Fragile discretion within a welter of gossip. Highly individualized blends of spirituality and superstition. A complex oral tradition, with long memories fuelled by a mix of responsible record keeping and nostalgia. And finally, a canny literacy and intelligence.
>
> (Putz 1984: 26)

There is one final element of islanders' supposed social personality that seems also to be reported persistently in the literature, namely the elevated regard for equality, even when this has negative features. The penchant for equality is a product of two quite divergent provenances. The first is a sentiment that all islanders have to face loneliness, isolation and vulnerability to the elements – an equality born of the need to rely on one another. The second is a post-slavery phenomenon, where newly emancipated slaves on the plantation islands were determined never to let one emerge from their number who would lord it over the others – an equality derived from resistance to oppression. The second form is classically described by Peter J. Wilson (1995) as 'crab antics'. Based on his ethnography of Providencia (an island close to Nicaragua), the title of his book alludes to crabs trying to crawl out of a barrel. As one crab gets to the top, it is dragged down by the weight of others pulling it down into the barrel again. This is equality of course, but one where it is seen as better that everyone fails rather than have some succeed.

Islands and creolization: the Caribbean example

While general observations on islands and islanders give us a few pointers, we need to turn more specifically to the Caribbean islands, which have provided one of the most important sites for the analysis of creolization with the concept becoming what Khan (2001) refers to as a 'master symbol' of Caribbeanness. Like Khan, we take issue with the delimiting of the creolization concept to one specific geographical location/moment and, indeed, with the ways in which as a 'model for' reality, it can become a 'fiction' which, as Khan argues, 'supports some of the very assumptions and approaches it is meant to dismantle' (p. 272).

While we believe that context is crucial, the very premises of our wider project are: first, that the concept of creolization is applicable to other spaces in which similar processes of relative isolation, colonization and slavery led to the emergence of new cultural forms and, second, that the term can perhaps usefully (though not unreflectively) be expanded to incorporate other phenomena related to processes of cultural globalization in the contemporary world. But we need to return to our current task and pose our question again. Does the fact that the creole society model, or rather, the very concept of creolization, has been so widely associated with the Caribbean (and beyond this with other island societies) suggest that there is some kind of 'elective affinity' between creolization and islandness? In other words, do islands – and perhaps again, we should clear that we mean relatively small islands with a number of shared or similar social, geographical and historical characteristics – provide fertile settings for the emergence of creolization?

Let us first consider some of the convergences between the term island and the concept of creolization. Both terms have con-tested meanings. They have both been used very specifically to refer to particular spaces or to particular moments in history. Yet they have also been used metaphorically: creolization as a meta-phor for cultural change and resistance, islandness as a metaphor for remoteness, insularity or detachment. Moreover, used metaphorically, both are often adopted to denote notions of liminality or in-betweenness, and of processes that are not yet complete. Indeed, while both have been used to refer to particu-lar, bounded processes and practices, they have also both been used to denote connectedness, openness to the world, what Glissant (1990) describes as a 'poetics of relation', a notion that is echoed in Benitez-Rojo's (1996) idea of a 'repeating island'.

Of course, this seems like a rather tenuous attempt to bring together a geographical term and a concept used to refer to social identities and processes. Yet perhaps these semantic similarities provide some clues as to why processes of creolization are par-ticularly striking in these oceanic spaces characterized by travel-ling, movement and 'routes' as opposed to 'roots' or origins. And indeed, why islands are so salient in the articulation of creolization processes. Here the insights of the spatial theorists (outlined above), who pointed to the dynamic relationship between the social and the spatial, are illuminating. The argument is not that islands necessarily provide environments for creolization. Again island space is not a blank page or tabula rasa for the emergent social relations, but rather constitutive of, and deeply embedded in, those social relations that are, in the case of the Caribbean and many other postcolonial island spaces, characterized by deeply unequal relations of power. As Stuart Hall (2003, 31) argues in his discussion of creolization, 'Questions of power, as well as issues of *entanglement*, are always at stake' (emphasis in the original).

If we take the islands of the French Caribbean – the Antilles – as an example, we can see that the concept of creolization has been highly contested. Moreover, scholars such as Richard Burton (1995) noted a tension between, on the one hand, a 'creole revivalism' and the valorisation (albeit highly contested) of creole language, culture and thought (famously expressed in the *Eloge de la Creolité*, 1989) and, concurrently, processes of what he describes as 'decreolization' resulting from the continuing relationship of dependence on France. Yet this is where the islandness of these French departments becomes relevant, and perhaps has been, in part, responsible for the resistance to the complete assimilation into French mainstream culture. On the one hand these islands, as French 'possessions' since colonization, have seemed to represent exoticized, precious, 'objects of desire' (McMusker 2011, 42), moulded by the French imagination. Yet on the other hand, while Antillean identity may be marked by a certain 'mimicry' of France and French culture, there is also little doubt that the Antilles have been exemplary examples of intense creolization, of expressions of difference and resistance to monochromatic identities, or to the French assimilationist project.

In his seminal work, *The Poetics of Relation* (1990), the Martinican writer and thinker, Edouard Glissant, pointed to the unpredictability, the creative chaos that characterizes Caribbean identity, born out of the trauma of its history and of the plantation. He suggested that, 'Within the space apart that it comprised, the always multilingual and frequently multiracial tangle created inextricable knots within the web of filiations, thereby breaking the clear, linear order to which Western thought had imparted such brilliance' (p. 71). For Glissant, the composite, rhizomic, nature of Caribbean identity, the creolized spaces that emerged out of traumatic historical experiences, present new ways of thinking about the world, a world of relation. In a more recent intervention, Glissant (2008: 89) wrote:

> Dare we suppose that there are some places that I shall call Archipelago places (in the Caribbean, in the Pacific, and in so many other areas ...) – where such a concept of the Relative, of the open links with the Other, of what I call a *Poetique de la Relation* shades or moderates the splendid and triumphant voice of what I call Continental thinking, the thought of systems? Most certainly, we cannot and must not propose and model, any pattern, available for all. But in such diffracted places – in these 'laboratories' of chaos, which are metaphors for our chaos-infested world – let us say that chaos is beautiful; not chaos born from hate and wars, but from the extraordinary complexity of the exchange between cultures, which may yet forge the Americans that are at last and for the first time both deeply unified and truly diversified.

As the above quotation suggests, there is a sense that creolized and archipelagic (or we might say 'islanded') identities, represent an ideal, a goal for contemporary societies. We are thus by no means arguing that creolization is *only* salient in islands.[1] We are, rather, suggesting that bringing 'islandness' into the equation can help us to identify distinctive forms of creolization and think through some of the processes, practices and environments through and in which creolization – both literally or metaphorically – becomes apparent.

Islands and diasporas: the example of Mauritius

At first sight it is counterintuitive to take Mauritius as an example of how diasporas are articulated on island settings as there is widespread agreement among scholars that Mauritius is an textbook case of creolization. For example, in her authoritative history of the island Megan Vaughan (2005, 2), avers that Mauritius is unambiguously a creole island in that 'without natives [it] has always been the product of multiple influences, multiple sources, which to different degrees merge, take root and 'naturalize' on this new soil'. All the additional markers congruent with creolization that we have identified are there. The island is relatively remote, small, colonialized (with the complication that once Dutch, then French, the island later become a British colony), and

---

1   It would indeed be reasonable to expect that creolization will assume different forms as it 'migrates' from island settings. This is argued, for example, by Benítez-Rojo (1996) who maintained that creolization on the mainland in Mesoamerica and South America was different because depopulation was incomplete, despite millions of deaths. As the indigenous populations gradually recovered demographically they allied with Spanish settlers to develop distinctive nationalist and creolized political movements. In the contemporary period, new forms of creolization, particularly at the level of popular culture, are emerging in globalized and 'super-diverse' metropolitan settings (Murdoch 2012).

developed a plantation society with imported slaves (later indentured labourers). The African, Malagasy, Chinese, French, Indian and mixed segments of the population were deeply riven by ethnicity, snobbery and social class, but they spoke a common Creole language, effected some common elements of popular culture (in cuisine, and sega dance and music) and had little connection, over extended periods, with their countries of heritage.

This disconnection with home promoted and consolidated creolization, though the reasons for it varied among the ethnic groups that constituted the Mauritian population. In the case of Franco-Mauritians, their link with France was effectively cut during the Napoleonic wars and the surrender to a British naval squadron on 3 December 1810. Thereafter the island became a British colony, though the French language and French-based Creole survived. Independence in 1968 coincided with the reassertion of French cultural power in the region (for example, TV channels beamed from Réunion are popular in Mauritius) and the renewed prestige of a French higher education. The majority Indo-Mauritian population was also only fitfully connected with India during the colonial period and this distance was strongly reinforced by Nehru after India's own independence in 1947. Concerned to ally himself with the non-aligned and anti-colonial movement, Nehru advised those of Indian ancestry living elsewhere to adopt local citizenships and identify with local issues and struggles.

This hands-off policy changed from the 1970s, slowly at first and then at a rush. In Mauritius it was marked by the construction of the lavishly funded Mahatma Gandhi Institute, designed to promote cultural, educational and literary links. Investment in the export-processing zone, Indian tourism to the island, the establishment of Indian banks (the Bank of Baroda alone has nine branches) and penetration by right-wing Indian political parties and conservative religious groups followed. As a result of this enhanced connectivity with 'mother India', Indo-Mauritians have become somewhat de-creolized with a greatly enhanced sense of their diasporic connections. This phenomenon has been acutely observed in the case of the language, notably the valorization of Hindu, in preference to Mauritian Bhojpuri and Creole. As Eisenlor (2007, 4–5) argues:

> Ancestral languages are emblems of group identification. ... Diasporic traditions among Indo-Mauritians cannot be understood as 'survivals' from a time before migration to Mauritius. ... Though relative latecomers in the process of settling the island, Hindu Mauritians ... have legitimated their central place in a Mauritian nation not in terms of an imagined state of indigenousness but by the construction of diasporic ancestral cultures.

The story of the tiny Sino-Mauritian community is similar. Once creolized, and indeed strongly represented in the mixed population, some Sino-Mauritians are now conduits for large Chinese investments – US$ 750 million in 2010 alone – on the island (Mandaro, 2010). The newly re-designated 'Creole population', which once embraced the island at large, has now effectively been reduced in government statistics and popular rhetoric to the 27 per cent of islanders of African and Malagasy heritage.

Before drawing more general inferences from this story, there is another aspect of diasporic identity politics that needs comment, namely the creation of UNESCO world heritage sites. As Boswell (2005) anticipated, in the context of a small island society these were highly likely to become highly controversial, amplifying ethnic and diasporic rhetoric and forms of protest. So when UNESCO recognized the Aapravasi Ghat in 2006, the site in Port Louis where nearly half a million Indian labourers were landed, those Mauritians of African-Malagasy origin were immediately aggrieved at their own lack of recognition. UNESCO responded two years later by identifying Le Morne Cultural Landscape, a mountainous area where escaped slaves created Maroon communities, as a world heritage site.

We can venture a number of generalizations derived from the Mauritian experience. First, even in one of the prototypical cases of creolization, nascent or vestigial diasporic associations can be 'switched on' at certain times and in certain circumstances. In the cases mentioned, we have highlighted changes in the countries of origin as significant, though of course there is an interaction between island-centred tensions expressed in the cut and thrust of identity politics and the reactivation of homeland connections and heritages. Second, while we can find cases of complete creolization, when creolization mutates into indigeneity – Jackson (2012) describes this outcome in Guyana – this is by no means a certain trajectory. Third, the effects of exogenous ambitions by powerful actors (the governments of China, India and France all share expansionist objectives in the ocean) are keenly felt and greatly magnified by the fact that they are played out in a small island setting.[2]

Conclusion

In this chapter we have alluded to general theories advanced by social geographers valorizing the salience of space and showing

---

2 Space forbears us saying much about US ambitions in the area, but it is pertinent to note that the USA has a massive military base on Diego Garcia (controversially leased by the British). The local Chagossian population was expelled and forms a diasporic exiled population living, for the most part, in the rough parts of the Mauritian capital, Port Louis.

how spatial and social relationships are mutually constitutive. We argue that this interactive process has particular bearing in island societies because of certain shared features we designate (with others) as 'islandness'. Vanini and Taggart (2012: 12) put this succinctly as follows: 'Islandness is … not simply the sense of place typical of islands, but also the multiple ways through which relations among inhabitants, and between islands and their dwellers, are practised.' In our paper, 'islandness' refers both to certain islands and to many islanders. 'Certain' islands because our sub-set of islands is limited to those that share elements like relative smallness, relative remoteness (notwithstanding intermittent connectedness), a subdued or absent indigenous population, settlement by mercantile powers, the establishment of dominant plantation economies, the importation of labourers from distant places, the imposition of a colonial government and the emergence of free workers/settlers from slavery or coercion. Such settings, we argue, provide a natural home or fertile breeding ground for the development of creole languages, and creolized social and cultural practices. That it not to say that creolization is uniformly emergent across such islands (only parts of islands may be affected) or that creolization cannot emerge in mainland settings. Rather we assert that islandness and creolization have an elective affinity – in particular that creolization has an intensity and near-pervasiveness that is both characteristic and normatively approved.

We say 'near-pervasive', as we venture to say that creolization is generally an incomplete process on the islands with which we are familiar; the possible manifestations of diasporic practice and consciousness seem ever present in the background. Négritude survived in the French Antilles. In 1970, Black Power – drawn from US examples – was asserted in Trinidad. Twenty years later a Muslim group took the Trinidad and Tobago cabinet hostage in a bizarre attempt at a coup. In our examples drawn from Mauritius we observed the destructive possibilities of diasporic links. Again, space matters. On the islands with which we are concerned, creolization occurs as a response to isolation, neglect, the capricious whims of colonial powers and the ups and downs of the markets for tropical commodities. In a quotidian way, islanders learn from each other, rely on each other and gradually share creolized folkways, because they have to.

However, there is no certainty here, no telos. The temporal dimension also matters. We argued earlier that vacillation between abandonment and reinsertion is a common feature of islands. At certain moments, islanders can be connected or reconnected to the circuits of capital, the vagaries of big-power politics and their culturally-specific ecumene. So long as creolization has not transmogrified into indigeneity, diasporic impulses can be switched on – perhaps for the good, when the sense of a common moral and social order with a shared future can override narrow ethnicities. However, we need also to recognize that islands are more vulnerable not only to natural disasters but also to those on the island and in heritage countries who may wish to manipulate diasporic filiations in more atavistic directions.

References

Benítez-Rojo, Antonio. 1996. *The repeating island: the Caribbean and the postmodern perspective*. Durham, NC: Duke University Press.

Benson, Michaela and Karen O'Reilly (eds.). 2009. *Lifestyle migration: expectations, aspirations and experiences*. Farnham, Surrey: Ashgate.

Bernabé, Jean, Patrick Chamoiseau and Raphaël Confiant. 1989. *Éloge de la créolité*. Paris: Gallimard.

Boswell, Rosabelle. 2005. 'Heritage tourism and identity in the Mauritian villages of Chamarel and Le Morne.', *Journal of Southern African Studies* 31(2): 283–95.

Burton, Richard. 1995. 'The French West Indies a l'heure de l'Europe: an overview'. In *French and West Indian: Martinique, Guadeloupe, and French Guiana Today*, eds R. Burton and F. Reno. London: Macmillan Press.

Eisenlohr, Patrick. 2007. *Little India: diaspora, time and ethnolinguistic belonging in Hindu Mauritius*. Berkeley: University of California Press.

Glissant, Edouard. 1990. *Poétique de la relation*. Paris: Gallimard (*Poetics of Relation*. 1997. translated by Betsy Wing, Ann Arbor: University of Michigan Press).

Glissant, Edouard. 2008. 'Creolization in the making of the Americas.', *Caribbean Quarterly* (54): 1/2: 81–9.

ISISA (International Small Islands Study Association, 2010) http://tech.groups.yahoo.com/group/ISISA/message/468

Jackson, Shona N. 2012. *Creole indigeneity: between myth and nation in the Caribbean*. Minneapolis: Minnesota Press.

Khan, Aisha. 2001. 'Journey to the center of the earth: the Caribbean as master symbol.', *Cultural Anthropology*, 16(3), 271–302.

Mandaro, Laura. 2010. 'Tiny Mauritius lures China with talent, Africa know-how.' *Market Watch, Wall Street Journal*, 29 June.

Massey, Doreen. 1993. 'Politics and space/time', *New Left Review* I/196: 65–84.

McCusker, Maeve and Anthony Soares (eds.). 2011. *Islanded identities: Constructions of postcolonial cultural insularity*. Amsterdam: Rodopi.

Murdoch, H. Adlai. 2012. *Creolizing the metropole: migrant Caribbean identities in literature and film*. Champaign, IL: University of Illinois Press.

Pitt, David. 1980. 'Sociology, islands and boundaries.', *World Development* 8(12), 1051–9.

Putz, G. 1984 'On islanders.', *Island Journal*, 1:26–9.

Thomas, W. I. and D. S. Thomas. 1928 *The child in America: behavior problems and programs.* New York: Knopf.

Vannini, Phillip. 2011. 'Constellations of ferry (im)mobility: islandness as the performance and politics of insulation and isolation.', *Cultural Geographies*, 18(2), 249–71.

Vannini, Phillip and Jonathan Taggart. 2012. 'Doing islandness: a non-representational approach to an island's sense of place.', *Cultural Geographies* Online early version, 22 March: 1–18.

Vaughan, Megan. 2005. *Creating the creole island: slavery in eighteenth-century Mauritius.* Durham, NC: Duke University Press.

Wilson, Peter J. 1973. *Crab antics: the social anthropology of English-speaking Negroes of the Caribbean.* New Haven: Yale University Press.

Addendum

This article started as a paper presented to a conference on 'Islands and identities: creolization and diaspora in comparative perspective', Queen Elizabeth House, University of Oxford, 6–7 December 2012. It was subsequently published in *Diaspora*, 17(1), 6–17.

Chapter 16

If you want to know about social identities, study the Caribbean

Robin Cohen

This is a pre-publication article, submitted to *Social Identities* for the 21st Anniversary edition of the journal (2017) doi: 10.1080/13504630.2017.1314909.

It is well-known that social theory has historically been dominated by European thinkers – from the founding figures like Marx, Weber, Durkheim and Simmel to more recent luminaries like Foucault, Beck, Habermas, Giddens and Baumann. They are fecund and important thinkers and, not surprisingly, many contemporary scholars turn to them when starting their investigations of social identity. Yet, this Eurocentric starting point has some limitations. The founding thinkers rarely used the word 'identity' and, arguably, contemporary European social theory is largely insulated from discussions of colonialism, post-colonialism, colour, race and racism, which often are significant components of felt identity, identity politics and discriminatory social practices. Bhambra (2014) has made a passionate plea for widening conventional epistemologies of social science to include voices from the periphery, a plea I have heartily endorsed in my Foreword to her book. But my entreaty here is more specific: if you are a researcher studying the question of social identity, I urge you to turn your attention to the Caribbean.

Why the Caribbean?

The poet William Blake thought that we might observe 'the world in a grain of sand'. My claim is more modest, yet still ambitious. Just about any major theory of social and cultural difference will find echoes in, and can draw major insights from, the Caribbean. Why that region? The Caribbean was a nexus of the intersections and contradictions of an early form of global capitalism, mercantilism. Here European settlers, African slaves, indigenous populations, indentured Indians and subsequent migrants from places as far afield as China and Syria, found themselves trying to make new lives in small, often hostile, settings. They spoke many languages – a number of European ones (like English, French, Dutch, Danish and Spanish), Asian ones (like Bhojpuri) and also developed shared Creole languages. The whole gamut of conventional religious identities are represented, while newer syncretic faiths like Shango, Santeria, Voudou and Rastafarianism flourish. The contemporary countries of the region are variously independent, dependencies, parts of France (Martinique, Guadeloupe and Guyane) and a territory appurtenant and belonging to, but not a part of, the United States (Puerto Rico). The Caribbean includes some of the most notorious tax havens (like the Caymans, Panama, the Bahamas, British Virgin Islands, Dominica and Anguilla) and a rare survivor of socialism (Cuba). The region also exhibits some intriguing gender anomalies. For example, the number of males enrolled at the three campuses of the University of the West Indies has been steadily declining since 1980; now over two-thirds of students are female. The Caribbean also has a large diaspora. Emigration from the Caribbean is normal – about half the populations in the cases of Monserrat, Guyana, Puerto Rico and Suriname. In short, everything one could desire in a living social science laboratory is present in the Caribbean. In a relatively small space, with a relatively small population, all the key complexities that underlie the study of social identities are visible and present.

Caribbean social theory

Assuming you are already interested, I hope you will be further enticed by the amazing array of social theory generated in the Caribbean or by scholars of the Caribbean. Let me provide an indicative list, including a few references to the literature:

Négritude

This literary and cultural intervention was initiated by francophone African intellectuals in Paris in the 1930s, notably by the Senegalese Léopold Senghor (later Senegal's president), and the poets Aimé Césaire and Léon Damas from the French Caribbean. Césaire's (1995/1937) prose poem *Return to my Native Land* is variously described as a surreal or seminal *chef-d'oeuvre*, celebrating the possibility of a transnational identity for black Africans and their descendants.

The lived experience of being black and post-colonialism

Césaire's student and fellow Martinican, Frantz Fanon (1986/68) both elaborated his work and developed new understandings of the psychological damage blacks had to endure and overcome as they sought to escape white domination. He was a vital influence on movements like Black Consciousness, Black Power (Stokely Carmichael was Trinidad-born) and the Black Panther Party. He also excoriated the new political leaders of African counties as they consolidated their own power at the expense of the 'wretched of the earth' (Fanon 1967), thus supplementing a race analysis with a powerful, though non-traditional, class analysis.

Social and cultural pluralism

In the 1950s and 1960s, 'pluralism' became the principal way of understanding societies that were artificially created by colonialism from people of different origins (Furnivall 1948). The Jamaican M. G. Smith (1965, 1974) developed and applied Furnivall's ideas on pluralism in the context of the Caribbean and more broadly. The governing notion was that parallel social institutions consolidated each segment making up colonial societies while only a few instrumental ties bound the segments together. His ideas were widely applied across the colonial and post-colonial world.

Matrifocality

M. G. Smith's near namesake, the anthropologist Raymond T. Smith, echoed some similar themes in his early work on Guyana, but more relevantly for contemporary social theory, he was among the first to develop a full account (descriptively and conceptually) of female-headed households (Smith 1996). Such households and matrifocality more generally have become increasingly important and much more common because of transnational migration, HIV/AIDs and the political assertion by women in a number of societies.

Transnationalism

Precursors of the idea of transnationalism can be found elsewhere, but many scholars credit the most salient exposition of transnationalism to Nina Glick Schiller and her colleagues. In their crucial work on *Nations Unbound* (1994) they argued that, in many cases, familial, social, political, organizational, economic and religious ties had spread across national borders. She drew on her doctoral work on Haiti, on Grenada and (outside the Caribbean) on the Philippines. In Europe, the most influential theorist of transnationalism is Steven Vertovec (2009) who, it is worth remembering, did his doctoral work on Indians in Trinidad.

Social remittances

Peggy Levitt (2001: 54–69) saw that 'transnational villagers', moving between the Dominican Republic and the USA were both 'cultural creators' and carriers of values and social practices to which they had been exposed at each end of the migration circuit. Their oscillating journeys expanded and transformed the repertoires of social interaction in which they participated – thus 'social remittances'. Levitt's writings on the theme have been widely cited by migration and social identity scholars in many parts of the world.

Transculturation

Transculturation is one of the great ideas that was articulated before its time and, one should probably add, failed to gain the attention it deserved because it was developed by a Cuban sociologist, unconnected to mainstream US sociology and writing in Spanish (Ortiz 1995/1940). Broadly, he was interested in the ways in which cultures and identities gradually mix and merge, though he was also aware of the brutality of one-way conquest over indigenous peoples (like the Spanish conquest of Cuba) and the possibilities of ethnic violence. Nowadays, the core of his argument has been refashioned in the concept of creolization (see below) and associated non-Caribbean ideas like hybridity and interculturalism. It is still, however, worth reading Ortiz for the many subtleties of his argument.

Creolité and creolization

The merging and mixing of cultures and identities is a constant theme in many Caribbean settings. Possibly the most ambitious plan to turn this common phenomenon into a political project was generated by three francophone Caribbean scholar-activists, who issued their 'manifesto' on créolité (loosely, 'creoleness') (Bernabé et al. 1989). They explicitly set their faces against négritude (see above) arguing that it was more important to celebrate the mélange of peoples at their points of settlement, rather than unearth their roots at their points of origin. Although often associated with the *créolité* movement, the eminent Caribbean cultural theorist, Edouard Glissant (1997/90, 2008), stressed that mixing was a process, not an outcome, and that the process had to have oppositional, creative and resistant elements. In elaborating this idea, Cohen (2007) and his co-author (Cohen and Sheringham 2016) largely aligned themselves with Glissant's views.

Diaspora (new versions) and the black Atlantic

Diaspora is, of course, a very old term, but it gathered steam and took on new life with the intervention of two major Caribbean intellectuals. The first was Jamaican-born Stuart Hall, especially in his crucial article on cultural identity and diaspora (Hall 1990). The second was Paul Gilroy, perhaps better considered a British social theorist, though his mother was Guyanese and he was close to his part-Caribbean origins. In his much-cited account of the *Black Atlantic* he adumbrated a deterritorialized, indeed oceanic, diasporic identity (Gilroy 1993). Both authors provided crucial reference points in the new understandings of global diasporas generated in the 1990s (Cohen 2008).

Conclusion

This short review of Caribbean social theory picks out some of the big blobs of paint on the intellectual palette, but there are many more colours and mixtures to discover. Cautious scholars do not like to stick their necks out, but I will. By understanding the Caribbean and the social theories developed there, any account of social identity will be conceptually enriched and massively enhanced. Gender-sensitive, emerging from a colonial and post-colonial experience, relevant to contemporary discussions on diversity, multiscalarity and intersectionality, Caribbean social theory can be seen as a 'master symbol' (Khan 2001), a mine of information and understanding that will help to create a truly global social science.

References

Bernabé, Jean, Patrick Chamoiseau and Raphaël Confiant. 1989. *Éloge de la créolité*, Paris: Gallimard.

Bhambra, Gurminder K. 2014. *Connected sociologies*, London: Bloomsbury.

Césaire, Aimé. 1995. *Notebook of a return to my native land*, Hexham, Northumberland: Bloodaxe Books (first published 1937).

Cohen, Robin. 2007. 'Creolization and cultural globalization: the soft sounds of fugitive power', *Globalizations*, 4(3), 369–84.

Cohen, Robin. 2008. *Global diasporas: an introduction*, 2nd edn, London: Routledge.

Cohen, Robin and Olivia Sheringham (2016) *Encountering difference: diasporic traces, creolizing places*, Cambridge: Polity.

Fanon, Frantz. 1986. *Black skin, white masks*, London: Pluto (first published in 1968).

Fanon, Frantz. 1967. *The wretched of the earth*, Harmondsworth: Penguin.

Furnivall, J. F. 1948. *Colonial policy and practice: a comparative study of Burma and Netherlands India*, Cambridge: Cambridge University Press.

Gilroy, Paul. 1993. *The Black Atlantic: modernity and double consciousness*, London: Verso.

Glissant, Edouard. 1997. *Poetics of relation*, Ann Arbor: University of Michigan Press (first published 1990).

Glissant, Edouard. 2008. 'Creolization in the making of the Americas.' *Caribbean Quarterly* 54(1/2), 81–9.

Hall, Stuart. 1990. 'Cultural identity and diaspora', in Jonathan Rutherford (ed.) *Identity: community, culture, difference*, London: Lawrence and Wishart, 222–37.

Khan, Aisha. 2001. 'Journey to the center of the earth: the Caribbean as master symbol', *Cultural Anthropology*, 16(3), 271–302.

Levitt, Peggy. 2001. *The transnational villagers*, Berkeley: University of California Press.

Ortiz, Fernando. 1995. *Cuban counterpoint: tobacco and sugar*, Durham, NC: Duke University Press (first published in 1940).

Schiller, Nina Glick, Linda Basch and Christina Blanc-Szanton. 1994. *Nations unbound: transnational projects, postcolonial predicaments and deterritorialized nation-states*, Newark, NJ: Gordon & Breach.

Smith, M. G. 1965. *Stratification in Grenada*, Berkeley: University of California Press.

Smith, M. G. 1974. *The plural society in the British West Indies*, Berkeley: University of California Press (first published 1965).

Smith, Raymond T. 1996. *The matrifocal family: power, pluralism and politics*, New York: Routledge.

Vertovec, Steven. 2009. *Transnationalism*, London: Routledge.